Identity and Change
in the Christian Tradition

Contributions to Philosophical Theology

Edited by Gijsbert van den Brink, Vincent Brümmer and Marcel Sarot

Vol. 2

PETER LANG

Frankfurt am Main · Berlin · Bern · New York · Paris · Wien

Marcel Sarot
Gijsbert van den Brink
(eds.)

Identity and Change
in the Christian Tradition

PETER LANG
Europäischer Verlag der Wissenschaften

BT
90
.I44
1999

Die Deutsche Bibliothek - CIP-Einheitsaufnahme

Identity and change in the Christian tradition / Marcel Sarot ;
Gijsbert van den Brink (eds.). - Frankfurt am Main ; Berlin ;
Bern ; New York ; Paris ; Wien : Lang, 1999
(Contributions to Philosophical Theology ; Vol. 2)
ISBN 3-631-35161-5

ISSN 1433-643X
ISBN 3-631-35161-5
US-ISBN 0-8204-4354-9

© Peter Lang GmbH
Europäischer Verlag der Wissenschaften
Frankfurt am Main 1999
All rights reserved.

Printed in Germany 1 2   4 5 6 7

Table of Contents

The Role of Authority in Religious Traditions

The Role of Theology in Religious Traditions

Hermeneutics and Change in Religious Traditions

Preface

In October 1997, the Research Group in Philosophy of Religion of Utrecht University organized an international research colloquium. The main papers presented at this colloquium are collected in this volume. By providing information about the backgrounds of the colloquium, this preface serves to put these papers into their context.

'Identity and Change in the Christian Tradition' was the title of the colloquium at which the Utrecht research group launched its new research programme on 'Philosophical Analysis and the Nature of Change in Religious Traditions.' The notion of a 'research programme' may require some explanation. In the sciences, the use of increasingly complex and expensive equipment and laboratories has made it imperative for scientists to cooperate. Nowadays, research is rarely executed by individual inventors in backyard sheds or in attic rooms; these individuals would not be able to come by the necessary equipment. Research in the sciences is organized in research programmes, where a number of scientists cooperate on several coherent projects. Only when scientists cooperate in this way, are the responsible authorities willing to grant them the subsidies required for their costly apparatus. However, the tendency to organize research in programmes is not just due to budgetary efficiency; it is also felt widely that by joining their forces, scientists are more likely to be successful in their research, and will be better able to instruct next generations of scientists. It is for this kind of reasons that in the Netherlands, and increasingly so in other European countries, especially in Scandinavia, not only scientific research, but *all* academic research is organized into research programmes.

In Utrecht, prof. Vincent Brümmer established and developed a research programme in philosophy of religion that concentrated on the philosophical analysis of conceptual issues in the Christian doctrine of God. Apart from a number of studies on the methodological problems involved in applying the tools of conceptual analysis to the field of theology and religion, this programme produced a number of essays, monographs and dissertations dealing with conceptual issues involved in various divine properties which have been attributed to God in the Christian tradition.[1] After more than a decade of research in philosophical

---

1. Among the main books produced in the context of the programme are: Vincent Brümmer, *Speaking of a Personal God* (Cambridge 1992); id., *The Model of Love* (Cambridge 1993); Gerrit Immink, *Divine Simplicity* (Kampen 1987); Marcel Sarot, *God, Possibility and Corporea-*

theology, however, the members of the programme decided that it would be good to take stock of the results of their joint research,[2] and to make a fresh start. It was decided to set up a new research programme, in which the kind of philosophical analysis developed in Utrecht in recent years will be applied to the study of theories concerning the nature of change in religion. Here, 'religion' will be taken broadly, so as to include secular views of life which function as alternatives for institutionalized religions.

Western society is going through a period of rapid cultural change. In periods like these, religious traditions tend to change more radically and diversify more rapidly than in times of cultural stability. They have to, in order to remain relevant and adequate for dealing with the changing demands of life which their adherents are required to face. The new Utrecht programme will concentrate on a number of central questions about the nature of change and continuity within religious traditions: What function is the conceptual system or 'language game' of religion required to fulfil within the context of human thought and life and in what ways and under what circumstances do such conceptual systems require innovative changes in order to remain adequate for fulfilling this function? How are the continuity and change within religious traditions related to these issues and what is the nature of such continuity and change within traditions? What role can theology play in initiating and directing such changes?

In order to sharpen the focus of the programme, *two restrictions* will be applied to it. *First* of all, the programme will adopt an explicitly *philosophical* approach. In this way the programme will apply the analytical methods in philosophical theology which have been developed with success in Utrecht in recent years.[3] Thus far, philosophers have paid relatively little attention to the conceptual issues concerning continuity and change in religious traditions. Most contemporary theories on these issues, have been developed from an historical, an empirical, or a theological perspective, rather than from that of philosophy. Furthermore, theologians, and especially contextual[4] theologians, have developed inno-

---

lity (Kampen 1992), Gijsbert van den Brink, *Almighty God* (Kampen 1993, ²1996); Gijsbert van den Brink & Marcel Sarot (eds.), *Understanding the Attributes of God* (Frankfurt aM 1999), Luco J. van den Brom, *Divine Presence in the World* (Kampen 1993).

2. See Van den Brink & Sarot, *Understanding the Attributes of God.*

3. On the specific characteristics of the Utrecht approach, see Gijsbert van den Brink & Marcel Sarot, 'Contemporary Philosophical Theology,' in: Van den Brink & Sarot (eds.), *Understanding the Attributes of God*, 9-32.

4. In a sense, *all* theology is contextual. By contextual theologians I mean only those theologians who are consciously contextual, and who consciously allow the context from which and for which they theologize to exert a decisive influence on their theologies, e.g., liberation theologians, black theologians, feminist theologians, womanist theologians, etc.

vative proposals aimed at keeping theology adequate for the changing demands of life and experience. Insofar as philosophers have developed theories and proposals that are relevant to the issues of religious change, this has mainly been done within other branches of philosophy, such as the philosophy of culture, philosophical hermeneutics and the philosophy of science. There, theories have been developed that are indirectly relevant to the issues of religious change and continuity, but this relevance still awaits explicit spelling out. The new Utrecht programme will try to employ the philosophical theories developed within these other branches of philosophy to illuminate certain aspects of religious change and continuity. Moreover, it will also provide a philosophical analysis of the ways in which (contextual) theologians try to initiate and direct such changes, and the criteria which are relevant for judging the innovative proposals of theologians.

A *second* restriction is the following. Since the issues to be explored derive much of their interest and actuality from developments within Western society, the programme will concentrate on *Western* religion. Although 'religion' will be taken in its widest sense – including secular views of life which function as alternatives for institutionalized religions – much attention will go to the main religious tradition within this society: Christianity. This will be the case especially in its second and third sections, on the philosophical analysis of continuity and change in religious traditions. In this way the new programme will also build upon the expertise developed by the Utrecht research group in the analysis of conceptual issues in Christian doctrine. In the new programme, however, Christianity will not only be studied for its own sake, but also as the main manifestation or example of religion in Western society.

That it is desirable that the tools of analytical philosophy be applied to this type of issues has recently been eloquently argued by Robert M. Adams, who claimed that by concentrating on the examination and defence of quite traditional conceptions of Christian doctrines, philosophical theology

may fail to make contact with one of the central preoccupations of many theologians and students of religion: the reinterpretation of religious traditions. Reinterpretation of tradition, arguably, is and always has been a feature of any living theology, or indeed of any living appropriation of religious tradition. In Western religious thought of the last two centuries this process has become especially self-conscious. Reinterpretation of religious traditions has taken place in a context of historical and theoretical study of tradition as such, of its symbolic and institutional embodiments, of culture (more broadly), and of processes of change in all these matters. In this context the study of religion has tended to focus on such questions as the following: What is a religious tradition? What is the essence of a given religious tradition? What are its boundaries (if it has any)? What is the role of belief, in religious traditions? What constitutes holding the same belief, in different historical and cultural contexts? What is the meaning of traditional texts, ceremonies and doctrines today? And in the light of such questions, what constitutes loyalty to a tradition?

And after mentioning the disciplines which have contributed to the study of these questions, Adams concludes:

> Analytical philosophers have contributed much less than others to these fields, and thus may seem ... to have relatively little to say about some of the philosophical issues that most interest them. This may change; analytical techniques might well be fruitfully applied to many of these issues, and the 21st century may see a development of analytical philosophy in these domains.[5]

We hope that it may be given to the Utrecht research programme to contribute to this development, and we are grateful for the support which our new programme received from January 1998 onwards from the Dutch Research Council NWO, and from the Board of Utrecht University.

The starting of a new research programme is in no way a *creatio ex nihilo*. In the first place, even now that flexibility has become the watchword, there will always be some continuity in the staff – though perhaps less so than one would sometimes wish. There is one person I would like to mention especially in this connection, prof. Vincent Brümmer. Though retiring as a professor in the philosophy of religion and as leader of the research programme, his keen interest in our efforts to renew the research programme have been crucial to the whole enterprise. It is not without reason that his valedictory lecture also functioned as the opening lecture of this colloquium, and is included in this volume.

The success of a research group does not only depend upon its members, but also on the participation and cooperation of scholars working in the same field internationally. In Utrecht we have been fortunate to enjoy the enthusiastic cooperation of many scholars in the Netherlands, in Europe (especially in Britain and in Scandinavia), and even in the USA. We have experienced it as a fortunate sign that so many of them were present at the launching of our new research prog-

---

5. Robert M. Adams, 'Analytical Philosophy and Theism,' in: William J. Wainwright (ed.), *God, Philosophy and Academic Culture* (Atlanta, Ga 1996), 79-87, quotation from 84-85.

ramme, and we are very grateful for their interest. The papers which some of them delivered greatly enhance the quality of the present volume, and gave an important stimulus for several of the research projects on which we have since then embarked. We owe a great debt to prof. Dewi Z. Phillips, who not only chaired the final plenary in his own magisterial way, but also contributed an Introduction to the present volume in which he introduces the contributions collected here.[6]

We are also grateful to the Board of Utrecht University, and to the Research Institute INTEGON of the Utrecht Faculty of Theology, for their financial support both for the colloquium and for the publication of its proceedings in this volume. Many thanks are due also to Gerrit Brand, Wybren de Jong and dr. Michael Scott, who helped the organizers of the colloquium and the editors of the present volume in several ways.

Marcel Sarot

---

6. Prof. Phillips does not introduce Mr. Wybren the Jong's article, because that was nog given as a main paper during the colloquium. A previous version of Mr. de Jong's paper was given as a small paper at the colloquium. Since the topic of his paper was closely related to the valedictory lecture of prof. Brümmer, and since we have clustered the other papers in pairs, we have after the colloquium asked Mr. de Jong to rewrite his paper so that it could form a pair with prof. Brümmer's.

1. Introduction

Reflecting on Identity and Change

Dewi Z. Phillips (Swansea, Wales & Claremont, California)

The papers in this collection are made up, in the main, of the symposia presented at the Research Colloquium on Identity and Change in the Christian Tradition at Utrecht and Soesterberg on 16-19 October 1997. As well as the symposia, the collection includes Vincent Brümmer's valedictory lecture as Professor of the Philosophy of Religion at Utrecht University. The topics are wide-ranging, and the treatments various. I shall not try to cover them all, but give some indications of some questions which should be borne in mind when we reflect on this central topic. The questions are my own. Some, but not all of them, are to be found in the collection. I hope that is all to the good, since this introduction can then serve, not simply to indicate directions already taken in the papers, but also to indicate further directions one might pursue.

The papers in the collection not only address identity and change in the Christian tradition, but write out of that tradition. This immediately introduces a complexity of considerable significance: the writers are part of the identity and change they are writing of - personally, theologically and philosophically part of it. It is easy to assume that we are agreed on our topic, identity and change, and only differ, perhaps, in the account we give of it. Even the most cursory examination of this collection should disabuse us of this assumption. Agreement on the concepts of 'identity' and 'change' cannot be taken for granted, for these will themselves be seen to be subject to theological and philosophical disagreement. For some, the task may be thought to be that of doing something about a situation we understand. For others, it is that situation itself which needs to be understood. It would seem that if the latter is not understood, 'doing something about it' will be no more than moving in a fog. More fundamentally, can we always assume that 'something can be done about it,' whatever the 'it' is?

The scene for the symposia is set, in many ways, by Brümmer's valedictory lecture. Many in the conference expressed their indebtedness to his theological and philosophical contributions over the years, so it is particularly fitting that this should be so. His address also raises the issue, for the reader, of the difference between a philosophical and theological concern with the issues of identity and change in religion. The theologian, it might be said, is a guardian of the grammar of Faith. Can the same be said of a philosopher?

Theological and philosophical concerns overlap Brümmer's lecture, but this fact itself raises interesting questions. Brümmer shows how a number of simplistic answers to problems of identity and change will not do, and insists that, at any time, in a culture, the Christian tradition must be relevant, adequate, intelligible and credible in its relation to its surroundings. But the crucial issue is whether, in meeting this situation, the identity of the Christian tradition is preserved. Brümmer concludes that the tradition's self-understanding makes this possible:

> We can now conclude that the unity and identity of the Christian tradition can be found in the narrative continuity of the historical process of interpretation which starts in the Bible itself and refers to the connected series of events telling of the impact of Jesus Christ, who is acknowledged by believers to be the fixed origin of the tradition as well as the original locus of meaning for human existence. The heritage which is passed down from generation to generation in this tradition is however by no means timelessly immutable but requires constant translation, re-conceptualization and reinterpretation in the light of the ever changing demands of life confronting participants in the tradition (see below, 41).

Looking down the heritage which has come to us, it is easy to locate agreed absurdities which have fallen by the wayside. But have there not been religious and theological gains and losses marked by differences over what is to count as gain or loss? And when those disagreements are deep enough, will they not include the answer to Jesus' question, 'Whom do you say that I am?'. If that is so, can 'the impact of Jesus Christ' be regarded as a *fixed* origin of a tradition, or as something which needs a tradition or a teaching to be understood? Could one determine who Jesus is and then use this to assess various responses to him, or is there an internal relation between the sense of the identity and the religious responses? When Peter responds to Jesus' question, Jesus tells him that flesh and blood did not reveal this to him.

At the opposite end of this emphasis is the view that religion is embedded, in some sense, in human thought and experience. It would then be a distinctively philosophical task to make explicit the notion of this embeddedness. In the symposium on 'The Function of Religion in Human Life and Thought,' Santiago Sia attempts to do this in the context of Whitehead's philosophy, a philosophy which does not reject metaphysics, but calls for a revision of what we take metaphysics to be. For Whitehead:

Religion is the vision of something which stands beyond, behind, and within the passing flux of immediate things; something which is real, and yet waiting to be realised, something which is a remote possibility, and yet the greatest of present facts; something that gives meaning to all that passes, and yet eludes apprehension; something whose possession is the final good, and yet is beyond all reach; something which is the ultimate ideal, and the hopeless quest.[1]

But, as Sia points out, Whitehead is wary of putting too much substantive content into these words lest it hinder the hope of future adventure. This raises two important questions. First, what is the relation of this philosophical conception of religion to the historic religions? Second, what is the relation of this account of 'the greatest of all facts' to secular accounts, such as those offered by Freud or Marx? According to Sia, the historical religions make the implications philosophically discerned more explicit. Can this be equated with Brümmer's notion of an evolving tradition? Presumably, alternative perspectives will have to be shown to be confused or inadequate in some way.

In his reply, Marcel Sarot, too, wants to insist that religion must be related to human concerns, and what greater concern can there be than the question of the meaning of life? I think he is sceptical of attempts to arrive at this meaning theoretically. One way in which the issue becomes resolved for people is in terms of finding something to emulate. In the Christian tradition that emulation is found in the ideal of *imitatio Christi*. Sarot is aware that this ideal itself can be subject to religious and theological controversy.

I would like to see more discussion of the difference between following Christ and following a good man. After all, Jesus does not die the death of a martyr. He is the Lamb of God slain for the sins of the world. How could I follow that? I do not mean, of course, that I'd be bound to fail. I mean: what sense would it make to try?[2]

An interesting philosophical question arises for Sia and Sarot. The former admits to there being secular accounts of what matters most in life, and the latter would not deny that different ideals are emulated. It seems to me that Sia would be committed to saying, from a Whiteheadian perspective, that the perspective he advances is underwritten by an adequate metaphysics, and that others would lack such support. I do not think Sarot would want to take that path. In any case, it is

1   A.N. Whitehead, *Science in the Modern World* (Cambridge 1926), 267-8.
2   On this whole question see Søren Kierkegaard's discussion of the difference between following Socrates and following Christ in *Philosophical Fragments* (Princeton 1994). On the difference between emulating a good man and following Christ see Rush Rhees, 'Living With Oneself,' in: D.Z. Phillips (ed.), *On Religion and Philosophy* (Cambridge 1997).

philosophically interesting to ask what the relation of their respective conclusions would be to philosophical traditions which promise to teach us differences.

For Keith Ward, in the symposium on 'The Nature of Change in Religious Traditions,' these differences are only too apparent in the explosion of scientific knowledge since the sixteenth century. A huge difference, apparently, is in the special status Christianity gives to human beings in the universe, compared to the insignificant place they have in the light of cosmology. Ward argues that the former emphasis is theologically inadequate, since God's creation involves the whole world. He argues that the imputation of insignificance in the latter emphasis comes from a faulty metaphysics or a world view, and is not itself a scientific conclusion.

Ward wants to explore whether dominant scientific theories, such as Darwinism, can be viewed in a way that enriches religion. Given that there is design in nature, is its presence better explained by chance than by belief in a Creator? In his reply, Scott is sceptical about the introduction of the notion of 'chance' in this context, arguing that Darwinism has intellectual resources to explain evidence of design in nature. In so far as religious belief is understood as challenging this adequacy, Darwinism will undermine its claims. In face of it, he believes 'that the drift towards ever more radical non-realism will continue.'

Both Ward and Scott speak of God's creation in terms of design. This, I agree, has been common in philosophical circles since the eighteenth century. But it is also associated with deism. Presumably, Scott would call any alternative 'non-realism.' But what if the alternative is a religious song of creation? I would like to have seen a discussion of whether Darwinism contradicts that song. Does it contradict Genesis? I want to relate the present discussion to a parallel discussion of that question by Peter Winch.[3]

Winch argues only against the view that there is a *necessary* contradiction between Genesis and Darwin, but he does so by concentrating on the notion of contradiction. He expounds Wittgenstein's remark that we deal with contradictions *when they arise.* He wants to combat the idea of a contradiction as something lurking undetected in a mode of discourse for ever threatening its intelligibility. People have worried over whether there could be a hidden contradiction in mathematics. But it is deeply confused to think that if one were to arise, it would render the whole of mathematics pointless, as this might occur for a simple game. In the game, we might discover that the game is always won if a certain second move is made. This would render the game pointless. Even here, it would not follow that the game was pointless before this is pointed out. The newly discovered move should not be

---

3   Peter Winch, 'Darwin, *Genesis* and Contradiction,' in: *Trying to Make Sense* (Oxford 1987).

thought of as latent in the old moves. But, once it is pointed out, we cannot go on in the same way.

Winch suggests that, by contrast, we would deal with a contradiction in mathematics in ways akin to the way we deal with the Liar Paradox. When we realise the problems caused by the first person use of the verb 'to lie' - 'I am lying' - we simply legislate against that use. It would be absurd to say that all our distinctions between truth and falsehood are undermined as a result.

Where does the relation between Genesis and Darwin fit in? Does Genesis become pointless in face of Darwinism, or is some specific provision made as with the Liar Paradox or mathematics? Winch insists that no general answer can be given. Everything depends on *whether a contradiction has arisen*, and that cannot be answered without reference to the significance of the beliefs in the lives of the people concerned.

For some, the song of creation, with its talk of the treasures of the snow, the trees clapping their hands, and the sons of God shouting for joy, is not something science could comment on one way or another. The religious response to the miracle of creation, though different, has far more in common with aesthetic responses than with scientific theories.[4]

But what if a contradiction does arise for someone? The consequences are unpredictable. One alternative may be abandoned in favour of the other. The problem may be accommodated by modifications of various kinds, or one might conclude that the contradiction is only apparent. For some, wanting to explain the raindances causally by reference to spirits, misses the spirit in the rain. For others, the scientific explanation of sunrises and sunsets makes these terms a piece of inaccurate folk-psychology that we tolerate until we speak a scientific language. For the elder Gosse, hanging on to his faith meant believing that God created the fossils looking that old. The price was that he was finished as a serious geologist.[5] The consequences of contradictions, as well as what they are, and whether they occur, depends on the significance of science and religion in people's lives. We should not ask, in the abstract, therefore, 'Does Genesis Contradict Darwin?'

If this conclusion is taken to heart, it will have interesting consequences for the question of how a religious tradition can exert an authority on us today. This is discussed by Paul Helm in the symposium, 'The Role of Authority in Religious Traditions': 'To think of the Christian tradition as presently exercising *de jure* authority one needs to be able to argue for the idea of the *de jure* authority of some-

---

4   For my elaboration of this view see my 'Is Hume's "True Religion" a Religious Belief?' in: D.Z. Phillips & Timothy Tessin (eds.), *Religion and Hume's Legacy* (London 1998).

5   Edmund Gosse, *Father and Son* (London 1912).

17

thing that existed two thousand years ago, the idea of the past exercising authority over the present.'

He considers two arguments against this, one of which he regards as less threatening than the other. The less threatening concerns the epistemic status of testimony. Helm criticises, effectively, Hume's claim that the value we place on testimony must be judged by our present beliefs. In relation to Hume's attack on miracles, he shows that his attack on testimony concerning miracles itself relies on testimony. I think Helm is right when he says that credence in relation to testimony is 'a primitive feature of the human cognitive situation,' but wrong in thinking that this is an extension of 'the principle of credulity.' This latter notion involves 'assumption' and 'probability,' terms which are more sophisticated than, and parasitic on, the primitive responses Helm wants to account for. Try accounting for a child's learning to speak in terms of the principle of credulity. One would assume the very capacities the child is acquiring.

What is needed to supplement this point is the relation of authority to testimony. In this connection, Helm considers the greater difficulty connected with the so-called scepticism Kripke claims to find in Wittgenstein's analysis of rule-following. If any interpretation can be given of any rule, how can we ever know that we are following the rule *in the same way*? It is easy to see how the same dilemma can be posed about the continuance of *the same tradition*.

Helm does not mention that Kripke ignores the fact that Wittgenstein says that at a certain point we are not *interpreting* the rule, but going on in the same way. The question of why this is called 'the same way' does not arise. People do not agree to go on in this way; their agreement is shown in the fact that they do. But, as Helm says, the agreement we find in following a mathematical rule is not present in religious matters. As a result, he concludes that 'the obstacles to the idea of a *de jure* Christian tradition are not so much philosophical as empirical in character.' But surely this calls for more *philosophical* discussion of authority in religion, since the disanalogy with authority in other areas, such as mathematics, is precisely what creates puzzles about the religious cases.

It is precisely these puzzles which are taken up by Luco Van den Brom in his reply. He is right to question the priority Helm gives to propositions in religion, on the ground that this does not do justice to propositions. It is not our propositions which give sense to our practices, but our practices, what we do, which give sense to our propositions. The same can be said of religious beliefs and traditions. But this point leads to the same question that faced Helm: what is to count as an authoritative tradition?

Van den Brom, at the end of his paper, rightly stresses the importance of authority in the conversations of the Christian community. He discusses the role of Scripture in that conversation. He is right to emphasise that Scripture cannot stand alone, since its authority is mediated through the religious community. He considers various views of this mediation. What seems to me to need further discussion is a claim that without *some* authoritative background, the religious discussions Van den Brom refers to would not make sense. This is an extremely important topic which has far-reaching consequences.[6]

The importance of these conclusions is borne out in the theological emphases found in Christoph Schwöbel's contribution to the symposium on 'The Role of Theology in Religious Traditions.' He insists that the notion of rationality in religion cannot be divorced from religious rituals and traditions which are handed down from generation to generation. But these traditions involve interpretation and personal appropriation in face of tensions created by features of human experience such as suffering. These emphases recall the tasks for theology emphasised in Brümmer's lecture.

Schwöbel emphasises that 'In Christianity tradition is from early on an essentially contested concept.' Yet, he also wants to say that tradition has its origin in a foundational disclosure of the divine. An old difficulty returns: does the disclosure give sense to the practice, or does the disclosure, like a gesture, require an audience for which it can be a disclosure?

For the most part, it is the discussion of tradition that holds centre stage, and certain models of tradition are discussed. All the models are normative, which again emphasises the importance of an authoritative background as a condition of the possibility of disagreement. But how is this notion of authority related to the changes which occur in Christian traditions? When Schwöbel describes 'the task of Christian theology as that of 'managing' the relationship of identity and change,' he may give the impression that the theologian enjoys an independence he does not possess. But this is wrong, since he makes it clear that theology is not an autonomous activity, and its problems are often not of its choosing. I do not think he would deny that there is an interaction between what a theologian may want to say, and what a religious community is prepared to accept. After all, a theologian is part of that community and regards, or should regard, his calling as a God-given privilege.

In his reply, Gijsbert van den Brink takes up the notion of a theologian being concerned with 'the management of change,' and stresses the interaction between it and the believing community. He considers in detail, as a case study, whether a theological proposal by the theologian Den Heyer was consistent with what he calls the traditional or classical doctrine of the atonement. There is no difficulty in saying

---

6   For discussions of authority closely related to this issue see Gareth Moore, 'Tradition, Authority and the Hiddenness of God' and 'Voices in Discussions,' in: Timothy Tessin & Mario von der Ruhr (eds.), *Philosophy and the Grammar of Religious Belief* (London 1995).

that Den Heyer tried to accommodate those who found the credibility of certain doctrines hard to accept, but in Van den Brink's opinion, too much that is essential is lost in the accommodation. He emphasises the seriousness of what is at stake. According to some, were Den Heyer's views to prevail, they would empty the Church. It is extremely important to remind ourselves, when we talk of theologians as managers of change that 'theologians are *themselves* involved in processes of change.' I think Van den Brink also reminds us of something extremely important when he says that theologians do not create their innovative proposals out of nothing: 'Rather, like other people, they *find themselves* believing or not believing or no longer believing particular things and doctrines.' His conclusion is that some common hermeneutical assumptions need to be reversed, since, in them, 'the conceptual categories of a specific culture or philosophy easily become the basic framework of interpretation.' By contrast, 'the primary way of transmitting the faith down through the centuries was not to accommodate the Christian message to contemporary sensibilities or to redescribe it into new concepts, but to teach the alien language and practices of the faith to potential adherents, and of course to enact these language and practices both in one's personal life as well as in the communal life.' Of course, this does not settle anything about competing understandings of traditional doctrines, but it warns against a too easy theological complacency about communicating these doctrines. Theology, in Lindbeck's words, 'should instead prepare for a future when continuing dechristianization will make greater Christian authenticity communally possible.'[7] But even this does not take seriously enough, it seems to me, the non-accidental difficulty cultural changes may create for the communal retention of certain Christian concepts.

This raises the whole question of whether optimism is a necessary feature of Christian hermeneutics. We can reflect on this question, usefully, when reading David Brown's contribution to the final symposium on 'Hermeneutics and Change in Religious Traditions.' With this symposium we have come full circle and returned to the issues with which we began. Brown begins with the words: 'Vincent Brümmer's valedictory lecture has two principal concerns, to locate some of the forces for change within a religious tradition and to reflect upon what then gives identity to the tradition over time.' Instead of discussing the issue in general terms, however, he presents us with two case studies, one of the suffering Job and the other of the Nativity stories. In each case, he is concerned to show 'why it is that communities of faith can come to form versions of a narrative that diverge substantially from what appears on the written page and make this the hermeneutical grid through

---

7   George Lindbeck, *The Nature of Doctrine: Religion and Theology in a Postliberal Age* (Philadelphia 1984), 134.

which that page is read.' In this the historical method is invaluable, in that it shows the nature of the pressures at any given time for going beyond the written word.

Brown's account of changes which actually took place is fascinating, and we can certainly learn from them. What we learn, however, is a complex question. I shall comment on some features of the understanding of Job in order to pose some philosophical (and perhaps theological) questions in the light of Brown's account. The fruition of the changes in our understanding of Job is said to show 'an initially self-satisfied Job presented as choosing to learn through his suffering and thus in this way become more Christ-like and so in deeper communion with God.' But suppose I have never thought of Job as self-satisfied, would I be told that this is because I have benefited from the changes Brown enumerates? What if I see Job's appeals to his own righteousness as a bewilderment which results from the apologetics of his Comforters? Job may be saying: *if you argue like this*, linking misfortune to deeds performed, then a comparison between us would show ... In other words, I have always read the Book of Job in ways closely related to the reading which Brown sees as imaginative growth. The issue is not whether I am right or wrong, but whether I *could* be right. In other words, is the picture more ragged than Brown suggests? Similar issues arise in the case studies Henk Vroom provides in his reply, regarding changing attitudes towards homosexuality and the place of women in one of the Reformed churches in the Netherlands.

Both writers would surely agree that the changes referred to have not been without friction. The picture is not one of an agreed unfolding of an ever richer story. At times, when the story takes a certain direction, some would speak of betrayal where others would speak of enrichment. It is no answer to tell the former that *their* preference was itself the product of change, since the whole issue concerns which changes are for the better or for the worse. Vroom is well aware of these complexities. How could he not be when some left the church over them? Discussing the language of God as Father, he rightly concludes that 'whether we use it or not says something about ourselves at the same time.' And we are a mixed bunch.

Going back to Job. Some have used the Book as a humanistic iconoclastic attack on religion which has hoodwinked the faithful into making this demolition job the corner-stone of their Faith![8] Brown insists that what he has been sketching 'is not at all the development of a philosophical solution to the problem of evil. That raises quite other issues.' But what if the issues it raises are the very ones that the Book of Job is protesting against, namely, the attempt to explain suffering in terms

---

8   See H. Tennessen, 'A Masterpiece of Existential Blasphemy: The Book of Job,' *The Human World* 13 (Nov. 1973). For my reply see 'On Not Understanding God,' in: *Wittgenstein and Religious Beliefs* (London 1993).

of theodicy, terms which, in one way or another, still dominate contemporary philosophy of religion? What is more, such theodicies enter into popular religion, practical pastoralia, etc. Are they imaginative extensions of a tradition or vulgarisations of the language of faith? In which way do most Christians think? Are we living at a time when religious language has been enriched by imaginative changes in this respect, or emaciated by disastrous accommodations? One need not deny that there have been imaginative changes, but do they predominate? It would be interesting, I suspect, to compare the answers Brown and Vroom would give to these questions, with the ways in which Van den Brink would answer them. What would the latter think of Sia's Whiteheadian proposals in the first symposium? Certainly, there is a great distance between them, but in which direction are we travelling: up or down?

The posing of this question brings us back to an observation we have made more than once: the theologian is part of the tradition and change he is reflecting on. Is this true of the philosopher too? A theologian, it seems to me, is a citizen of a community of ideas, whereas it has been claimed that a philosopher is not, and that is what makes him or her a philosopher. Some theologians in the conference balked at this suggestion, reluctant to let philosophy exist beyond their hermeneutic grasp, even a philosophy which teaches differences. This issue cannot be taken further here, but it is one which repays serious study, especially in a context in which theologians and philosophers come together to reflect on tradition and change. Whatever our view of their respective tasks, we need to proceed with caution for, adopting what has been said in a related, but different, context: if the very light by which we theologise or philosophise be darkness, how great is that darkness.

2. The Identity of the Christian Tradition

Vincent Brümmer (Utrecht)

1 Pluralism and Change

One of the five domes of St. Mark's cathedral in Venice is adorned on the inside by a magnificent mosaic representing the descent of the Holy Spirit at Pentecost. Around the rim of the mosaic there is a procession of exotic figures, each distinguished from the others by his or her own characteristic style of dress, headgear, beard, etc. These represent the Parthians, Medes, Elamites, Mesopotamians, Cappadocians, Phrygians, Cretans, etc. who, according to Acts 2:5f, were all amazed on that day by the fact that each of them could hear the message of the apostles in his or her own language. It became clear to them that the Christian message was not bound to one single language or culture, but could be expressed in all languages and in the conceptual forms of every culture. According to the Gambian theologian Lamin Sanneh,[1] this is a distinguishing feature of Christianity when compared to Islam. While in Islam the Koran is claimed to have been dictated word for word in Arabic to Mohammed, the New Testament message was written in Greek by Aramaic speaking Jews whose holy books were in Hebrew. Furthermore, while the Koran was written down by one single author, the New Testament message was witnessed to by a number of evangelists and apostles, each of whom expressed it in his own words, from his own perspective and in terms which were intelligible and relevant to his own specific audience.

Each author listened to God's Word in Christ from a particular viewpoint, largely determined by the spiritual-cultural situation of the Christian community to which he belonged. Each author preached the Good News with the focus required for making it God's Word of salvation to his people. The several focal points in the books of the New Testament explain why it is impossible to reconcile the various positions into a single consistent system of thought. ... To proclaim the Gospel in a manner comprehensible to her age, the Church must translate her message into the language and the concepts of the culture in which she lives and reply to the questions which are being asked in her day.[2]

---

1 Lamin D. Sanneh, *Translating the Message* (Maryknoll, NY 1989).
2 Gregory Baum, *The Credibility of the Church Today* (New York 1968), 154.

23

Clearly then, plurality of expression was a characteristic feature of the Christian message from its very beginnings.

Clearly, this plurality is not only synchronic at any given time but also diachronic through the course of history. Religious traditions like Christianity are not timelessly immutable but constantly require translation, re-conceptualization and re-interpretation in order to maintain their relevance and adequacy, as well as their intelligibility and credibility. Let me briefly elaborate on these four requirements.

1. *Relevance.* Even those religious beliefs which are claimed to be true at all times, are not thereby also automatically relevant at all times.[3] In the words of Jesus, 'a teacher of the law ... is like a householder who can produce from his store things new and old' (Matth. 13:52), and what the teacher produces depends in the end on what is relevant to the situation and to the audience for whom it is produced. In order to be relevant, every expression of the faith within a religious tradition is therefore necessarily one-sided and selective,[4] and in different situations and different periods in history different aspects are emphasized as especially relevant and of central importance to the demands of the day whereas others are overlooked or ignored as irrelevant or peripheral.

> Every age has its central questions; every age has its own way of being threatened and its own aspirations for a more human form of existence. ... Since the divine self-revelation in Christ is the Good News for every age, the same and identical message will be focalized differently in different ages, depending on the principle problems of men and their deep aspirations. ... As the Church enters a new spiritual-cultural environment in which people see life differently, have new questions and new ideals, she seeks to proclaim the Gospel with a new central message and thrust as the divine response to the central problems of the age.[5]

This has important implications for the nature of doctrinal development in a religious tradition. The way in which systematic theologians present the faith of the religious community as a coherent whole, depends in the end on the 'key model' or central focus in terms of which such a synthesis is constructed.[6] Changing the key

---

3   Cf. Maurice Wiles, *The Making of Christian Doctrine* (Cambridge 1967), 9.
4   Elsewhere I have argued that this selectivity and one-sidedness is a necessary effect of the metaphorical nature of religious language. See chapter 1 of my *The Model of Love* (Cambridge 1993).
5   Baum, *Credibility*, 152-153.
6   On the role of 'key models' in theology, see chapter 1 of my *Model of Love.*

model, can have far reaching effects on the doctrinal synthesis which is proposed. 'As the old focus gives way to the new, the entire doctrinal synthesis of the past falls apart in order to be made anew in the light of the new focus. The old way of seeing doctrines together in unity is dissolved: what is required in the new situation is their re-interpretation in the light of the new focal point.'[7] Clearly then, the faith of a religious tradition needs to be continually re-interpreted and re-conceptualized in different ways in order to remain relevant for the changing demands of life. But relevance is not enough.

2. *Adequacy.* Even if we were to select and highlight only those aspects of the faith which are relevant to the situation in which we find ourselves, this does not automatically mean that these aspects are conceptualized or developed in ways which are adequate for dealing with the demands of this situation. In order to be adequate, the faith which is handed down in a religious tradition needs to be developed creatively in ways which address the issues and demands which arise in the ever changing situations in which believers find themselves. It is therefore not enough merely to repeat the relevant aspects of what was said in the past in the way in which these were conceptualized in the past.

> Listening to the divine Word in Scripture and in the Church's past tradition has its limitations. Salvational questions may arise in a new spiritual-cultural environment which cannot be answered by a fresh return to Scripture and past tradition. These may be questions which the ancients did not ask, or could not, in their cultural context, have asked; and if these questions were foreign to them it is impossible to find a definite answer to them in the literature which expresses their faith. There may be hints in this literature, marginal remarks and suggestions which could be helpful to the Christian in search of God's message, but these remain too vague and too inconclusive for formulating the reply of faith with assurance.[8]

It is clear that the doctrines of faith developed by theologians in the course of the Christian tradition were not derived from the biblical writings by a mere exegetical reconstruction of what the biblical authors were intending to say. Nor were they the result of making explicit propositions which were implicitly intended by these authors all along. 'It is clearly impossible (if one accepts historical evidence as relevant at all) to escape the claim that the later formulations of dogma cannot be

---

7   Baum, *Credibility*, 153.
8   Baum, *Credibility*, 161.

reached by a process of deductive logic from the original propositions and must contain an element of novelty.'[9] Christian doctrine arises through the creative development by later theologians of what was often no more than 'hints, marginal remarks and suggestions' (Baum) which the original biblical authors could not possibly have conceived of thus in their time and circumstances. Thus the innovative development which is characteristic of a religious tradition will always involve the introduction of new elements which were not there before. In the words of my late Utrecht colleague Arnold van Ruler: 'Is it possible that no new things and no new truths and no new realities are being revealed? Is it not precisely one of the secrets of history that it is being wholly renewed over and over again in an incomprehensible spontaneity and creativity? ... This evolution embraces constantly renewed integration of new elements which arise in the historical process.[10] A case in point is the doctrine of atonement. My late Oxford tutor professor Ian Ramsey pointed out that

> in the earliest preaching of the gospel the Crucifixion had little significance of its own, and figured in the kerygma only in so far as the apostles proclaimed that God had now raised up him who earlier had been crucified. ... The Crucifixion was thus something which the kerygma presupposed, as that which preceded the raising up. The climax of Peter's speech at Pentecost was that 'God hath made him both Lord and Christ, this Jesus whom ye crucified' (Acts 2.36). In this way the Crucifixion figured only indirectly in the earliest apostolic preaching.[11]

Nevertheless, Ramsey argues, the Biblical writings do provide a variety of metaphors (justification, substitution, satisfaction, reconciliation, redemption, propitiation, sacrifice, love, etc.) in terms of which the religious meaning which the Crucifixion has for believers, can be explained. By creatively developing these metaphors into systematic models of atonement, theologians have in the course of the Christian tradition proposed various versions of the doctrine of atonement,[12] each of which has to be judged on its adequacy for the situation in which believers find themselves. There is therefore nothing surprising in the claim recently defended by the Dutch New Testament scholar C.J. den Heyer that the traditional substitution-

---

9 Wiles, *Making of Christian Doctrine*, 4.
10 A.A. van Ruler, 'The Evolution of Dogma,' in: D.J. Callahan, H.A. Oberman & D.J. O'Hanlon (eds.), *Christianity Divided* (New York 1961), 100.
11 Ian T. Ramsey, *Christian Discourse* (Oxford 1965), 30.
12 Ramsey, 31-60. See also my own proposal (*The Model of Love* chapter 8) to develop this doctrine in terms of a model of love.

ary doctrine of atonement cannot be found as such in the New Testament writings.[13]

3. *Intelligibility*. People derive their own categories of understanding from the culture into which they have themselves been socialized. The message of a religious tradition can therefore only be intelligible to them to the extent that it can be translated into these categories or is expressed in terms which show some recognizable continuity with them.[14] Since cultures are not static and categories of understanding are not timeless, the Church must always translate her message anew into the categories and concepts which are current in the culture of her day or familiar to the audience to whom she addresses her message. This kind of translation can already be found in the Bible itself. A good example is Jesus's remark about the necessity of our lamp not being hid under a bushel. Of this David Brown points out that

the phraseology in Matthew's version ('put it on a stand and it will give light to all in the house') assumes the typical one-roomed Palestinian house, and so must be original; whereas Luke alters what were almost certainly Jesus's actual words to reflect the larger Hellenistic house of the day, with its separate entrance passage from which light would shine on those entering it ('put it on a stand so that those who enter may see it'). ... Luke was clearly determined that the illustration should immediately come alive, as it were, for his non-Jewish readers, and so does not hesitate to alter the words actually spoken.[15]

The Ghanaian theologian Kwame Bediako has carefully analyzed the way in which the church fathers transposed the Christian message from its original Jewish matrix into the categories of understanding of Hellenistic culture, and argued persuasively that an analogous kind of re-conceptualization is required to make the Gospel intelligible in an African context today.[16] In this connection he quotes the words of bishop Bengt Sundkler: 'A theologian who with the Apostle is prepared to become to the Jews as a Jew, to them that are without law, as without law, and *therefore* unto Africans as an African, must needs start with the fundamental facts of the African interpretation of existence and the universe.'[17]

---

13   C.J. den Heyer, *Verzoening: Bijbelse notities bij een omstreden thema* (Kampen 1997).

14   Cf. Denis Nineham, *The Use and Abuse of the Bible* (London 1976), chapter 1 for an extended and illuminating explanation of these points.

15   David Brown, 'Did Revelation Cease?' in: A.G. Padgett (ed.), *Reason and the Christian Religion* (Oxford 1994), 126.

16   Kwame Bediako, *Theology and Identity* (Oxford 1992).

17   Bengt Sundkler, *The Christian Ministry in Africa* (London 1962), 100.

4. *Credibility.* A religious tradition requires continuous re-conceptualization not only in order to remain relevant, adequate and intelligible, but also to maintain its credibility. It can happen that generally accepted ways of understanding the Christian message are falsified by new developments in our scientific knowledge of the world or by new insights about the actual course of history. In this situation believers can choose between three responses. They could retreat into obscurantism and deny or ignore the outcome of scientific inquiry. When the scientific evidence is overwhelming, this is a quite irrational way of dealing with the problem. 'One thing is certain: it can never be a Christian's duty to deny what he knows to be true or affirm what he knows to be false; and there are some things which no modern human being can affirm or deny with integrity.'[18] Secondly, believers could admit that the claims of the Christian faith have been definitely falsified by scientific or historical inquiry. This could lead them to abandon the faith or, like my Leiden colleague Han Adriaanse, claim that the progress of scientific knowledge seriously erodes the credibility of the faith and is therefore an unhappy 'thorn in the flesh' which believers will have to put up with.[19] Finally they could hold that the results of scientific inquiry falsifies our understanding of the claims of faith but not necessarily these claims themselves. What is required therefore is a reinterpretation of these claims in ways which are consistent with the incontrovertible evidence of scientific inquiry. Thus in 1996, as far as I know, no celebrations occurred anywhere to mark the sixth millennium of the creation of the world! This merely shows the universal acceptance among believers today that scientific inquiry has definitely falsified the dating by archbishop James Ussher (1581-1656) of the earth's creation on the basis of biblical genealogy tables, even though this was at one time commonly accepted among Christian apologists. Believers today will tend rather to reinterpret the biblical message of creation in ways which are consistent with current scientific knowledge. I think that this response is in accordance with the actual dynamics of change in religious traditions. Furthermore, this strategy of reinterpretation can already be found in the Bible itself. David Brown points out that 'Mark, in common with the early Paul, seems to have thought that the world would soon end, and that this was somehow bound up with the impending destruction of Jerusalem. ... By the time Luke came to write, Jerusalem had in fact been destroyed in the great revolt of AD 70. So he rewrites Jesus's words to make clear that they referred to this recent destruction, thereby, of course, divorcing the event from any connection with the end of the world.'[20]

---

18 Nineham, *Use and Abuse,* 31.
19 H.J. Adriaanse, *Vom Christentum aus* (Kampen 1995), chapter 5.
20 Brown, 126-127. In this example Brown contrasts Luke 21:20-24 (esp. v.24) with Mark 13:14-20 and I Cor. 7:29.

All these considerations make it clear that pluralism of interpretation and change in conceptualization are characteristic features of the Christian tradition, not only in the course of its history, but also in its very beginnings in the Bible itself.

2   Unity and Identity

The reality of pluralism and change in the Christian tradition raises a serious problem regarding the unity and identity of this tradition. How can we maintain that the various and changing conceptualizations of the faith within the Christian tradition, are all forms or expressions of *the same* faith? As Nicholas Lash explains,

> the difficulty arises from the conviction of Christian belief that the message proclaimed in the life, death and glorification of Jesus Christ is God's definitive word to mankind. Therefore unless the word proclaimed to men of every successive age and culture is in some significant sense, the *same* word, God's promise is not fulfilled. And yet it is clear that what Christians do, and think, and say today is very different from what they did, and thought, and said yesterday – or the day before. Therefore, we need some 'theory' or 'hypothesis' which can, so far as possible, reconcile our conviction concerning the continual availability in history of the unchanging gospel with our recognition of the extent, variety and complexity of historical change.[21]

This problem does not only regard the unity of faith but also the identity of the community of believers throughout the Christian tradition. In the words of Arnold van Ruler, 'the question at stake is whether and how we can prove that we are still the selfsame Church.'[22] Let us therefore now turn to an analysis of some of the most significant theories of identity and see which of them provides the most satisfactory solution to the problem of Christian identity.

1. *Identity and essence.* The identity of the Christian tradition is often explained in terms of the Aristotelian distinction between substantial and accidental change. Thus a tree can grow over the years, loose its leaves in the autumn and grow new leaves in spring etc. and still maintain its identity as a tree. Such changes are accidental since they affect only its accidental properties. If however it were to catch fire and be reduced to ashes, it would no longer be a tree. This would be a substantial change

---

21   Nicholas Lash, *Change in Focus* (London 1973), 59.
22   Van Ruler, 'Evolution of Dogma,' 91.

affecting its essential properties, i.e. those properties which make it to be what it is: a tree. Similarly one could distinguish between the accidental features of the Christian faith which could vary and change without the tradition ceasing to be the same Christian tradition, and those essential features of the Christian faith which make the tradition to be the Christian tradition it is. These have to remain the same throughout the history of the tradition. If they were to be modified, the tradition would lose its identity as the Christian tradition. In this way, for example, Origen in *De Principiis* distinguished between articles of faith which are essential to salvation and those which may legitimately be regarded as speculative.[23] A more recent example is Helmut Thielicke's contribution to the demythologization debate, where he asserts that 'every theologian ... must decide what is the kernel of the gospel, and what is merely the outward husk which has been shaped by human imagination, by traditional interpretation, by the tendency to produce credal formulae, by the subsequent historical consolidation of the truths of faith. What is 'truth' and what is 'mythology'? What is divine and what is human?'[24] The difficulty with this distinction is that we have no obvious or universally recognized criteria for distinguishing between essential and accidental properties, between the kernel and the husk. For this reason none of the ways in which people tend to draw this distinction, seem to be satisfactory.

Sometimes the distinction has been interpreted as one between features which are common to all instances of a phenomenon and those which vary between instances. Thus in the fifth century Vincent of Lerins[25] referred to the essential and invariable elements of the faith as 'what has been believed everywhere, always and by all' (*quod ubique, quod semper, quod ab omnibus creditum est*). In the nineteenth century Schleiermacher argued that 'the only pertinent way of discovering the peculiar essence of any particular faith and reducing it as far as possible to a formula is by showing the elements which remain constant throughout the most diverse religious affections within the same communion, while it is absent from analogous affections within other communions.'[26] This strategy fails for two important reasons. First of all, trying to identify Christianity in this way by its lowest common denominator, would entail an unacceptable reduction, since it excludes as unessential or irrelevant whatever is particular or special or unique for any specific expression of the Christian tradition. 'Is a student to dismiss as no part of Christianity anything in the Puritan movement that Mexican villagers do not share? – or any-

23 Cf. Stephen Sykes, *The Identity of Christianity* (London 1984), 232.
24 Helmut Thielicke, 'The Restatement of New Testament Mythology,' in: H.W. Bartsch (ed.), *Kerygma and Myth* (London 1957), 139-140.
25 *Commonitorium* II, 1-3.
26 F. Schleiermacher, *The Christian Faith* (London 1968), 52.

thing that Aquinas thought, with which the mystic Meister Eckhart and the evangelist Billy Sunday do not both agree. ... By this definition, the more elaborate and varied a tradition historically becomes, the thinner becomes the religion of which it is the embodiment. Sufficient external variety could reduce internal meaning to zero.'[27] In fact, we will have a hard time finding any tenets of the Christian faith which have been invariable in the strict sense of being free from all re-interpretation throughout the history of Christianity. Secondly, this strategy fails because it begs the question. In order to determine which elements are common to all instances of Christianity, we first have to decide what counts as an instance and that in turn requires us already to know the common elements which we are seeking to determine. Neither are we able to break out of this circle by limiting ourselves to those elements which are typical of mainstream Christianity throughout history. For who decides what is to count as 'mainstream'? In fact, all talk of 'mainstream Christianity' has usually been a rather eurocentric pre-occupation which has by now become totally implausible since the vast majority of Christians in the world today come from Asia, Africa and South America.

An alternative way of distinguishing the essential from the variable features of the Christian tradition, is suggested by John Hick's remark that the quest for the 'essence of Christianity' is ambiguous: 'There are two different things we might be looking for. We might be looking for *that which is most important in Christianity.* Or we might be looking for *that which is uniquely Christian* and not paralleled in any other faith.'[28] Thus the 'essence' of the Christian tradition can not only refer, as in the previous paragraph, to that which is uniquely common to all instances of Christianity, but also to those elements of the Christian faith which believers consider to be of fundamental importance and are therefore not willing to subject to re-interpretation or modification. Unfortunately this way of distinguishing the kernel from the husk does not provide us with anything which necessarily remains immutably the same throughout all time, since believers differ as to which elements of faith they consider fundamental and beyond dispute. Furthermore, aspects of the faith which at one time were generally considered indisputable within the community of believers, could nevertheless be modified and re-interpreted in various ways or even abandoned altogether at a later date. Thus for example, Marcel Sarot has shown how the doctrine of divine impassibility, according to which God is by nature unable to suffer, was universally accepted in the early church. Even the patripassianists and the theopaschitists are mistakenly trotted out as examples to the contrary.[29]

---

27 W. Cantwell Smith, *The Meaning and End of Religion* (London 1978), 149.
28 John Hick, *God and the Universe of Faiths* (London 1973), 108.
29 Marcel Sarot, 'Patripassianism, Theopaschitism and the Suffering of God,' *Religious Studies* 26 (1990), 363-375.

If anything, this was a fundamental tenet of faith 'believed everywhere, always and by all,' and nobody in the community of believers would even have contemplated to contest it. In contemporary theology, however, as Ronald Goetz points out, 'the rejection of the ancient doctrine of divine impassibility has become a theological commonplace.'[30]

Which elements of faith require modification or re-interpretation depends on the actual circumstances in which believers find themselves and on whether their relevance, adequacy, intelligibility or credibility are in any way called into question by these circumstances. It is however impossible for all aspects of someone's faith to be modified at the same time. 'Those who have new things to communicate do so by means of modifications of previously held beliefs. The modifications may be slight, or they may be far-reaching; but they can never be total.'[31] The total body of beliefs maintained by an individual or by a community of believers, can be compared to a raft afloat at sea. At any one time one or more planks in the raft may require to be repaired or replaced. It is however impossible to repair or replace all the planks at the same time. Most of them have to remain in place since we need to stand on these while repairing the others. At any one time every believer or community of believers will necessarily have to treat most of their beliefs as the undisputed foundations of faith on which they stand. But this is no guarantee that these same beliefs may not be questioned, re-interpreted, modified or even rejected by believers at some other time in the future. Many religious beliefs may be paradigmatic for the believers who hold them. But then, as Thomas Kuhn has shown, even paradigms are subject to shifts and therefore not timelessly immutable. Believers must claim that their beliefs are true, but this does not entail the claim that they are also infallible! The Cartesian ideal of indubitable first principles and the Hegelian ideal of attainable Absolute Knowledge are no more than chimaera's. 'No one at any stage can ever rule out the future possibility of their present beliefs and judgements being shown to be inadequate in a variety of ways.'[32]

Christians may respond to this by pointing out that the identity of the Christian tradition is guaranteed by the abiding presence throughout the ages of the Spirit of God within the community of faith. But then, the Spirit of God is like the wind which 'blows where it wills; you hear the sound of it, but you do not know where it comes from or where it is going' (John 3:8). The abiding presence of the Spirit is therefore not necessarily manifested by the presence of an immutable essence discernable in the faith or in the life of the community of believers. Essentialist definitions of the identity of the Christian tradition are clearly faced by insurmount-

---

30   Ronald Goetz, 'The Suffering God,' *The Christian Century* 103 (1986), 385.
31   Sykes, *Identity*, 18.
32   Alasdair MacIntyre, *Whose Justice? Which Rationality?* (London 1988), 361.

able difficulties. Would it not be more satisfactory rather to understand the identity of the tradition in terms of the continuity of its history? Could this continuity not also be taken as a sign of the abiding presence of the Spirit of God?

2. *Identity and continuity.* A popular example sometimes employed in discussions of identity theory, is that of the ship built by Theseus[33] which, after its first voyage, returned to its home port battered by the storms it had endured. After repairs in which all the broken planks were replaced by new ones, it left on its second voyage in which it again had to weather the storms. After fifty voyages followed each time by repairs, there was no single plank left of the original ship. Nevertheless, we would still tend to call it the 'same ship,' which we would not have done if the ship had been destroyed in a storm and replaced by an exact replica called 'Theseus II.' The identity of the ship is located in the recognizable continuity of its history rather than in any of its parts which remain immutably the same throughout this history. In Wittgensteinian terms, we might say that its identity is found in the family resemblance between all the stages in its history.

This form of identity can be applied to cultural traditions in general and to religious traditions in particular. Contrary to what Plato thought, the conceptual forms of human thinking are not timelessly immutable. They have what in contemporary German hermeneutical theory is called a *Wirkungsgeschichte* within the continuous historical process of a cultural tradition. This also applies to religious forms of thought and life and the religious traditions in which they are embedded. A religious tradition is not an immutable set of religious forms of thought and practice, but a process with a *Wirkungsgeschichte* in which religious faith is handed down from one person to another and from generation to generation. Wilfred Cantwell Smith emphasizes the 'cumulative character' of this process:[34] In a process of socialization religious believers receive from the past a heritage in the form of rites, ideas, group pressures, family influences, vocabulary, social institutions, etc. This heritage includes the totality of forms in which their predecessors had expressed in thought and action the faith which they in turn had received from their predecessors. What they handed down in this way was however not identical to what they had received. By making the faith their own and by expressing it authentically in ways which were relevant, adequate, intelligible and credible in their own changing circumstances, they had added their own form to it. In the same way the present generation of believers will hand down the religious heritage which they

---

33   This example comes from Thomas Hobbes, *De Corpore* 11.7 and has been popularized in recent discussions of identity theory by David Wiggins, *Sameness and Substance* (Oxford 1980).
34   Cantwell Smith, *Meaning and End*, chapter 6.

have received in a modified form to those who come after them. Thus a religious tradition is a cumulative process of interactions between the religious heritage which is handed down and the personal faith of those who make this heritage authentically their own. The heritage which has been handed down does not include the later expressions of faith. On the contrary, these are added to it cumulatively. The faith of later generations is conditioned by the heritage but not completely determined by it. The personal faith of every believer adds his or her own authentic expression to it. The later history of the tradition is the prolongation and enrichment of its earlier existence as modified by the intervention of the personal faith and activities of countless members of the community of believers.

Thus understood, a religious tradition consists of a series of overlapping chains of events. Although no longer identical, consecutive chains do have much in common. The further such chains are historically removed from each other, however, the less they have in common. In fact, there is no guarantee that all the varying chains which make up the tradition will share any identical and unchanging elements. In this way a religious tradition is identified with its history. In the words of Cantwell Smith, 'the thread running through all the diverse phenomena of any tradition, linking them together, would thus be simply that of continuity, some being related to others only in that they have grown out of them. This does justice to the richness and complexity of the traditions, ever growing, ever changing; to their humanity; and to their openness towards the future.'[35] Cantwell Smith doubts, however, whether this view can satisfy the believer. 'One has misunderstood a people if one does not sense that their faith is greater than its history, is above the sins and foibles and distractions of those who profess it. ... What have been called man's religions, then, are as any historian can see involved in history; that is, in change, in imperfection, in the hurly-burly of the mundane. Yet also, as any participant can testify, they involve the transcendent – the abiding, the ideal.'[36] For Cantwell Smith, then, the identity of a religious tradition is not found merely in the continuity of its history, but above all in the abiding Transcendent to whom all believers respond in the ever varying expressions of their personal faith. The trouble with this view is that it makes the identity of a religious tradition a matter of faith rather than of sight. Participants in a tradition may believe that they are all responding to the same abiding Transcendent, but they lack the phenomenological criteria to show that this is indeed the case. They may all believe that their faith has been inspired by the Spirit of the Transcendent, but they lack a procedure 'to test the spirits, to see whether they are from God' (I John 4:1). Thus, if we are to determine

---

35 Cantwell Smith, *Meaning and End*, 152.
36 Cantwell Smith, *Meaning and End*, 153.

the identity of the Christian tradition, we cannot avoid 'looking for *that which is uniquely Christian* and not paralleled in any other faith' (Hick). This cannot itself be merely a matter of faith but must also be manifested in the phenomena which constitute the Christian tradition.

At this point someone might raise some doubts about whether we have done justice to the actual phenomenological unity displayed by a religious tradition. Alasdair MacIntyre has argued persuasively that a tradition is more than a mere complex sequence of overlapping but distinct episodes. It is a unified whole which provides the context within which alone these various episodes are intelligible.

> A course of human events ... is a complex sequence of individual actions. ... The point about such a sequence is that each element in them is intelligible as an action only as a-possible-element-in-a-sequence. Moreover even such a sequence requires a context to be intelligible. If in the middle of my lecture on Kant's ethics I suddenly broke six eggs into a bowl and added flower and sugar, proceeding all the while with my Kantian exegesis, I have *not*, simply by virtue of the fact that I was following a sequence prescribed [in the cookery book] by Fanny Farmer, performed an intelligible action.[37]

According to MacIntyre, this is also the way in which speech-acts are related to the conversations which provide the context of their intelligibility.

> Consider what is involved in following a conversation and finding it intelligible or unintelligible. ... If I listen to a conversation between two other people my ability to grasp the thread of the conversation will involve an ability to bring it under one out of a set of descriptions in which the degree and kind of coherence in the conversation is brought out: 'a drunken, rambling quarrel,' 'a serious intellectual disagreement,' 'a tragic misunderstanding of each other' ..., 'a struggle to dominate each other.' ... We allocate conversations to genres, just as we do with literary narratives. Indeed a conversation is a dramatic work ..., in which the participants are not only the actors, but also the joint authors, ... working out in agreement and disagreement the mode of their production. ... Conversation, understood widely enough, is the form of human transactions in general.'[38]

---

37   MacIntyre, *After Virtue* (London ²1985), 209.
38   MacIntyre, *After Virtue*, 211.

The unity and coherence of conversations and human transactions is therefore the unity and coherence of 'enacted narratives' within which individual human activities and speech-acts are intelligible. It is only within the context of a conversation that a speech-act can be understood as a challenge or response, agreement or disagreement, consensus or conflict, raising a new point, changing the subject, joking, misunderstanding, etc. Divorced from the context, speech-acts are not intelligible at all.[39]

Similarly the unity and coherence of a religious tradition is that of an 'enacted narrative.' Religious traditions can be understood as a genre of conversation carried on through time. In this sense G.K. Chesterton is correct that 'tradition is only democracy extended through time... Tradition may be defined as an extension of franchise. Tradition means giving votes to the most obscure of all classes, our ancestors.'[40] The narrative unity of the tradition does not require any *a priori* points of agreement shared by all participants. Engaging together in a conversation does not necessarily entail an invariable consensus between all partners. On the contrary,

> traditions, when vital, embody continuities of conflict. ... A living tradition then is an historically extended, socially embodied argument, and an argument precisely in part about the goods which constitute that tradition. Within a tradition the pursuit of goods extends through generations. ... Once again the narrative phenomenon of embedding is crucial: the history of a practice in our time is generally and characteristically embedded in and made intelligible in terms of the larger and longer history of the tradition through which the practice in its present form was conveyed to us.[41]

These considerations are helpful in explaining the unified and coherent nature of the continuity of religious traditions. But does this *continuity*, however unified and coherent it may be, suffice to explain the *identity* of the tradition? Do these considerations remove the doubts which we expressed above? The unity of a conversation is given in the interaction between its participants. Similarly the unity of the Christian tradition is given in the interaction between members of the community of believers throughout the ages. But who is to count as a member of this community? Do all those involved in the conversation count as such? 'A religious tradition ... is the historical construct, in continuous and continuing construction, of those

---

39 On this point see my paper on 'Wittgenstein and the Irrationality of Rational Theology,' in: J.M. Byrne (ed.), *The Christian Understanding of God Today* (Dublin 1993), 88-102.
40 G.K. Chesterton, *Orthodoxy* (London 1957), 69-70.
41 MacIntyre, *After Virtue*, 222.

who participate in it. These are in interaction also ... with those who do not participate [as well as] with a total environment that may include earthquakes or modern medicines, moonlit lakes or tyrannous governments.'[42] Thus MacIntyre also points out that 'the traditions through which particular practices are transmitted and reshaped never exist in isolation from larger social traditions.'[43] How are we to distinguish a tradition from the larger one in which it is embedded? Clearly, the metaphor of a conversation can help us to understand the continuity and unity of a religious tradition, but more is required if we are to determine its limits or identity. How is the Christian conversation to be distinguished from others with which it interacts or in which it is embedded? Here again we cannot avoid 'looking for *that which is uniquely Christian* and not paralleled in any other faith' (Hick). Let us consider whether this has something to do with the source or point of origin of the tradition.

3. *Identity and origin*. At this point Saul Kripke's theory of proper names[44] might provide a useful clue. According to Kripke, proper names are 'rigid designators' in the sense that, once a name has been attached to someone or something, the name sticks despite all changes or modifications which the person or entity might undergo in the course of time. Thus a speaker uses a name correctly if there is a suitable chain of communication linking *his* use of the name with the individual designated by the name in an initial 'baptism.' Naming an entity can be compared to fixing a harpoon to a whale:[45] The line connecting the harpoon to the ship, maintains the link between the whale and the whaler in spite of all the irregularities of the route along which the whale chooses to swim. Thus there are two necessary conditions for something to maintain its identity as the entity to which the name refers: the continuity of its history as well as the fixed origin to which it is linked by this continuous history. Continuity is not enough. Without the unbroken link with the same origin, something cannot remain the same entity it originally was. In this sense Kripke claims that 'the *origin* of an object is essential to it.'[46] If the historical chain of communication no longer links something with the same origin, it loses its identity as the same object. Thus Kripke points out that 'obviously the name passes on from link to link. But of course not every sort of causal chain reaching from me to a certain man will do for me to make a reference. There may be a causal chain from

42   Cantwell Smith, *Meaning and End*, 165-166.
43   MacIntyre, *After Virtue*, 221. Cf. his remarks on the ways in which 'one narrative may be embedded in another' 213.
44   Saul Kripke, *Naming and Necessity* (Oxford 1980).
45   For this metaphor, see Susan Haack, *Philosophy of Logics* (Cambridge 1978), 64.
46   Kripke, *Naming and Necessity*, 114.

our use of the term 'Santa Claus' to a certain historical saint, but still the children, when they use this, by this time probably do not refer to that saint.'[47] Unlike the Dutch Sinterklaas, the American Santa Clause is no longer identical with St. Nicholas, since the name has now come to refer to someone coming at Christmas time with his reindeer sleigh from Greenland and no longer to the original Bishop of Myra whose birthday is on December 6th.

Understood in this way, the unity of the Christian tradition may be determined by its narrative continuity, but its identity depends also on its recognizable link with a fixed point of origin: the life and death of Jesus Christ. However, this is not merely a neutral event in which the Christian tradition happens to find its starting-point, but also an event which has a special significance within the Christian tradition. The Christian conversation throughout its history is embedded in the broader religious conversation about the meaning of human existence in which many others besides Christians alone are involved. This context determines the nature and meaning (or what MacIntyre calls the 'genre') of the Christian conversation as such. The identity of the Christian tradition embedded within this broader conversation, is therefore to be found not merely in the Christian's acknowledgement of the Christ event as the fixed origin of the tradition but also in the recognition of it as the original locus of meaning for human existence. Other religious traditions participating in the broader conversation, find this original locus of meaning elsewhere. As Nicholas Lash explains,

the Christian's basic question is: 'Whether or not the meaning of human existence is to be worked out in view of the Christ event?.' What differentiates the Christian from the non-Christian is that the former is the man who, in the concrete, has been brought personally face-to-face with that question (albeit often in a very existential, unacademic, 'simple' way), and has answered: 'Yes.' The form of his response, his 'Yes,' will be his confession of faith and a life lived in obedience to that commitment. In other words, although the answers which the church gives to the question about Christ, and to all the other questions which flow from it, may vary considerably from one historical and cultural context to another, the question to which they are forms of affirmative response is perennial and unchanging.[48]

---

47 Kripke, *Naming and Necessity*, 93.
48 Lash, *Change in Focus*, 178.

'Christianity' is what Stephen Sykes calls an 'essentially contested concept'[49] in the sense that the Christian tradition is an ongoing dispute about the meaning and interpretation of this term. The unity and identity of the dispute is constituted by the shared reference to the achievement of a single original exemplar acknowledged by all participants as original locus of meaning. For all of them the nature and interpretation of this exemplar is the subject of dispute. The primary condition for such disputes about 'essentially contested concepts' is therefore 'that there must be an acknowledgement by all the contestants of the authority of the original exemplar. Although the achievement is from the first variously describable, the contestants are held together by the conviction that the contest has a single origin in a single, albeit internally complex, performance. ... The contestants who disagree about what Christianity is, are, despite their differences, disagreeing about the nature of a single 'performance' ... the connected series of events telling of the impact of Jesus Christ.'[50]

From this Sykes concludes that 'formally speaking, a Christian is defined as one who gives attention to Jesus whose achievement is contextualized by God.'[51] According to Sykes, this formal definition involves two essential elements. On the one hand, the kind of attention which Christians pay to Jesus entails that the performance or achievement of Jesus is for them the authoritative exemplar which determines the ultimate meaning of human life and experience. On the other hand, the quality of this attention is that which is due to something of ultimate and universal significance and which in this sense has divine authority. Hence, as Sykes points out, God is taken to be the context of the Christ event in the sense that from start to finish God is spoken of as initiating, accompanying and bringing to completion Jesus's achievement. To this we might add a third element: Jesus is not an arbitrary focus of attention and authority for Christians. On the contrary, they experience the Christ event as inspiring in a way which calls for it to be accorded such exemplary authority and they attribute this inspiration to the Spirit of God.

In calling this a 'formal definition,' Sykes emphasizes three things. First of all, the definition permits terms like 'Christian,' 'Christianity' and so forth to be used intelligibly by both spectators of and participants in the Christian tradition. As such it merely lays down the minimum conditions of intelligibility required for the common use of such terms. If these conditions are not met, we are no longer disputing about the same terms. Secondly, though the definition lays down hermeneutical constraints[52] on what can count as a plausible interpretation of the terms in ques-

49   Sykes, *Identity*, 251-252. Sykes makes use here of the term developed by W.B. Gallie, *Philosophy and the Historical Understanding* (London 1964).
50   Sykes, *Identity*, 254.
51   Sykes, *Identity*, 255.
52   On hermeneutical constraints, see my 'Philosophy, Theology and the Reading of Texts,' *Relig-*

tion, it nevertheless allows for a large variety of alternative interpretations. In this sense the definition does not foreclose the question of the inherent contestability of these terms, but merely provides a formal indication of the area in which the contest about their interpretation takes place. Thirdly, 'a formal definition is both banal and boring. Christianity only becomes interesting as a concept when someone has the courage to spell out in greater or lesser detail one or other of the contestable possibilities which the definition permits.'[53] The history of Christian theology is the history of the various attempts to spell out these possibilities and to argue for or against alternative proposals to do so.

In this way, for example, the trinitarian structure of most early Christian creeds reflects and develops the three essential elements of the formal definition of Christianity noted above: Christ as exemplary authority, God as the transcendent context for understanding the Christ event, and the Spirit as the inspiring source of the acknowledgement which the Christian bestows on Christ. Such creeds provide summaries of the faith in which 'we are not dealing with a condensation of the whole content of Christian believing, but with a slightly elaborated version of a formal definition of the area which believing occupies. ... They are a Christian, that is, an insider's depiction of the area of contest. They are thus characteristically fuller than a merely formal definition. At the same time they permit a wide variety of arguments to be developed both about the content of Christian belief and the norms for deciding what constitutes Christian belief.'[54] However, these early creeds are not the first attempt at elaborating the meaning of this formal definition. The contest about how to interpret the Christ event starts in the Bible itself. In fact we have no direct unambiguous access to this event itself. Our only access to it is found in the (for believers paradigmatic) attempts by the biblical authors to witness to and explain the meaning which this event is to have for the followers of Jesus. Since these attempts are themselves interpretations, the process of interpretation begins within the Bible itself. Thus Stephen Sykes points out that 'we are already, in the first decades after Jesus' life and death, embroiled in the problems of conflicting interpretations of his teaching. Paul himself is already a commentator lodged in the history of tradition. There is no primitive period of immediate and unambiguous clarity.'[55] In fact, 'internal conflict between Christians with differing apprehensions of the gospel is not an anomalous or unusual phenomenon. On the contrary,

---

ious Studies 27 (1991), 451-462 and chapter 5 of my *Wijsgerige Begripsanalyse* (Kampen ⁴1995).

53   Sykes, *Identity*, 256.
54   Sykes, *Identity*, 257-258.
55   Sykes, *Identity*, 15.

it is, and always has been normal. Unity, peace and love are achieved by the containment of conflict within bound, not by its elimination.'[56]

We can now conclude that the unity and identity of the Christian tradition can be found in the narrative continuity of the historical process of interpretation which starts in the Bible itself and refers to the connected series of events telling of the impact of Jesus Christ, who is acknowledged by believers to be the fixed origin of the tradition as well as the original locus of meaning for human existence. The heritage which is passed down from generation to generation in this tradition is however by no means timelessly immutable but requires constant translation, re-conceptualization and re-interpretation in the light of the ever changing demands of life confronting participants in the tradition.

In his parable *Haroen and the Sea of Stories*, Salman Rushdie describes how the little boy Haroen accompanied by Iff, the Water Genie, was adrift in the Ocean of the Streams of Story on the back of the mechanical hoopoe bird Butt.

> He [Haroen] looked into the water and saw that it was made up of a thousand thousand thousand and one different currents, each one a different colour, weaving in and out of one another like a liquid tapestry of breathtaking complexity; and Iff explained that these were the Streams of Story, that each coloured strand represented and contained a single tale. Different parts of the Ocean contained different sorts of stories, and as all the stories that had ever been told and many that were still in the process of being invented could be found here, the Ocean of the Streams of Story was in fact the biggest library in the universe. And because the stories were held here in fluid form, they retained the ability to change, to become new versions of themselves, to join up with other stories and so become yet other stories; so that unlike a library of books, the Ocean of the Streams of Story was much more than a storeroom of yarns. It was not dead but alive.[57]

Like the Streams of Story, the Christian heritage is handed down to us in fluid form, retaining the ability to change and to become new versions of itself. For this reason the Christian tradition is not dead but alive. It is the task of theologians to keep it so by creatively sustaining and developing our understanding of the original exemplar's achievement in ways which remain relevant, adequate, intelligible and credible in the ever changing context where we humans are called upon to live and move and have our being.

---

56   Sykes, *Identity*, 212. Cf. MacIntyre's remark that 'traditions, when vital, embody continuities of conflict' (*After Virtue*, 222). See footnote 41 above.

57   Salman Rushdie, *Haroen and the Sea of Stories* (London 1990), 72.

3. The Finality of Christ and the Authenticity of Creative Developments

Wybren de Jong (Utrecht)

1 Introduction

Christians believe that God's revelation in Christ was final. Jesus Christ is God's definitive word to mankind. This claim is central in Christian faith; it is what binds many Christians together, and it distinguishes their religion from others, like Judaism and Islam. But what is meant by such a claim? I think we can analyse it into four different subclaims: those of uniqueness, truth, completeness and decisive importance.

First, it is claimed that Christ is *unique* in comparison with various others who preached God's word, e.g. the Old Testament prophets. Jesus not only taught about the Kingdom of God, He was and is its concrete embodiment. He is God's Word become flesh, the Son of God, the second person of the Trinity, etc. Thus, Christ's uniqueness warrants the confession that He is our only Lord or that He is the ultimate source of meaning.

Second, it is believed that, in so far as God's revelation in Christ involves a propositional or ethical element, this message is unqualifiedly *true*: it does not need changes or additions in order to correct a falsity or one-sidedness.[1] This belief is a further consequence of the claim that in Christ God revealed Himself: in Him we see the Father, and whatever can be said of the Son can also truly be said of the Father (except that the Son is not the Father). Moreover, it also follows from the Christian concept of God: someone who reveals falsehoods cannot be God, since God is omniscient and perfectly good. Of course, every revelation must be interpreted by its receivers if they are to understand it as a message, and such interpretations may be false or one-sided. However, it is claimed that there are interpretations of the Christ event which yield true religious insight, and which together comprise the message which God intends to reveal.

Third, Christians claim that this was a *complete* or sufficient revelation, at least when taken in conjunction with God's revelations to the Israelites before Christ and

---

1   Of course, God's revelation in Christ is not limited to a propositional message: the message is only one aspect of this revelation amongst others.

43

to the Apostles. No further revelations are necessary to the knowledge of our salvation. Thus, in the early church Montanism was rejected, because it affirmed the necessity of new revelations by prophets after Christ.

Fourth and last, the Christ event is held to be of *decisive importance*: God once for all accomplished our salvation in His life, death and resurrection. This decisive importance of Christ for salvation is a recurrent theme both in the New Testament (e.g. John 14:6; Rom. 3:21-26), the ecumenical creeds (e.g. the Nicene) and later confessional documents. Moreover, this redemption concerns not only human individuals, but also social, economic and political structures, i.e. it encompasses the renewal of our whole culture. This has been stressed especially by liberation theologians. And finally, salvation in Christ might even extend to the earth's flora and fauna, and more widely to the cosmos as a whole. This is an emphasis which we find in contemporary ecological theologies. In sum, the finality of Christ involves the belief that He is our Lord and Saviour, and that His life and death reveal a message which is complete and unqualifiedly true.

It seems obvious that maintaining these four claims has consequences for the way in which the Christian tradition may and may not be reinterpreted in the course of history. First, if Christ's uniqueness warrants His ultimate authority, then our practices and institutions should not be incompatible with His lordship. Second, later developments in doctrine and ethics should not change or contradict the gospel, if the latter is unqualifiedly true. Third, if the revelation in Christ is complete, then every belief we hold about our salvation should be derivable from it. And finally, if the Christ event was of decisive importance, then we should always put our trust in Christ's redemptive work. In sum, the claim of Christ's finality entails at least four criteria for evaluating developments in the Christian tradition. I will call them criteria of authenticity, for they can be used to distinguish true developments from corruptions of the gospel.

In this paper, these criteria will be elaborated. In order to do so, I must first make a clear distinction between authenticity and identity. Then I will show that, at least *prima facie*, these criteria are in conflict with the universal significance of Christ, because they do not seem to allow creative developments. But finally, I will argue that there is an application of these criteria which does not have this unfortunate consequence.

2   The Distinction between Authenticity and Identity

Authenticity should not be confused with identity. Criteria of identity do not determine the truthfulness of developments, but instead they distinguish between Christianity and other religions; they demarcate the boundaries of the Christian tradition.

They distinguish between those religious movements which fall inside, and those which fall outside Christianity. Thus, they spell out the minimum conditions of intelligibility required for the common use (by believers and unbelievers) of the terms 'Christianity,' 'Christians,' etc. According to Vincent Brümmer,[2] there are only two criteria for Christian identity. The first determines the kind of continuity which is shared by all Christian movements. And the second determines what the uniqueness of Christianity is when compared to other religions.

The difference between criteria of identity and authenticity becomes clear when we realise that a development can be characteristically Christian but nevertheless unfaithful to Christ. For example, the crusades were a series of events within Christian history, and the theology which legitimated these religious wars forms an undeniable part of the Christian tradition. However, though these theologians claimed to reinterpret the significance of the Christ event, it is now clear to most Christians that they did not fully understand the Gospel. The crusades were not in line with God's revelation in Christ; they were even incompatible with it. They were a corruption that turns the Gospel into its opposite. In short, the fact that a development belongs to the Christian tradition does not imply that it satisfies the criteria of authenticity.

Similarly, the institution of slavery not only existed among Christian communities for long periods, but it was also defended by theologians on the basis of the Bible. For example, in the apostolic letters we find instructions to Christian slaves that they should obey their masters, e.g. 1 Tim. 6:1-2. Moreover, Christian slaveholders are neither reproached by the Apostles nor expelled from the church for having slaves. Advocates of slavery took such texts as signifying that God approves of this institution. However, their opponents pointed to God's deliverance of Israel from its slavery in Egypt, and argued that this proves His abhorrence of it.[3] Most Christians today would agree that advocating slavery in God's name is irreconcilable with the commandment to love one's neighbour as oneself and, even more, with God's partiality towards poor and miserable people. Thus, though the defense and promotion of slavery occurred in the Christian tradition, such developments cannot be regarded as authentic.

The theological legitimation of the crusades and of slavery are two examples of unauthentic developments within the Christian tradition, and obviously we can find many other instances of unfaithfulness to the gospel. Antisemitism, patriarchal power structures and androcentrism have all been legitimated by appealing to biblical texts. In the Gospel of John, for example, the Jews are portrayed as the main opponents and enemies of Jesus. And the twelve disciples who are called by Jesus

---

2   Vincent Brümmer, 'The Identity of the Christian Tradition,' in this volume.
3   Cf. Willard M. Swartley, *Slavery, Sabbath, War and Women: Case Issues in Biblical Interpretation* (Ontario 1983), 31-45.

are all male, according to the New Testament. Thus, we cannot deny that such ideologies have been able to find support in the Christian tradition, and even in the Bible. However, what we can and should deny is that these views are authentically Christian: it has become clear that they are incompatible with the good news about Jesus Christ.

The difference between Christian identity and authenticity is analogous to the difference between 'identity as object' and 'identity as person.' A person can be identified, i.e. distinguished from other objects and persons, if one knows a unique description of how he or she looks and behaves. Such a unique description constitutes one's identity as an object: it consists of one's actual characteristics, wishes, desires, etc. However, as a person one has the capacity for evaluating this actuality. In other words, human beings have second-order volitions.[4] They approve of some of their own volitions and character traits, and repudiate others; when these are revealed they feel ashamed. Such evaluations are based on a comparison of my actuality with an ideal picture which I make of myself. This ideal picture constitutes my identity as a person; it can be regarded as the ultimate good which I am called upon to actualize in my life. Moreover, when I claim a personal identity, I ask others to recognize this ideal as my individual and ultimate good, and to treat me accordingly. Since my existence as a person is not solipsistic, my identity claim can only be upheld to the extent that others endorse it and recognize me as the person I claim to be. Thus, whereas my identity as object is simply given by the actual state of affairs, my identity as a person depends on a consensus in which the identity which I choose as my ultimate good is endorsed by others.[5]

Analogously, a church can transcend the actual developments in its history. Some are endorsed as authentic, but others are repudiated; their occurrence is regrettable because they are instances of unfaithfulness to Christ. The actual history of the church is compared to an ideal picture of the community of the Lord: the latter is made explicit in an ecclesiology. In this way we can reinterpret the traditional distinction between the visible and the invisible church. The invisible or ideal church is a genuine follower of Christ, though the visible or actual churches fall short of this ideal. Thus, believers claim that there is more to their church than the imperfect actuality which historians can observe. Wilfred Cantwell Smith has stated this point somewhat more generally: 'one has misunderstood a people if one does not sense that their faith is greater than its history, is above the sins and foibles and

---

4   This term was introduced by Harry G. Frankfurt, *The Importance of What We Care about* (Cambridge 1988), 16.
5   For this exposition of the difference between 'identity as object' and 'identity as person' I depend on Vincent Brümmer, 'Religious Belief and Personal Identity,' *Neue Zeitschrift für Systematische Theologie und Religionsphilosophie* 38 (1996), 155-165.

distractions of those who profess it.' This sentence might be interpreted as a general injunction to acknowledge and identify with the ultimate good of religious communities: it is claimed that their religions 'involve the transcendent – the abiding, the ideal.'[6] However, the identity of a religious community does not depend on the recognition of outsiders: as long as it has enough members its claim can be upheld in the face of widespread disagreement. Its identity does, however, depend on the recognition of God, because its relationship with Him constitutes its ultimate good.

The examples of unauthentic developments which we have discussed show that there could be controversy on the question of how the criteria of authenticity should be applied. Each criterion raises its own difficulties. First, what kind of authority does Christ have over us? What does His authority mean for our practices and institutions? Are there any authorities which are entitled to speak in His name? Second, what is the message which may not be contradicted? Does it contain timelessly valid ethical rules, e.g. prohibitions against euthanasia, homosexuality and the use of contraceptives? Third, what kinds of derivation from the gospel are allowed? For instance, is Anselm's doctrine of atonement, i.e. that Jesus vicariously suffered our punishment, a valid derivation? And finally, might not trust in Christ lead to the neglect of one's own responsibility, to 'cheap grace'? When is it appropriate to trust and submit ourselves to our government as a God-given institution, and when do we have to resist?[7]

These questions show that the criteria of authenticity cannot be applied independently of a certain standpoint within the Christian tradition. They do not provide a neutral point outside the context of the faith of the church, from which this faith could be evaluated as true or false. Rather, given a contemporary theological account of the significance of Christ, these criteria offer a means for evaluating developments in the past. Since there are many conflicting contemporary theologies, we cannot assume that one can give definitive answers to the theological questions which are raised by these criteria. That may only be possible in the eschaton. Although this diminishes the usefulness of these criteria for reaching future theological agreement, nevertheless they can stimulate the ecumenical discussion about Christian authenticity, because they indicate the crucial issues in this debate. Moreover, since they provide a means for evaluating the past, they can help churches to develop a historically informed self-consciousness. However, instead of developing these points further, I will concentrate on the question of how these criteria relate to the phenomenon of change in the Christian tradition.

---

6   Wilfred Cantwell Smith, *The Meaning and End of Religion* (London 1978), 153.
7   Cf. Dietrich Bonhoeffer, *Letters and Papers from Prison* (London [12]1970).

Brümmer has argued that a religious tradition must always be developed in creative ways in order to remain relevant for and adequate to the changing problems of the age, and to be intelligible and credible within various cultural contexts.[8] But, one might ask, are not such creative developments ruled out by the criteria of authenticity? Does not every innovation change the message to a certain extent? Moreover, if a development is creative, then it cannot merely be derived from earlier stages of the tradition. And finally, are there not circumstances in which both trust in Christ's reconciliation and obedience to Him seem to exclude adequate ways of dealing with the problems of our world?

However, it might be that the criteria of authenticity are actually less stringent than they seem. For example, the completeness of the original revelation does not imply that there cannot occur any revelations after Christ, e.g. in other religions. It merely implies that the salvational content of such revelations should also be derivable from the Christian revelation. From a Christian perspective, all aspects of salvation known in other religions are in the end related to Christ. Not everything which is claimed to be salvation can be accepted as such by Christians. In order to test whether a certain religion leads to salvation, we must compare it with what we know of salvation in Christ.

The same point is made by Brümmer in his book *The Model of Love*. He argues that knowing God is of paramount importance to human salvation, and continues: 'we can only "know God" to the extent that we have fellowship with God and achieve a "union of wills" with God, and this will manifest itself in the Christlike character of our lives.... But then it is only possible in the light of our knowledge of God as revealed in Christ for us to discern that others (and ourselves) inside and outside the church can be said to "know God".'[9]

Moreover, the completeness of God's revelation in Christ also does not imply the further claim that in addition to our beliefs about our *salvation* also all our beliefs about *God* should be derivable from it. Here, we should distinguish between 'knowing God,' which is necessary for salvation, and 'knowledge about God': we may know a lot about a person without knowing her personally, i.e. being in a relation of mutual trust with her, and conversely, we can trust a person without knowing every available piece of information about her.[10] Thus, knowledge about salvation cannot simply be equated with knowledge about God. Besides, the claim

---

8   Brümmer, 'Identity of the Christian Tradition.'
9   Vincent Brümmer, *The Model of Love: A Study in Philosophical Theology* (Cambridge 1993), 205.
10   Cf. Ilham Dilman, *Love and Human Separateness* (Oxford 1987), 121.

that the latter should also be derivable from the Christ event would render impossible any beliefs about unforeseen acts of God after the Christ event. For example,
it would then become impossible to believe that God called you yesterday to
become a minister in the church, because that belief could not be derived from the
original revelation in Christ. This is clearly not what is meant by the finality of
Christ. Thus, the third criterion of authenticity proves to be much less stringent than
it seems: we argued that it does not exclude other revelations which may yield
additional knowledge about God.

What is more, we have already seen that there is much disagreement about the
way in which the criteria of authenticity should be applied. It might be the case that
even though many kinds of application exclude creative developments, there are
nevertheless certain other applications which do not. In my view, such non-exclusive applications are the only acceptable ones, because a Christian is committed to
the (nearly) universal significance of the Christ event: Christ is the ultimate source
of meaning, not just for first-century Jews, but for everyone in every circumstance.
Therefore, the criteria of authenticity should admit adequate reinterpretations of the
Christian tradition in almost every situation. (One might of course hold that there
are people or cultures who have cut themselves off from salvation, effectively
barring the adequacy of Christianity for their lives, but we cannot play this card too
often).

In the following section, I will show that such non-exclusive applications of the
criteria of authenticity are possible. I will do this by developing them in a non-
exclusive way. I will not claim that this is their only possible or only acceptable
interpretation. The mere fact that they admit of a non-exclusive construal, however,
implies that these criteria of authenticity do not *in principle* exclude creative developments.

4 The Authenticity of Creative Developments

In order to show that each of the criteria of authenticity admits of a non-exclusive
interpretation, I will discuss them one by one. Let us start with the first criterion: our
practices and institutions should be compatible with Christ's lordship. In this connection, the question arose what kind of authority Christ holds over us and what the
acknowledgement of this authority should imply for our practices and institutions.
This has been the subject of intensive ecumenical debate. However, here it is not
necessary to give a definitive answer to this question, but merely to show that there
is a non-exclusive answer. Now, according to the New Testament witness, obedi-

ence to Christ's authority is found primarily in the church[11] when it allows itself to be guided by the activity and inspiration of the Holy Spirit.[12] Thus, the acknowledgement of Christ's lordship should generally (but not invariably) lead to the creation or continuation of churches which are open to the presence of the Holy Spirit within the community of faith. But, we are bound to ask, which communities qualify as church? In answer, we might propose that the church exists wherever the gospel[13] is proclaimed and the sacraments[14] duly administered. These criteria do not exclude reinterpretations of the meaning of the gospel and the sacraments, as long as these do not conflict with the uniqueness and ultimate authority of Christ. In other words, the only condition is that the proclamation and the rituals of the church should encourage us to confess Christ as our only Lord. And finally, practices and institutions outside the boundaries of the church are not prohibited, as long as these do not conflict with full membership in the church. Therefore, the first criterion does not necessarily exclude creative developments.

The second criterion stated that, since the gospel is unqualifiedly true, its message should not be changed or modified by developments in doctrine and ethics. The problem here was to find the content of the message. Now, a revelation must always be received by someone, and the Apostles are the most obvious candidates for being the addressees of the gospel. But if they are the receivers, then the gospel must be bound up with their cultural framework, and with the problems they had to face in their lives. Thus, it might not be intelligible in other cultures nor adequate to their changing problems.

However, it is possible to hold that, even though Christ founded a living *community* in His relationship with the Apostles, nevertheless they were not the only

---

11 The church is the body of Christ (e.g. 1 Cor. 12:12-31; Eph. 4:12); it is founded and sustained by His flesh and blood (Eph. 2:13-16); and He is also the head of this body (Col. 1:18). But obedience to Christ is not found exclusively in the church: it may occasionally also be found outside the church (cf. Mark 9:38f and parallels).

12 After His resurrection, Jesus orders His disciples to wait for the Holy Spirit, in whom they must be baptized (Acts 1:4-5). Only after they have received this inspiration, do they begin to preach the Gospel (Acts 2:1-4). Throughout the Acts of the Apostles baptism, the initiation rite of the new community of Christ, is followed by the gift of the Holy Spirit. Moreover, in his letters, Paul often stresses that we should live by the Spirit (e.g. Gal. 5:5, 16ff), that the Spirit joins and unites us with Christ (e.g. Rom. 8:1-17), and that we can only confess Christ as Lord through the Spirit (1 Cor. 12:3).

13 Here, the term 'gospel' means 'the good news about Jesus Christ,' as it was preached by the Apostles and later written down in various writings, which were, finally, canonized by the church to form the New Testament.

14 Disputes might arise as to how many sacraments there are; I would propose, again without claiming to give a definitive answer, that there are two sacraments, i.e. Baptism and Holy Communion.

receivers of the *message*. The church of later ages might also be involved in its reception. There might be a time lapse between the time of sending and that of receiving the message, as when somebody writes a letter which is only read by another after several years. Thus, it might be that some aspects of this revelation were only fully understood in later ages, so that the understanding of the Apostles was only partial: they did not and could not understand the significance the Christ event was to have for later ages. So our second criterion does not necessarily imply that we should not modify or add to the understanding of the Apostles. What it does imply, however, is that the witness of the Apostles cannot be rejected out of hand, and that any modification of and addition to it should enjoy recognition in the church in which Christ exercises His authority. But even this does not guarantee the truth of such reinterpretations, as is amply illustrated by the crusades.

In other words, we might hold that God's revelation is a process, rather than a single event. The sending of the message by God has been achieved, namely in the Christ event, but the reception by the church remains an ongoing process. Moreover, through the Holy Spirit, God is also involved in this reception process. This does not necessarily imply new emissions. Revelation can occur not only by the manifestation of something new, but also by a transformation of the receiver which enables him to understand certain aspects of the message. Thus the inspired understanding of the church might discover ever new depths[15] in the original revelation.[16]

If revelation is an enduring process, then also those aspects which were revealed in the tradition of the church should not be contradicted. For example, gradually it has become clear that practices like slavery and conversion by force are incompatible with the ethic of the gospel. Therefore, every development which introduced such practices or defends their maintenance must be regarded as unauthentic. This does not mean, however, that genuine developments cannot occur in cultures where these practices are commonplace, but merely that a certain kind of development is excluded.

Moreover, it also does not imply that we have to adopt the entire doctrinal synthesis of earlier ages. We can hold that the meaning of the Christ event can never

---

15   On the concept of 'revelation of depth' see Luco J. van den Brom, 'Models of Revelation and Language,' in: Vincent Brümmer & Marcel Sarot (eds.), *Revelation and Experience: Proceedings of the 11th Biennial European Conference on the Philosophy of Religion* (Utrecht 1996), 56-71, esp. 68-71.

16   It is not a good idea to consider the tradition of the church as itself part of the Christ event, because then one neglects the distinction between the work of Christ and that of the Holy Spirit. This is not to deny that the Christ event was a relational act, in which Christ founded a living community, which required the participation of the Apostles. But I would propose that the continuation of this community is a work of the Holy Spirit, which involves directing the attention of Christians back to the Christ event.

be grasped in its entirety by such a system. The ecclesial understanding is always partial and contextualized. Christians may later come to realise that certain traditional beliefs were false, even those which have been held almost unanimously during long periods of Christian history, e.g., the doctrine of God's impassibility. And finally, the criterion of non-contradiction does not rule out that certain aspects which were crucially relevant in one context may fade into the background in other circumstances. Therefore, it does not exclude changes in focus: in every age God's Word in Christ is heard 'from a particular viewpoint, largely determined by the spiritual-cultural situation of the Christian community.'[17]

Obviously, this conception of revelation as a process is also very important with respect to our third criterion, viz. that every belief about our salvation should be derivable from the original revelation. Again this does not necessarily imply that all these beliefs should be derivable from the witness of the Apostles. What it does imply, however, is that they should be derivable from the signs and events which occurred in the lives of Christ, the Apostles and the Israelites before Christ. But how can we derive a belief from an event? In general, every revelatory occurrence can be interpreted in many different ways, unless there is an unambiguous agreement between God and the receiver about its meaning. For example, in Judges 6:36-40 God and Gideon agree that the presence of dew on a fleece of wool will stand for the statement 'God is trustworthy and keeps His promises,' but in the absence of such an agreement this sign would have been open to various other interpretations.[18] In the case of Christ's life and death there was no clear antecedent consensus about the meaning of these events. Indeed if, as I propose, God's revelation in Christ is an enduring process, then searching for the God-given significance of this event will also be an ongoing practice. Therefore, every interpretation of the Christ event can in principle reflect the message which God wants to convey to the church. But of course not every interpretation is approved by God. As Christians we know that God is benevolent, and that, therefore, He wants us to achieve insight into those aspects of salvation which are relevant for us in dealing with our contemporary problems. Therefore, I would propose that only those interpretations are to be accepted which reveal depth in the context of the interpreter: those which enable him or her to grasp the meaning or significance of events in human life. Such depth may be discovered when the circumstances in which we live are seen in the light of the biblical history of salvation, and vice versa: when this history is reinterpreted in terms of our conceptual framework. In sum: I would propose that beliefs about salvation are derived (derivable) from the Christ event if they are (can be) based on

---

17   Gregory Baum, *The Credibility of the Church Today* (New York 1968), 154.
18   Cf. Van den Brom, 'Models of Revelation and Language,' 56-71, esp. 66.

an 'interpretation of depth.' Thus, this construction of the third criterion does not rule out adequate and credible reinterpretations of the Christian tradition. However, its context-dependent nature makes the cross-cultural application of this criterion very difficult.

Every interpretation of depth must be 'natural' in a certain sense: it must not violate what actually happened in Jesus' life and death, because otherwise it could not be said to be derived from these events. Hans Küng has argued that, on the basis of historical critical exegesis of the New Testament, we can exclude many views about Jesus' message as historically false.

He was a man who exploded the usual schemes and would not be enlisted on any front. He was in conflict with the political-religious establishment (not a priest or theologian), yet no political revolutionary either (rather, a preacher of non-violence). He was no advocate of migration, either physical or spiritual (he was not an ascetic or a Qumran monk), nor was he a pious casuistic lawyer (not a Pharisee full of 'joy in the commandment'). To this extent Jesus of Nazareth differed not only from the great representatives of the Indian-mystic and Chinese-wisdom traditions (Buddha and Confucius) but also from the two other Near Eastern Semitic religions (Moses and Muhammad).[19]

On the basis of this knowledge of Jesus' history, we can exclude certain beliefs about salvation in Christ as unauthentic. For example, Jesus may not be seen as a military leader like Mohammed, who will lead Christian armies to conquer their enemies, as in the crusades. Nor can we hold that Christ simply taught a certain kind of legalism as a way to salvation. Further, Jesus also did not believe in an endless cycle of reincarnations, nor can His death and resurrection be understood as a kind of deliverance from this cycle. As far as we know, these views cannot be derived from the Christ event. Instead, they are distortions of history. Therefore, they are excluded by the third criterion.

However, though Christian accounts of salvation in Christ should not distort history, they do not have to be limited to historical accounts either. We can distinguish between the facts of history on the one hand, and their significance in a certain

---

19 Hans Küng, *Christianity: Its Essence and History* (London 1995), 34-35. Küng summarizes here what he developed at length in *On Being a Christian* (London 1976). The results of his historical investigation are to a certain extent dependent on the exegetical tradition in which he stands. Nevertheless, he (and I) have certain beliefs about who Jesus really was, and if these beliefs are true, then certain developments should be excluded as unauthentic. This dependence on exegetical traditions merely illustrates the fact that the criteria of authenticity can only be applied from a certain standpoint within the tradition.

situation on the other (even though we cannot separate them in a neat way). Moreover, the significance which we attribute to these events does not have to be the same as the one which the Apostles conceived of. Of course, their (disciples') faithful witnesses in the New Testament provide our only access to the original events, and these texts are the starting point for Christian theology which has been authorised by the tradition of the church. Nevertheless, our interpretation can go beyond the message which the authors intended to convey. According to Brümmer,[20] the goal of interpretation is often not primarily to reflect the intention of the author, but rather to enter into a dialogue with the text, and to arrive at a critical innovation of our concepts and ideas. Thus, we can distinguish between intentional and rational interpretations. The latter are attempts to render the witness of the Apostles more fruitful, significant or meaningful in our own situation.

Summarizing, we have argued that the process of revelation proceeds by means of ever new interpretations of depth, and that these interpretations must not violate the events as they actually occurred. However, Christian theologians do not have to limit themselves to the intentional interpretation of scripture. On the contrary, I fully agree with David Brown that 'the historical is by no means all that matters. No less relevant is the question of what the text itself can say to us today, and the power of its narrative to engage our attention.'[21] In some cases, even an unhistorical story can teach us something about the significance of Christ. For example, it is frequently argued nowadays that the birth narratives of Matthew and Luke are legendary. Nevertheless, they make an important point, namely that the whole life of Jesus (i.e. what really happened) is to be seen as the definitive act of God.[22] In my view the historical events are the signs which can become revelatory to us in a dialogue with the biblical text.

In fact, David Brown[23] has shown that this process has been going on throughout Christian history: beliefs are often based on interpretations of a scriptural text which do not reflect the intention of its author. For example, Luther based his theology of justification by faith on Roman 1:17, but many theologians now argue that it rests on a narrowing of focus unknown to Paul. Thus, Brown argues that there occurs an inspired imposition of meaning rather than a discovery. I would suggest

---

20   Cf. Vincent Brümmer, *Wijsgerige Begripsanalyse* (Kampen 1989³), Ch. 5; id., 'Philosophy, Theology and the Reading of Texts,' *Religious Studies* 27 (1991), 451-462.

21   David Brown, 'Tradition as a Dynamic Force for Positive Change,' in this volume.

22   Cf. Maurice Wiles, 'Divine Action: Some Moral Considerations,' in: T.F. Tracy (ed.), *The God who Acts: Philosophical and Theological Explorations* (Pennsylvania 1994), 13-29, esp. 27-28.

23   David Brown, 'Did Revelation Cease?', in: Alan G. Padgett (ed.), *Reason and the Christian Religion: Essays in Honour of Richard Swinburne* (Oxford 1994), 121-142.

that such a reinterpretation of the significance of Christ should not be excluded, as long as it does not violate the historical facts to which Paul was testifying.

The last criterion which we have to discuss, is that, because the Christ event is of decisive importance, we should always put our trust in Christ's redemptive work. The difficulty here was that, seemingly, under certain circumstances trust in Christ might exclude any possibility of facing up to the problems of the world and dealing with them in adequate ways. Does not this faith weaken our sense of human responsibility for the world? And does not the extent of human influence on the continued existence of life on this planet nowadays make a strong awareness of responsibility indispensable?

In response, I think, we should argue that this kind of reasoning is misleading: putting our trust in Christ does not exclude human responsibility for the world, but rather strengthens our awareness of it. In order to substantiate this claim, we might suggest that Christ's life and work was of decisive importance for two reasons. First, it showed us the full extent of our human alienation from God. Without this revelation, we would be ignorant of our sinful condition, and thus we could never begin to ask for forgiveness. Moreover, by His deeds of loving sacrifice He offered reconciliation and provided the strongest possible incentive to return the love of God. Such an account of Christ's decisive importance does not deny our human responsibility for God's creation, but rather presupposes personal relationships between people and their God in which both sides are responsible for their own deeds.

Second, the Christ event was also decisive in that it revealed how unjust and godless our socio-political institutions can become if they are not continually renewed by the Holy Spirit. Moreover, by His proclamation of the Kingdom of God which is both present and yet to come, Christ assured us that our attempts to sanctify the structures of our society are not in vain. Similarly for the earth and the cosmos as a whole: we might propose that Christ's resurrection signifies that they will not end in utter destruction, but that they will be transformed into a new creation. These considerations show that, contrary to appearance, genuine trust in Christ does not weaken our sense of human responsibility, but strengthens it.

More generally, we might argue in favour of the enduring relevance and adequacy of Christian faith in the following way. Although the problems which people have to deal with are subject to change, they are not wholly arbitrary either. For example, there will always be resemblances between the forms in which the questions of life and death, of guilt and meaninglessness are asked. And Christians hold that the problem of how to live a good life *coram Deo* will always be relevant, because ultimately humans can only find meaning in their relation with God. Moreover, if the meaning of life is determined by our relation with God, then we cannot ignore our alienation from Him and the reconciliation He has offered. (Indeed, every development which leads us to ignore these issues is excluded by this criterion). Thus, we may expect that salvation in Christ can always be reconceptualized in adequate ways. Finally, one could add that putting our trust in Christ will always be relevant because it is constitutive of living communities, which the Holy Spirit can use as means to renew the structures of the world.

In sum, I have shown how the four criteria of authenticity could be developed in ways which do not exclude creative developments in the Christian tradition. To recapitulate, I do not claim that this is the only possible application of these criteria. Rather the aim was to show that the four criteria of authenticity do not in principle exclude such developments. As I have shown, we would have to abandon the universal significance of the Christ event, if they did. Fortunately, Christians do not have to pay this conceptual price. Thus, this analysis has shown that there is no inconsistency in claiming both that Christ is God's definitive word to humankind, and that creative developments in the Christian tradition are necessary.

4. The Function of Religion in Human Life and Thought

A Whiteheadian Exploration

Santiago Sia (Los Angeles)

1   *Introduction*

Any attempt to discuss the function of religion in human life and thought – the title assigned to me – will inevitably call for some preliminary comments. For one thing, there is the obvious need for an initial explanation of how 'religion' is to be used in the present context. This is to be expected because that term has been, and is frequently, defined and developed in many ways. It has even been suggested that 'religion' itself is a historical invention. In addition, the term 'religion' carries such a variety, sometimes even a divergence, of connotations that it would be more misleading rather than helpful to talk about its function since its so-called function would be dependent on the particular understanding of religion that one has. Moreover, certain manifestations, expressions, or practices which are alleged to be 'religious' would be regarded as questionable or even objectionable by those who do regard themselves as sincere believers or practitioners of religion.

The word 'function' can be just as problematic here. For in ordinary contexts one gives it a rather pragmatic or utilitarian meaning as when one talks about the function of the motorcar or even the function of an association. To link religion with such a usage of the word is not only to devalue religion, giving it a subservient role, but is also to be rightly accused of perpetuating the objectivist understanding of religion. After all, it is claimed by many, if not most, religious followers that a more appropriate way of appreciating the connection between religion and human life and thought would be to discuss it in terms of 'the relationship to' or 'the significance for' or even 'the role of,' rather than in terms of 'function in,' human life and thought. It is a claim that should alert us to the existence of much subjectivity and of the personal dimension in religion, which makes an exploration such as the one we are undertaking more difficult or even doubtful.

There is still another consideration that needs to be addressed at this stage. Despite the variety of understandings and connotations, religion seems to be so intimately related to human life and thought that it would appear to be superfluous to discuss this topic. In fact, some would even claim that religion is not just about a particular way of living and thinking but it is human life itself (which implies

57

practice and thought). Consequently, there has always been a very close connection between religion and morals, between religious belief and human hopes, between religions and world-views. Given this assumption it would seem odd to still talk of the function of religion in human life and thought. At most, one would be expected merely to provide a version of how religion – in whatever way it is understood – and human life and thought are significantly associated rather than still defend the argument that religion has any close links with human life and thought.[1] It is an issue that is somehow related to the debate as to whether religion can be explained or only interpreted.[2]

In this essay, taking these preliminary remarks into account but without being side-tracked by the controversies, I want to explore a specific philosophical conception of religion. Religion here will be understood as arising from our experience but grounded in rational reflection. It is a conception that highlights the need for a response, and the kind of response one makes will determine how religion helps to make sense of human living. Furthermore, since a significant factor in our consideration of religion in human life and thought is the extent to which a specific understanding of religion can support the integration of these two, it will be necessary to show how this is possible.

2   Whitehead's Conception of 'Religion'

We have noted already that the use of the term 'religion,' given the complexity of its meaning and use, requires some clarification. A popular illustration of this complexity can be seen in discussions as to whether Buddhism should be regarded as a religion insofar as – at least as generally understood – it does not believe in a transcendent god. Compounding that difficulty of classifying Buddhism as a religion is the fact that there are different kinds of Buddhism. Again, as is well known, there has been some claim that Marxism, because of its demands on its followers, is a religion except in name. Additionally, the sophistication of the more established religions such as Christianity or Islam has led at times to the suspicion that native religions found in Africa or Asia are nothing more than superstitious beliefs – to the annoyance of those who regard them as genuine, if undeveloped, religions. More recently, we have been faced with the rise of what is labelled as cults rather than

---

1   This would seem to be in line with the task of philosophical theology discussed by Vincent Brümmer in his *Speaking of a Personal God: An Essay in Philosophical Theology* (Cambridge 1992), Ch.1. He adds, however, that philosophical reflection is not merely descriptive but also innovative.

2   Robert A. Segal, *Explaining and Interpreting Religion: Essays on the Issue* (Frankfurt aM 1992).

religions despite the fact that in some cases their present development appears to parallel the early stages in the growth of the more established religions. It is not surprising therefore that Wilfred Cantwell Smith would question the validity and the helpfulness of the concepts 'religion' and 'religions.' Because the concept of religion in the West has evolved and because religion itself has been reified, he claims that these concepts are not only unnecessary but also much less serviceable and legitimate than they once seemed.[3]

The existence of many general interpretations of religion leads John Hick in his recent book *An Interpretation of Religion* to opt for dividing them into naturalistic, i.e. religion as a purely human phenomenon, or religious, i.e. confessional. In contrast to these two groups Hick offers what he considers to be a theory of religion that is not confessional but one that acknowledges its plurality of forms. Focusing on belief in the transcendent, he bases his interpretation on 'a family-resemblance understanding' of religion.[4] Likewise, the variety of competing definitions of religion and the difficulty of judging their correctness cause Peter Clarke and Peter Byrne to turn to the 'family resemblance definition' of religion as a looser, more informal mode of definition. They believe that there can be no finality in the definition of religion because the phenomenon of religion keeps developing as illustrated by the New Religions, which have disclosed fresh insights into the relationship between religion and our present culture.[5]

The 'family-resemblance understanding or definition' of religion can be useful in stressing the commonality amidst the diversity of religions. At a time when interreligious dialogue is particularly called for, such an understanding of religion can help set the appropriate context. It is also important in distilling what is essential in the different religions. But it seems to me that Alfred North Whitehead's understanding of religion has the advantage of being more directly relevant to the topic under discussion. As Dorothy Emmet observes, religion for Whitehead has great significance for the ordering of life: it inevitably issues in propositions with a bearing upon the conduct of life.[6] It is therefore his definition of religion which will serve as the focus of this exploration.

Whitehead's account of religion is contained principally in his *Religion in the Making*. But this is complemented by shorter discussions in *Science in the Modern World*, *Adventures of Ideas* and other writings. Commenting on Whitehead's discussion of religion, John Cobb notes that Whitehead depended heavily on secondary

3   Wilfred Cantwell Smith, *The Meaning and End of Religion: A Revolutionary Approach to the Great Religious Traditions* (London 1978), 121.
4   John Hick, *An Interpretation of Religion: Human Responses to the Transcendent* (London 1989).
5   Peter B. Clarke & Peter Byrne, *Religion Defined and Explained* (London 1993).
6   Dorothy Emmet, *Whitehead's Philosophy of Organism* (London 2nd ed. 1966), 245.

sources with which he had limited familiarity. Nevertheless, he adds that Whitehead's discussion is valuable not only because it throws light on his philosophy but also because he develops his understanding of the relationship between philosophy and religion, a point that will be of particular interest to us here.[7] Cobb also observes that Whitehead was not really preoccupied with religion, despite returning to this topic again and again. Whitehead's attention was more focused on what have become known as penultimate questions. But religion remains in the background, securing the importance of these questions; however, it is rarely itself at the centre of the stage.[8] Thus, it seems even more worthwhile to explore his conception of religion further.

Religion, Whitehead writes, is 'what the individual does with his own solitariness.'[9] He states that the essence of religion is to be discovered, not in public dogmas, practices, or institutions, but in confrontation with 'the awful ultimate fact, which is the human being, consciously alone with itself, for its own sake.'[10] This association of religion with solitariness will no doubt strike many as highly suspect and therefore unlikely to be of much help to us after all. Indeed in an article developing this definition of religion, Donald Crosby observes that Whitehead's description of religion has been frequently quoted and usually disparaged. However, he argues – and I agree with him – that it is seldom understood in anything like the way Whitehead intended.[11]

One of the misconceptions of Whitehead's definition of religion is that he is championing an individualistic interpretation of religion, which seems to contradict the teaching of many an established religion. Admittedly, Whitehead does place great importance on individuality in so far as he maintains that religious consciousness does not arise until one has risen above what he calls 'communal religion,' that is, beyond the stage in one's development that is informed by the myths, collective rituals, emotions and beliefs of one's society. As Whitehead puts it, 'The moment of religious consciousness starts from self-valuation.'[12] One becomes 'religious' when one stands out as an individual, breaking out of the confines of the traditions and mores of inherited culture. One needs to loosen the strong grip of tradition upon oneself, thereby removing the sense of being at the mercy of arbitrary power.[13]

---

7   John Cobb, Jr., *A Christian Natural Theology: Based on the Thought of A.N. Whitehead* (London 1966), 216.

8   Cobb, *Christian Natural Theology*, 223.

9   Alfred North Whitehead, *Religion in the Making* (=RM) (Cambridge 1926), 17; also, 47.

10   RM, 16.

11   Donald A. Crosby, 'Religion and Solitariness,' in: Lewis Ford & George Kline (eds.), *Explorations in Whitehead's Philosophy* (New York 1983), 149.

12   RM, 59.

13   RM, 39-40.

Only then will that individual be confronted with the concerns which are of utmost importance and depth. Only then will he or she become aware of the inadequacy of social custom and authority to answer the most fundamental of questions and be forced to turn elsewhere. Stripped of one's sense of belongingness, experiencing solitariness, one begins to ask: 'What, in the way of value, is the attainment of life?'[14] One discovers then one's uniqueness rather than one's society as the focus and source of freedom and value. For Whitehead religiosity, it would seem, really stems from the exercise of one's individuality, particularly as experienced in solitariness.

It is important, however, to contextualise what Whitehead says regarding solitariness. Although Whitehead does stress that religion is primarily individual, the solitariness that one experiences is due to the detachment from one's immediate surroundings. This in turn leads one to search for something permanent and intelligible to throw light on one's immediate environment.[15] Religion expresses, according to Whitehead, 'the longing of the spirit that the facts of existence should find their justification in the nature of existence.'[16] The detachment or disconnection from immediate surroundings is thus a prerequisite for 'the emergence of a religious consciousness which is universal, as distinguished from tribal, or even social.'[17] Whitehead in fact sees a close connection between solitariness and universality. Although the moment of religious consciousness starts from self-valuations, as we have already noted, 'it broadens into the concept of the world as a realm of adjusted values, mutually intensifying or mutually destructive.'[18] Whitehead denies that there is such a thing as absolute solitariness: 'Each entity requires its environment. Thus man cannot seclude himself from society.... But further, what is known in secret must be enjoyed in common, and must be verified in common.'[19]

Elsewhere Whitehead describes religion as 'the reaction of human nature to its search for God.'[20] I will return to Whitehead's conception of God later. But at this point, it is worth noting, by way of explaining the phrase 'reaction of human nature,' that Whitehead does not believe human nature to have a separate function which could be regarded as a special religious sense. Nor does he hold that religious truth is something other than the highest form of knowledge, which had been first

---

14   RM, 60.
15   RM, 47.
16   RM, 85.
17   RM, 47.
18   RM, 59.
19   RM, 137-138. It should also be borne in mind that Whitehead's metaphysics regards 'relatedness' or 'the social' as more fundamental and inclusive compared to individuality.
20   A.N. Whitehead, *Science in the Modern World* (Cambridge 1926) (= SMW), 266.

acquired with our ordinary senses and then developed by our intellectual operations. As he puts it succinctly, 'religion starts from the generalisation of final truths first perceived as exemplified in particular instances.'[21] What follows then is the amplification of these truths into a coherent system and the application of them to the interpretation of life. This interpretation serves as the criterion for the success of these truths. Although in this matter religious truths can be judged like any other truth, they are peculiar in that they explicitly deal with values. By this claim Whitehead means that religious truths make us conscious of what he calls the permanent side of the universe which we can care for. In this way religion enables us to discover meaning in our own existence against the background of the meaning of the wider scheme of things.[22]

Inasmuch as Whitehead's description of religion as 'a human reaction' involves knowledge, it invites comparison with Plato's. Plato, it will be recalled, regarded religion as the culmination of the search for truth. Plato differentiated and distanced his conception of religion from the more anthropomorphic versions, which were prevalent in his time. In contrast, Whitehead, while regarding 'communal religion' with its myths, practices and beliefs as merely a stage in the development of religious consciousness, nevertheless prefers to discuss religion in the context of what he refers to as 'the great rational religions.' For him these religions are 'the outcome of religious consciousness which is universal, as distinguished from tribal, or even social.'[23] Furthermore, Whitehead's definition needs to be qualified by what he says elsewhere; namely, that the immediate reaction of human nature to God is worship.[24] In this sense it is much closer – and further removed from Plato – to Charles Hartshorne's conception of religion as essentially worship by which Hartshorne means 'devoted love for a being regarded as superlatively worthy of love.' Hartshorne maintains that what distinguishes true religion from primitive ones is the worshipful attitude which it inspires.[25]

Although the definitions from Whitehead provided thus far do not explicitly mention human life, there is no doubt but that Whitehead sees an intimate link between it and religion. In fact, Whitehead claims that 'justification' is the basis of religion. By justification he means that one's character is developed according to one's faith. For him this is the primary inescapable truth. 'Religion is force of belief

21   RM, 124.
22   RM, 124.
23   RM, 47.
24   SMW, 192.
25   See, among others, Charles Hartshorne, *A Natural Theology for Our Time* (La Salle, Ill. 1967). I have discussed this point in some detail in my *God in Process Thought: A Study in Charles Hartshorne's Concept of God* (The Hague 1985), 9-18.

cleansing the inward parts.'[26] Consequently, he maintains that sincerity is the primary religious virtue. In terms reminiscent of Kant, Whitehead holds that even the doctrinal side of religion, i.e. the system of general truths, will transform one's character so long as these truths are sincerely held and vividly apprehended. Religion also promotes the transformation of society through its moral energy.[27] On the other hand, unlike Kant, Whitehead also maintains that while religion is valuable for ordering one's life, conduct is merely an inevitable by-product. It is not the mainstay of religion. In fact, the overemphasis on rules of conduct can be detrimental to religion. What should emerge from religion is individual worth of character. But Whitehead warns us that worth is positive or negative, good or bad. Thus, in a rather startling observation, but perhaps a more realistic one, he points out that religion is by no means necessarily good and therefore that it may be very evil.[28] Along similar lines Hartshorne, who describes human beings as fragments of reality, maintains that our reaction to that fragmentariness is what characterises our religion. Our religion is good if we accept our relative insignificance in the best possible way, poor or non-existent if we close our eyes to this situation. We could persuade ourselves into thinking that our limitation in space and time is only of slight importance or we could consider ourselves the centre of the universe, with everything else revolving around us.[29]

Whitehead's conception of religion also clearly establishes its link with human thought not only because of his constant recourse to the word 'rational' but also because of his distinction between religion and mere sociability. Religion, he says, emerges from ritual, emotion, belief, and rationalisation. But it is only when belief and rationalisation are well established that solitariness itself is discernible as of essential religious importance.[30] Without these, religion is in decay and returns to mere sociability.[31] Thus, religion as a human reaction is a conscious reaction. Furthermore, it is a conscious reaction to the world we find ourselves in. While religion appeals to the direct intuition of special occasions and emanates from what is special, it encompasses everything through conceptualisation.[32] This is accomplished with the help of human reason. Progress in religious truth, Whitehead tells us, is 'mainly a progress in the framing of concepts, in discarding artificial abstrac-

---

26   RM, 15.
27   RM, 15.
28   RM, 17.
29   Charles Hartshorne, 'The Modern World and the Modern View of God,' *Crane Review* 4/2 (Winter 1962), 73. Cf. also his 'Man's Fragmentariness,' *Wesleyan Studies in Religion* 41/6 (1963-64), 17-28.
30   RM, 18-19.
31   RM, 23. Also, his *Adventures of Ideas* (= AI) (Cambridge 1942), 207.
32   RM, 32.

tions or partial metaphors, and in evolving notions which strike more deeply into the root of reality.'[33]

For this reason, Whitehead shares the tendency, rooted in Western philosophical tradition but criticised in some quarters, to connect religion with a metaphysics. It must be noted, however, that metaphysics for Whitehead is understood and developed differently from the dominant metaphysical schools of thought in the West. He describes metaphysics as 'the science which seeks to discover the general ideas which are indispensably relevant to the analysis of everything that happens.'[34] Whitehead argues that rational religion – and as we have already noted, rationality for Whitehead is an integral part of religion – must have recourse to metaphysics.

Metaphysics enables religion to scrutinise itself. Whitehead regards the dispassionate criticism by metaphysics of religious beliefs to be of utmost necessity. 'Religion will not regain its old power,' he points out, 'until it can face change in the same spirit as does science. Its principles may be eternal, but the expression of these principles requires continual development.'[35] He strongly insists that the foundations of dogma must be laid in a rational metaphysics which criticises meanings, and endeavours to express the most general concepts adequate for the all-inclusive universe.[36] Moreover, for Whitehead the dogmas of religion are 'clarifying modes of external expression,' signalling the return of individuals from solitariness to society. Since there is no absolute solitariness, everything taking place in an environment, religious dogmas as modes of expression are thus important. The interaction between religion and metaphysics is regarded by Whitehead as one great factor in promoting the development in religion of an increasing accuracy of expression, disengaged from adventitious imagery.[37]

At the same time, however, metaphysics can benefit from its connection with religion by taking into account the evidence furnished by religion. While religion must reckon with metaphysics in formulating and developing its teachings, it makes its own contribution of immediate experience to that pool of knowledge.[38] In this way, metaphysical knowledge becomes truly all-inclusive. Thus, metaphysics and religion are not only related but also, and more importantly, mutually beneficial.

Whitehead offers yet another definition of religion, which incorporates what has been presented so far and adds another dimension:

---

33   RM, 131.
34   RM, 84. See also, 88-89.
35   SMW, 189.
36   RM, 83.
37   SMW, 266. Whitehead adds that the interaction between religion and science also promotes religion's development.
38   RM, 79.

Religion is the vision of something which stands beyond, behind, and within, the passing flux of immediate things; something which is real, and yet waiting to be realised, something which is a remote possibility, and yet the greatest of present facts; something that gives meaning to all that passes, and yet eludes apprehension; something whose possession is the final good, and yet is beyond all reach; something which is the ultimate ideal, and the hopeless quest.[39]

John Cobb explains that religion for Whitehead is not a means to any end beyond itself, not even to the good of society. Instead religion is a vision of that whose possession, although unattainable, is the final good. Cobb adds that the reason for worshipping – we have already heard that the reaction to this vision is worship – is not to achieve some good, but because that which one dimly apprehends evokes worship.[40] In other words, religion is the attempt to see behind the ephemeral, and what one sees, although not too clearly, inspires a worshipful attitude.

This last definition also gives us an indication of how Whitehead conceives the object of religion to be. God is the object of that vision. Yet Whitehead, not just in this passage but generally, is quite reluctant to refer to God in his discussions on religion. Lewis Ford offers an explanation: 'Whitehead accords great importance to religious vision, but at the same time finds a great hindrance in the particular image of God being proposed in the existing religious community, on two grounds: it stifles the adventure of inquiry, it perpetuates an outworn psychology of tyranny.'[41] Ford observes that Whitehead presumably did not yet have a clear idea of God at the time of his writings. Consequently, Whitehead's description is 'an intuitive, proleptic statement of what he was searching for, deliberately couched in paradoxical terms since he did not yet have the conceptual warrants to justify these claims.'[42] But, Ford points out, they serve as a lure towards which his thought was moving.[43]

This vision of God has an effect on one's life. John Cobb makes the observation that Whitehead's own general mood in life was of quiet confidence in the worthwhileness of living. But this confidence was not derived from any assurance about history or about nature.[44] Indeed, Whitehead maintains that the worship of God, which is the outcome of this vision, is 'not a rule of safety – it is an adventure of the spirit, a flight after the unattainable. The death of religion comes with the repression

---

39   SMW, 267-268.
40   Cobb, *A Christian Natural Theology*, 216-217.
41   Lewis Ford, *The Emergence of Whitehead's Metaphysics 1925-1929* (New York 1984), 107-108.
42   Ford, *Emergence*, 108.
43   See the last chapter of *Process and Reality* (= PR) with the title 'God and the World.'
44   Cobb, *Christian Natural Theology*, 218.

of the high hope of adventure.'[45] He accepted that there is perpetual perishing, loss as well as gain, sorrow as well as joy. In rather poetic terms, he refers to human life 'as a flash of occasional enjoyments lighting up a mass of pain and misery, a bagatelle of transient experience.'[46] And yet, whatever may be its temporal outcome, what guarantees the worthwhileness of life for Whitehead, remarks Cobb, is the vision of God. When we respond positively to that vision, contributing our share to the world, then it is a vision that indeed can give meaning to life. 'The vision of God was for Whitehead,' as Cobb sums it up, 'the basis for all reality of meaning and all depth of feeling.'[47]

3   *Religion and Experience*

No doubt, Whitehead's conception of religion raises some important questions: To what extent is this helpful in determining what could be classified a religion? Does it nullify the claim that special experiences are themselves religious? Is religion a merely human phenomenon? Does this mean that while solitariness is universal, religion itself is not so in so far as one may not reach, for whatever reason, that stage of doing something about one's solitariness? How does this conception of religion relate to the major religions of the world? These are fundamental concerns which need to be addressed carefully. However, in exploring Whitehead's under-standing of religion, my present interest has to be limited to dealing with the specific issue – the question assigned to me – as to how religion can help in our attempts to grasp the meaning or significance of human life.

Although Whitehead accepts that there are special occasions which can lead to religious consciousness, religion as far as he is concerned emerges from ordinary human experience.[48] He refers to 'the human search' or 'the longing of the spirit' for something which transcends everything, but the search or the longing for it is rooted in mundane matters, in everyday experience. This search or longing results in solitariness. Solitariness, however, is more than just the common experience of loneliness. Solitariness is the sense of separateness, the initial experience having been that of belongingness. It enables one to become aware of one's individuality, which is a further stage from one's previous preconscious experience of sociality

---

45   SMW, 276.
46   SMW, 275.
47   Cobb, *Christian Natural Theology*, 223.
48   According to Whitehead, 'experience' is one of the most deceitful words in philosophy. He provides a brief analysis of it in his *Symbolism: Its Meaning and Effect* (Cambridge 1928), 19f. For a more extensive and technical discussion, see his PR, particularly Part III.

and relatedness. Since religion is a response to solitariness, it means that solitariness itself is actually 'prereligious,' despite being a further stage in one's search for the transcendent. Strictly speaking then, religion is not to be equated with individuality. And unlike the sense of solitariness, religion is more than a stage. There has been an evolution in one's experience and not just a prolongation. In addition, there has been a development since there is an active element: religion after all is what one does with one's own solitariness. It is the response to one's search or longing. There is a purposeful consciousness in religion that is merely latent in solitariness but is developing as one becomes aware of one's individuality.

It is interesting that Whitehead should regard the human experience of longing and searching, which leads to solitariness, as the fundamental context in which religion can emerge. Some of the modern critics of religion had attacked it for preying, as it were, on such experiences. Freud, tracing religion back to the human need for emotional comfort, especially relief from disasters, accidents, sickness, and other natural evils that surround us, accused religion of perpetuating human immaturity through its teachings and practices. He regarded religion as an infantile neurosis that ought to be cured before we can grow into mature, healthy adults. Once cured of such a sickness, human beings, he alleged, can achieve maturity as a race. It will then no longer be necessary to invent fanciful beings personalised by religion for us to be able to face this impersonal and at times brutal world of ours. Marx criticised religion for enslaving people through its preaching of acceptance of one's miserable lot in life and its championing the virtues of patience, humility and self-denial. Religion, he claimed, misleads us in not recognising the real causes of our alienation and suppresses our desire to improve the economic and political conditions of life. Both of these influential thinkers would hardly agree with Whitehead that true religion stems from the human experience of longing and searching. If anything, such an experience in their view is being misinterpreted and misled by religion.

But these experiences of life, as our prereflexive starting point, are part and parcel of human life itself. While agreeing with Freud that religion is based on emotional needs, Jung rightly criticised him for not taking into account that they are basic to human nature and that we cannot deny them without inducing neurosis. What is called for therefore is not the abandonment of religion as demanded by Freud. Rather, it is our response to those needs that is really in question. It will determine the kind of religion that we have in mind, as Whitehead clearly states. Our response to human longing or yearning for something more does not have to be, and should not be, in the form severely criticised by Freud and Marx.

Unless religion embarks on its journey with our everyday experiences, including emotional ones, as the place of departure, it can easily become so abstract as to be rendered irrelevant. Worse, it makes nonsense of many religious practices and customs, which have arisen in response to specific life-situations. Religion cannot ignore deep-felt hunger or yearning for 'something more' even if it is not always clear what that 'something more' is or even if the expression of this desire is simplistic or unreflective. Whitehead correctly underscores this point whereas Plato neglects it. In the Western world Plato led the way in freeing religion from the particularistic, anthropomorphic expressions of it as exemplified by the Greek divinities. He insisted that true religion is concerned with fundamental and comprehensive questions rather than with emotional concerns. His own theory of religion was grounded in his desire to understand the universal attributes of reality, far removed from the transient, ever-changing environment which surrounded him. But by sharply establishing a line of demarcation between the established interpretation of religion in his day – understandably so given its crudities – and his own one, Plato unfortunately cut off an important link with concrete life. He wanted to construct a theory of religion that had left behind the world of sense experience. While there were good reasons for dissociating genuine religion from the so-called religious practices and beliefs of his time, Plato's hard-line attitude resulted in a rather intellectualised, and even elitist, version of religion. Whitehead's conception of religion, on the other hand, rightly shows that it is in the midst of everyday life, experienced in various fashions and expressed in concrete ways, that we begin to ask questions which take us beyond the particular situation that we find ourselves in and lead us to what he refers to as 'solitariness.' And our reaction, also part of human living, to that solitariness shapes religious thought.[49]

Our further attempts to make sense of our experiences of and in life lead to something more general and more complex as we yield to the urge for something more. There is in human life what Whitehead calls 'a noble discontent,' which is 'the gradual emergence into prominence of a sense of criticism, founded upon appreciations of beauty, and of intellectual distinction, and of duty.'[50] Such a discontent distances us from particular experiences and inevitably prods us to seek conceptual expressions and rational support. Whitehead outlines the process in this particularly helpful passage:

> Our consciousness does not initiate our modes of functionings. We awake to find ourselves engaged in process, immersed in satisfactions and dissatisfactions, and actively modifying, either by intensification, or by attenuation, or by the introduction of novel purposes. This primary procedure which is presupposed in consciousness I will term Instinct. It is the mode of experience directly

---

49 In a book, titled *From Suffering to God* (London 1994), I tried to illustrate how the experience of suffering leads to the question regarding what we can say about God.
50 AI, 12.

arising out of the urge of inheritance, individual and environmental. Also, after instinct and intellectual ferment have their work, there is a decision which determines the mode of coalescence of instinct with intelligence. I will term this factor Wisdom. It is the function of wisdom to act as a modifying agency on the intellectual ferment so as to produce a self-determined issue from the given conditions.[51]

Whitehead reminds us that 'religion is concerned with our reactions of purpose and emotion due to our personal measure of intuition into the ultimate mystery of the universe,' and that here we must 'not postulate simplicity.'[52] Rational thinking has a major contribution to religion. Situations in life have a way of pressing challenging questions on us, and for the sake of intellectual credibility in religion, these questions cannot remain ignored. While religion is not, and should not be, a purely rational enterprise, it does involve careful, deliberate and logical thinking. Whitehead frequently uses the phrase 'rational religion.' On this point his reference to the obvious link between religion and metaphysics is especially notable. It is obvious not in the sense that the link is generally accepted since there are those who not only do not wish to associate religion with metaphysics or with any other kind of philosophical trappings but even argue that such an association is detrimental and dangerous. Rather, there is a clearly recognisable tradition which closely connects the two even if the kind of connection is variously interpreted. As we have already seen, Whitehead, following in that tradition, accepts and defends that linkage. For him both religion and metaphysics are based on human experience and represent a common search for ultimacy. They help shape human thought and influence human life. Whitehead's understanding of the relationship between the two indicates that for him the formation of religious thought is inevitably connected to a metaphysical view of reality.[53]

---

51 AI, 58. Whitehead sets this out for the purpose of understanding social institutions, but I have used it in this context because it also shows how he understands the process from experience to conceptualisation. He does add that this division must not be made too sharply.

52 AI, 207. Whitehead maintains that history and common sense have testified that systematic formulations are potent engines of emphasis, of purification, and of stability. Without resorting to reason Christianity would have sunk into superstition.

53 It is also grounded in his theory of knowledge. Whitehead rejects 'mere knowledge.' He claims that knowledge is always accompanied with accessories of emotion and purpose and that there are grades in the generality of ideas (Cf. AI, 5). All knowledge, according to him, is derived from, and verified by, intuitive observation. All knowledge is conscious discrimination of objects experienced (Cf. AI, 227-228). He regards ideas as explanatory of modes of behaviour and of inrushes of emotion dominating our lives. Although ideas do modify practice, practice mainly precedes thought; and thought is mainly concerned with the justification or the modification of

One area where metaphysics features in religion is in the development of religious doctrines.[54] We have seen that Whitehead maintains that progress in religious truth comes about 'in the framing of concepts, in discarding artificial abstractions or partial metaphors, and in evolving notions which strike more deeply into the root of reality,'[55] all of which are achieved with the aid of metaphysics. But it is also useful to recall that for Whitehead religious truths are generalised truths, which originated in particular instances, expanded into a coherent system and *then applied to the interpretation of life*. The criterion for acceptance or rejection of these truths is their success in the interpretation of life.[56] Whitehead's well-known metaphor to describe speculative philosophy as the flight of the aeroplane is equally applicable to the discovery and formulation of religious truths: after taking off from life's experiences and being borne aloft by rational thinking, religion must touch down in life's fields again.

Religious doctrines represent a further stage in the process of making more explicit what one has held implicitly or has experienced. Ideally, they should express faithfully these prereflexive experiences. If they do, then one's appreciation of religion becomes richer and possibly more profound. But sometimes the process of conceptualisation does not do justice to the earlier stage; hence, the need to rethink and re-interpret doctrines. As Vincent Brümmer observes, 'Changes in the circumstances and demands of life bring about changes in cultural and hence also in the conceptual forms that people find adequate, including the concomitant beliefs that they hold to be true. Because of changes in the demands of life, our conceptual forms cannot remain eternally adequate.'[57] This is why the task of formulating religious doctrines is an on-going one. It is not surprising then that an urgent challenge today is to formulate religious doctrines which are not only based on concrete life but also, in an intellectual and systematised manner, express adequately the

---

a preexisting situation (cf. AI, 140; also, 127).

54 There has been of course talk of the demise of metaphysics, particularly during the era of logical positivism. However, it is probably more accurate to speak of the decline of certain metaphysical ways of philosophising rather than of metaphysical thinking itself. It should be noted that Whitehead's notion of metaphysics and his metaphysical view of reality are quite distinctive. Cf. PR. Because of its emphasis on becoming (as well as relatedness and events), his metaphysical system has been referred to, among other descriptions, as 'process metaphysics' although he himself referred to it as the 'philosophy of organism.'

55 RM, 131. Cf. my 'Process Thought as Conceptual Framework,' *Process Studies* 19/4 (Winter 1990), 248-255. For a very useful discussion, based on Whitehead's thought, on the relationship between doctrinal beliefs and experience, see John B. Cobb, Jr. & David Ray Griffin, *Process Theology: An Introductory Exposition* (Philadelphia 1977), 30-40.

56 RM, 124.

57 Brümmer, *Speaking of a Personal God*, 20.

realities of life. What is called for therefore is the integration of religion with both human thought and life. The following quotation from Whitehead is particularly appropriate here:

> Religion is an ultimate craving to infuse into the insistent particularity of emotion that non-temporal generality which primarily belongs to conceptual thought alone. In the higher organisms the differences of tempo between the mere emotions and the conceptual experiences produce a life-tedium, unless this supreme fusion has been effected. The two sides of the organism require *a reconciliation* (italics mine – SS) in which emotional experiences illustrate a conceptual justification, and conceptual experiences find an emotional justification.[58]

Despite some questions which will remain, Whitehead's conception of religion does, in my view, result in a clearer understanding of the role of religion in human life by showing how religion arises in the first place and how it also serves as the criterion for religious truths. At the same time it underlines the need to transcend our experiential starting point through rational thinking and to integrate the doctrinal expression with concrete human life. In this paper – in the light of my preliminary comments – I have tried to show through an exploration of Whitehead's conception of religion how a particular understanding of religion can in itself disclose its close connection with human life and thought. Also, taking into account the other papers which follow and the topics that they propose to develop, I have limited myself to a more philosophical discussion of the fundamental concept of religion.

---

58   PR, 16.

5. Religion, Meaning and Imitation

The Christian Ideal of *Imitatio Christi* as a Way of Making Sense of Life

Marcel Sarot (Utrecht)

1 *Preliminary Remarks: The Function of Religion*

Speaking about the 'function of religion' is not without problems. As Santiago Sia has pointed out,[1] the word 'function' usually has 'a rather pragmatic or utilitarian meaning as when one talks about the function of the motorcar ...' And he continues: 'To link religion with such a usage of the word is ... to devalue religion, giving it a subservient role...' Since it is not my intention to devalue religion, or to give it a subservient role, I will start by briefly discussing the use of the term 'function' in this connection. 'Function' is a notoriously slippery term; it has many different shades of meaning, and it is easy to slip from one of these meanings into one of the others. Here, I will merely distinguish between two different, but related, meanings: the meaning in which Santiago Sia uses the term in the above quotation, and the meaning in which I will use it in this article. Sia uses the term in a 'utilitarian' sense, so that it becomes more or less equivalent to 'goal.' In this sense, it is the function of a motorcar to make it easier for us to travel from A to B. And it is this function that justifies the existence of motorcars. If cars would not facilitate travelling, there would be no point in their existence. If we would use the expression 'function of religion' in this sense, that would imply that religion would be subservient to a higher goal. And if religion would be seen as subservient to a higher goal, its value would be dependent upon that. Such a view of religion, it might be argued, would devaluate religion. It would devaluate religion by acknowledging merely instrumental value in religion, and denying the intrinsic value of religion. This is not the sense in which I will use the phrase 'function of religion' here.

'Function' can also be taken in another, closely related but nevertheless very different sense, namely that of 'proper activity,' 'appropriate behaviour,' or 'role.' The example of 'the function of a motorcar' can also be interpreted in this way. It is not only the goal of a motorcar to facilitate travelling, but also its 'proper activity'

---

1   In the present volume, 57.

or 'role.' In the case of motorcars, proper activity and goal coincide. This is merely a contingent fact about motorcars, however; there is no necessary conceptual connection between proper activity, goal, and justification of existence. To illustrate this by means of an example, it has often been held by philosophers that theoretical thinking, or, in other words, philosophising, is the proper activity of human beings. But this need not imply that it also is the justification for the existence of human beings! Even when they are born philosophers, human beings may be taken to be goals-in-themselves! Similarly, religion may have a role or proper activity of its own, without its being implied that religion needs a non-religious justification.

I do not think that there are serious objections to asking what the functions of religion are in this sense. Asking this question is asking for the proper object of religion, asking what religion is intended to do and what it is not intended to do. It does not imply the imposition of alien criteria on religion, but merely asks what religion itself aims to do. In this sense, it might be part of the function of religion to mediate the vision of God that was so important to Whitehead.[2] And it is not the function of religion, contrary to what some caricatures of Transcendent Meditation take it to be, to enable us to become weightless and thus to facilitate travelling through the air.

It is in this sense, that I will inquire about the function(s) of religion. More precisely, I will ask whether it is among the functions of religion to enable us to make sense of our lives. Is it a characteristic feature of religion that it helps us to discover the meaning of life?

2 More Preliminary Remarks: The Meaning of Life

In his *Theology and Philosophical Inquiry*, Vincent Brümmer defines 'the *meaning* of something as the totality of prescriptive properties of that thing.' He explains: 'We thus know the meaning of something when we know what attitude we ought to have towards it. We know the *meaning* of a situation when we know what we ought to do in that situation. We know the *meaning* of life when we know what ideal or objectives we ought to pursue in life' (121).[3] According to Brümmer, it is the task of *views of life* to confer meaning on life. He defines a view of life as 'the total set of norms, ideals, and eschatological expectations in terms of which someone directs and assesses his way of life' (132-133). As a rule, a view of life confers

---

2   Sia, 'Function of Religion,' in this volume, 65.
3   In this paragraph, the numbers between brackets in the text refer to pages of *Theology and Philosophical Inquiry* (London 1981).

meaning on life by proposing what Brümmer calls a 'primary determinant of meaning' (PDM). Each religion asserts of its own PDM (a) that it is factually unique; (b) that 'the attitude appropriate to it differs from attitudes appropriate to any other reality,' and (c) that 'the attitude we ought to adopt to any other thing or event, etc., is ultimately determined by its relation to' this PDM (133-134). As examples of PDMs Brümmer mentions the God of the Bible, Nirvana, Allah, the Absolute, Ideas, Nature, Mankind and Reason (134). It is clear, then, that by 'view of life' Brümmer understands religion, or its secular functional equivalent.

In this way, Brümmer clearly subscribes to the following propositions: (a) It is clear what the phrase 'meaning of life' means; (b) It is the function of religion[4] to determine the meaning of life. These convictions, though widely held, have recently come under severe attack. It is argued, more concretely, (1) that the phrase 'meaning of life' and the corresponding concern are of recent origin, (2) that by interpreting the function of religion in terms of 'providing meaning for life,' one necessarily misinterprets religion, and (3) that it is so unclear what is meant by the phrase 'meaning of life' (because the concept of meaningfulness is not well understood), that we should rather avoid it. I will now address each of these three issues in turn, propose a specific interpretation of the phrase 'meaning of life' and advocate that it is one of the functions of religion to satisfy the corresponding concern. Finally, I will substantiate some of my suggestions by analyzing a specific way in which religion sometimes provides life with a meaning, viz. by upholding the life of a concrete person as an ideal worth emulating.

3   The 'Meaning of Life': Questioning the Concept

The history of the concept of 'meaning of life' often figures in arguments about its meaning and use. It is frequently argued that the expression 'meaning of life' is of recent origin, and that the coining of this expression reflects certain important developments within our culture. This sometimes leads to the conclusion that the meaning of life cannot be the main focus of religion, because religion was there before the meaning of life was even thought about.[5] Moreover, it is sometimes

---

4   Here, I will use the term 'religion' in a general sense so as to include secular views of life which function as alternatives to religion.

5   It has recently been argued that the present use of the term 'religion' is also of recent origin. It appears, however, that while the use of *this* term for the concept of religion is relatively new, in the past other terms (*secta*, *lex*) were used for this concept. That is to say, it is not the *concept* that is of recent origin, but only the *use of this term* for this concept. Cf. Ernst Feil, *Religio I* (Göttingen 1986), *II* (Göttingen 1997). Moreover, even if the *concept* of religion had

argued that the history of the expression 'meaning of life' shows that the corresponding concept is beyond clarification. In this paragraph I will put forward these doubts concerning the value of the concept of meaning of life in some more detail, basing my exposition mainly on Gerhard Sauter's *The Question of Meaning*, that has only recently been published in English.[6] Whenever this seems useful, however, I will also draw upon other literature in which claims similar to those of Sauter are defended.

Discussions about the history of the concept of 'meaning of life' suffer from the fact that different languages use different expressions for this concept. The most frequently used French expression is 'sens de la vie,' German 'Sinn des Lebens,' Dutch 'zin van het leven.' Of the German 'Sinn des Lebens' and the Dutch 'zin van het leven' it is often claimed that they came into use only at the end of the nineteenth century.[7] The words 'Sinn' and 'zin' (in old Dutch: 'sin') were already in use before that time, but were not used for the meaning *of life*. The original meaning of 'Sinn' and 'zin' might be connected with 'direction' (cf. old German 'sinnan,' travel and the Latin 'sensus'); another important meaning of the terms was that of 'meaning' (the 'Sinn' of a text or of a gesture).[8] That the expression 'Sinn des Lebens' was coined at the end of the nineteenth century, is explained by the influence of Nietzsche and his nihilism.[9] As Helmut Gollwitzer explains: 'Das muß mit der Krise des europäischen Geistes zu tun haben, die sich im Nihilismus äußert. Erst

---

not existed in the past, it could hardly be seriously argued that *religions themselves* did not exist. Thus, the recent introduction of the term 'religion' in its present meaning cannot count as an counter-argument against the arguments presented in the main text against the application of meaning-terminology to religion.

6   Gerhard Sauter, *The Question of Meaning: A Theological and Philosophical Orientation* (Cambridge 1995). The German original dates from 1982.

7   Sauter, *Question of Meaning*, ch.2. Odo Marquard, 'Wider die allzu laute Klage vom Sinnverlust: Philosophische Bemerkungen und eine Fürsprache fürs Unsensationelle,' *Frankfurter Allgemeine Zeitung* 253 (31.10.1983), 9-10; revd. version 'Zur Diätetik der Sinnerwartung: Philosophische Bemerkungen,' in: id., *Apologie des Zufälligen: Philosophische Studien* (Leipzig 1986), 33-53, asserts that the term first appears in a piece by Dilthey published in 1883. Hermann Lübbe, 'Theodizee und Lebenssinn,' *Archivio di Filosofia* 56 (1988), states that 'Erst Wilhelm Dilthey – so der gegenwärtige Stand einschlägiger Bemühungen zur Erforschung der Geschichte der Formel "Sinn des Lebens" – hat diese Formel gebraucht, nämlich in den achtziger Jahrendes vorigen Jahrhunderts,' but fails to mention his sources. On the corresponding Dutch expression, H.H. Berger makes similar claims – again without mentioning sources – in 'Zin,' in: Harry Willemsen (ed.), *Woordenboek filosofie* (Assen 1992), 493-494.

8   See, e.g., Helmut Gollwitzer, *Krummes Holz – aufrechter Gang: Zur Frage nach dem Sinn des Lebens* (München 1970), 46-47: Sauter, *Question of Meaning*, 5-6.

9   K.H. Miskotte, *Kennis en bevinding* (Haarlem 1969), 157, however, suspects here the influence of philosophical idealism rather than nihilism, and claims that the term 'meaning of life' presupposes a cosmic view of life.

indem dieser die Frage allgemein bewußt machte, hat man sich aus einem Wort durch Bedeutungswandel ein Ausdrucksmittel für die neue Problematik geschaffen, das nun rasch ins allgemeine Bewußtsein einging.'[10] Thus, the coining of the phrase 'Sinn des Lebens' would reflect a growing consciousness that it is doubtful that life has a meaning; it is only by the introduction of the term 'Sinn' into this new context that the possibility that life is devoid of meaning ('sinnlos,' meaningless) becomes expressible in language. The other side of the coin is, then, that whenever the term 'Sinn' is used in this new context, the possibility that life is 'sinnlos' always resonates or is suggested as well. The use of terms like 'Sinn,' 'Sinnfrage,' 'sinnlos,' 'Sinnlosigkeit,' and 'Sinneskrise'[11] in this connection reflects the rise of nihilism in European culture, and may itself even be an obstacle to the satisfaction of the question of meaning. Whenever the value or purpose or sense of life is discussed in terms of meaning, it is implicitly supposed that this meaning is threatened or questioned. The concept of the meaning of life itself and the context which resonates in it are such, that the mere use of this concept makes it impossible to assert the meaning of life as a matter-of-course.[12] As Gerhard Sauter states:

> Human history has undoubtedly always seen and will always see experiences of futility, times of basic doubt, crises of orientation. But between these and the question of meaning that has been with us for the last century and a half there is a gap. Answers that were previously given to the questions of meaning will no longer speak to us so long as we do not pay attention to the uniqueness of these questions and measure our own questions by them. We have to begin ... at the gap that separates the absolute question of meaning from all that went before.[13]

So much for the recent origin of the phrase 'meaning of life' and the corresponding concern. If this concern is indeed new, we should be careful to note that religions

---

10 Gollwitzer, *Krummes Holz*, 49; cf. Gollwitzer's analysis in Ch.4: 'Die Sinnfrage im Nihilismus,' ibid. 83-175 and Marquard, 'Diätetiek,' 37-38.

11 In contemporary German, the word 'Sinn' is used in an amazing number of compounds. Apart from those mentioned in the main text, I have come across: 'Lebenssinn(frage),' 'Sinnantwort,' 'Sinnbeweis,' 'Sinndebatte,' 'Sinndefizit,' 'Sinndimension,' 'Sinnerwartung,' 'Sinnfindung,' 'Sinnfragenverbot,' 'Sinngarantie,' 'Sinngebung,' 'Sinnintention,' 'Sinnkriterium,' 'Sinnleere,' 'Sinnlosigkeitserfahrung,' 'Sinnlosigkeitsgefühl,' 'Sinnlosigkeitsverdacht,' 'Sinnmasochist,' 'Sinn-Negation,' 'Sinnproblem,' 'Sinnproduzent,' 'Sinnsetzung,' 'Sinnstiftung,' 'Sinnsuchbewegung,' 'Sinnsurrogat,' 'Sinnverlust(klage),' 'Sinnvermisser,' 'Sinnvermissung,' 'Sinnvermittler,' 'Sinnverwaltung(smonopol),' 'Widersinn.'

12 Cf. Gollwitzer, *Krummes Holz*, *passim*; Sauter, *Question of Meaning*, 17.

13 Sauter, *Question of Meaning*, 11.

and religious texts dating from before the rise of this concern (in the second half of the 19th century) cannot be intended as answers to or solutions of this concern. 'We shall not be open to Job and Old Testament scepticism, ... to mystics in the autumn of the Middle Ages, if all we catch in them is ... an echo of the crisis of meaning.'[14] The danger of interpreting longstanding religions and religious texts in categories that have arisen only recently, is that we make them ventriloquize, and loose the sensitivity for their strangeness, and thus for what they really have to say.

Moreover, as I have mentioned above, it is especially Nietzsche who is held responsible for raising the new question of the meaning of life. If I may summarize Sauter's discussion, he interprets Nietzsche as follows. According to Nietzsche, nature itself is without purpose, but the powerful will be able to survive in a meaningless world by themselves dominating a little part of it. Thus, meaning is created by those who master the outward world. Because this option is not open to those without will and power, Christianity, the religion of the powerless, tries to give the world meaning by mastering it *inwardly*, that is by *interpreting* the world as meaningful. The meaning which Christianity thus offers is a counterfeit, a trick whereby meaning is read into a meaningless world. Real meaning is not given, it is self-imposed! 'Only on the basis of the experience that the whole is without meaning is history possible as the giving of meaning to what is meaningless.'[15] Thus, the Nietzschean question of meaning rules out creation by God and makes us creators.

Meaning, then, is 'always ... manufactured and thus bears the mark of what we ourselves produce.'[16] If it is true that 'meaning' is thus intrinsically connected with the meaningless-in-itself that is being given meaning *by human beings*, interpreting traditional religions like Christianity as providers of meaning must necessarily go against the self-understanding of these religions. The question of meaning taken as a category of interpretation for theism is not merely anachronistic, it is also materially incompatible with theism. As Sauter has it, 'The question of God, when translated into the question of meaning, leaves no place for talk of the revelation and

---

14 Sauter, *Question of Meaning*, 11.

15 Sauter, *Question of Meaning*, 61-71 (quotation 67).

16 Sauter, *Question of Meaning*, 128, cf. 13; cf. Lübbe, 'Theodizee und Lebenssinn,' 407-414. This claim sounds less plausible when phrased in English than when made in German or Dutch, because these languages very frequently use 'Sinn' and 'zin' in the composites 'Sinngebung' and 'zingeving,' thus presupposing meaninglessness as coming before meaning. See H.J. Adriaanse, 'Het lichtend wereldbouwwerk,' in: G.A. van der Wal & F.C.L.M. Jacobs (eds.), *Vragen naar zin: Beschouwingen over zingevingsproblematiek* (Baarn 1992), 161, and cf. the title of a a recent Utrecht inaugural oration of Susan Wolf, *Meaningful Lives in a Meaningless World* (Utrecht 1997). See also G.M. van Asperen, 'Één temidden van velen: Zingeving en ethiek,' Van der Wal & Jacobs, *Vragen naar zin*, 88.

silence of God.'[17] The question of meaning leads to 'a positing of meaning instead of to openness to given meaning.'[18] And that, of course, is not intended as a recommendation for the translation of the question of God into that of meaning.

But it is not only that by phrasing the human quest in terms of meaning we run the risk of substituting our own action for God's action. It is also the case that by thus phrasing this quest and by consequently presupposing the nihilistic position that the world-in-itself is meaningless, we become so anxious for some stronghold that we run the risk of projecting it where it in fact is absent. This happens when we read into religion 'the wishful thinking of an all-embracing security.'[19]

It follows that the term 'meaning' is sometimes taken to have overtones that those who use the term innocently, do not intend. Though the term may be used in the – in German – more or less original sense of 'direction,' and then be almost equivalent to 'purpose' of life, it seems to be almost unavoidable that the idea of an interpretation (cf. the meaning of a text) given to an in itself meaningless life by a human being also resonates. If that is the case, if the meaning of this term is so complex, should we use the expression 'meaning of life' at all? Gerhard Sauter seems to be of the opinion that the expression is so tainted by its history that it is beyond clarification. As the term stands, it is of 'dubious significance,' and 'there is no adequate terminology clarification.'[20] These objections to the expression 'meaning of life' are reminiscent of the complaints which philosophers coming from the analytic tradition have expressed about this phrase, such as that 'Even if this ... question is not unintelligible, as the logical positivists thought, its obscurity and its scope are such as to make the risk of finding oneself talking pompous nonsense fairly great.'[21]

17   Sauter, Question of Meaning, 81.
18   Sauter, Question of Meaning, 150.
19   Sauter, Question of Meaning, 144. Sauter sees this danger exemplified in Hans Küng.
20   Sauter, Question of Meaning, 9.
21   Wolf, Meaningful Lives, 4. Cf. Kai Nielsen, 'Linguistic Philosophy and "The Meaning of Life,"' in: Elmar D. Klemke (ed.), The Meaning of Life (Oxford 1981), 177-204; John Wisdom, 'The Meanings of the Question of Life,' in: Klemke (ed.), Meaning of Life, 205-208; R.W. Hepburn, 'Questions about the Meaning of Life,' in: Klemke (ed.), 209-226; W.D. Joske, 'Philosophy and the Meaning of Life,' in: Klemke (ed.), Meaning of Life, 248-261; Rudolf Wohlgennant, 'Has the Question about the Meaning of Life any Meaning?' in: Oswalf Hanfling (ed.), Life and Meaning: A Reader (rpt. Oxford 1992), 34-38.

In the previous section I have at some length presented the misgivings of Gerhard Sauter and others about the continual use of the expression 'meaning of life.' In this section I will explain why I am not convinced by the arguments that have been given that we should not use this expression as a hermeneutical category in interpreting religion.

Firstly, as regards the history of the expression 'meaning of life,' recent research has shown that, though the expression has no ancient history, it is not as contemporaneous as has been supposed by Sauter and Marquard. It has especially been Volker Gerhardt who has shown that this term was frequently used some decades before 1883, the year in which Odo Marquard dates the 'birth' of this expression.[22] Even if we pay no attention to an occasional use of the term by Johann Wolfgang von Goethe in a letter dating from 1796,[23] we should certainly mention the use of the phrase 'Sinn seines Daseins' by J.G. Fichte in 1812.[24]After Fichte, Ludwig Feuerbach (1846) and Arthur Schopenhauer (1851)[25] were among those who used the expression 'Sinn des Lebens'; it may have been through Schopenhauer that the expression became more widely known.[26] It appears that also in other languages, such as English, the meaning and meaninglessness of life were being talked about before 1883.[27]

All this renders the connection which Gollwitzer, Sauter and others see between the coming into use of the expression 'meaning of life' and Nietzschean nihilism very doubtful; Nietzsche was born only in 1844 and thus can hardly have influenced the use which Goethe, Fichte, Feuerbach and Schopenhauer made of the expression.

---

22 Gerhardt, 'Sinn des Lebens,' in: Joachim Ritter & Karlfried Gründer (eds.), *Historisches Wörterbuch der Philosophie* Vol.9 (Darmstadt 1995), cols.815-824; id., 'Sinn des Lebens: Über einen Zusammenhang zwischen antiker und moderner Philosophie,' in: V. Caysa & K.D. Eichler (eds.), *Praxis – Vernunft – Gemeinschaft* (1994), 371-386. To the first of these articles I owe most of the information in this paragraph.

23 Johann Wolfgang von Goethe, 'Brief an Friedrich Schiller (9.7.1796),' in: Hermann Dollinger (ed.), *Der Briefwechsel zwischen Schiller und Goethe* (Stuttgart 1948), 82 uses 'Leben und Lebenssinn' as a parallel to 'Kunst and Kunstsinn.'

24 Johann Gottlieb Fichte, *Das System der Sittenlehre*, in: J.H. Fichte (ed.), *Johann Gottlieb Fichte's Nachgelassene Werke* Vol.3 (Bonn 1835), 23.

25 Ludwig Feuerbach, 'Die Unsterblichkeitsfrage vom Standpunkte der Anthropologie,' in: W. Schuffenhauer (ed.), *Gesammelte Werke* Vol.10 (1971), 282; A. Schopenhauer, 'Aphorismen zur Lebensweisheit,' VI, in: A. Hübschner (ed.), *Sämtliche Werke* 1 (1938), 523. These citations are given by Gerhardt, 'Sinn des Lebens,' and I have not been able to verify them.

26 Gerhardt, 'Sinn des Lebens,' 816.

27 *Lloyd's Encyclopaedic Dictionary* Vol.4 (London 1895) quotes an example from *Scribner's Magazine* June 1877, 216: 'This life of meaninglessness and idleness.'

If it was not nihilism which led to the use of the expression, what was it? Here Odo Marquard comes with a helpful hypothesis, by suggesting that

> Sinn ist eine Deckname für Glück. Es ist plausibel, daß er – als Begriff für das Lohnen des Lebens – gerade im 19. Jahrhundert ins Spiel kommt: zu einer Zeit, wo – als Folge des Erfolgs der kantischen Pflichtethik des kategorischen Imperativs und ihrer sogenannten Eudämonismuskritik, ihrer Kritik der Glücksethik – das Glücksproblem als zentrales Positivproblem aus der Philosophie verbannt war, und zwar so sehr, daß auch noch dort, wo – weil man das Glücksproblem als zentrales Positivproblem nicht auf Dauer aus der Philosophie verbannen kann – das Glücksproblem wiederkehrte, das Problem des Glücks nicht mehr unter seinem eigenen Namen auftreten dürfte, sondern nur unter Decknamen: dann also – zunächst und seither immer wieder – als Problem des Sinns.[28]

In other words: when 'happiness' ceased to be an acceptable term for the good life among the philosophical intelligentsia, 'meaning of life' was used to fill the vacuum. The Kantian critique of eudemonism may indeed have played a role here – especially in the German-speaking world – but it may also have played a role that the predominant philosophical use of 'happiness' in the sense of the Greek *eudaimonia* differed too much from the common use of 'happiness' as 'contentment, satisfaction, pleasure.'[29] It can easily lead to misunderstandings when the technical use of a term differs too much from its use in ordinary language; once there is a satisfactory alternative, it may be well-advised to use that. In this case, 'meaning of life' was such a satisfactory alternative for the existing term.

All in all, though the expression 'meaning of life' is of relatively recent origin, there seems to be reason to suppose that this new expression does not denote a new concept. This is corroborated by the investigations of Volker Gerhardt, who notes that 'Sinn des Lebens' is used without much difference in meaning besides earlier expressions such as 'Zweck des Lebens' and 'Wert des Lebens,'[30] and by Odo Marquard, who mentions some of the parallel terms that have come into use more recently, such as 'self-realisation' and 'quality of life.'[31] The concept of 'meaning

---

28   Marquard, 'Diätetik,' 42-43.
29   On the difference between happiness in this sense and *eudaimonia*, see my 'Introduction: Happiness, Well-being and the Meaning of Life,' in: Vincent Brümmer & Marcel Sarot (eds.), *Happiness, Well-being and the Meaning of Life: A Dialogue of Social Science and Religion* (Kampen 1996), esp. 3-13.
30   Gerhardt, 'Sinn des Lebens,' 815-816; see also the other article by Gerhardt.
31   Marquard, 'Diätetik,' 43.

of life,' then, does not seem to differ categorically from many of the other concepts that have been used to discuss the good life.

If that is the case, how does one account for the popularity of the expression? According to Gerhardt 'kann nur die Übernahme alter philosophischer und literarische Topoi erklären, daß sich die Sinnfrage in der Mitte des 19. Jh. ganz selbstverständlich einstellt.' It is precisely the continuity with questions that have been discussed by philosophers through all ages, that explains why the introduction of the expression 'meaning of life' has been so successful.[32] However, while this continuity may explain why the new expression was used without objections, it does not make clear why it was often preferred above standing expressions, sometimes to such an extent that it has almost driven these out of use. May it not be the case, that the neutrality and comprehensiveness of the new expression account for that? By comprehensiveness I mean that 'meaning of life' certainly has a wider connotation than many of its rivals, such as, e.g., 'aim of life' and 'purpose of life.' Such expressions seem to suggest that it is not up to human beings to decide what the meaning of life is; this meaning is put before them by, usually, God. And when Christian catechisms start with the question 'What is the aim of human life,' characteristic answers are 'To know God, by whom we have been created' (Calvin's Geneva Catechism) and 'To serve God, and thereby to enter into heaven' (a Dutch Roman Catholic Catechism). That leads me to the second advantage of 'meaning of life' over its rivals: this new expression is not commonly associated with a long tradition of Christian answers, and therefore is more neutral in the sense that it does not seem to limit the possible answers to questions about the meaning of life to Christian ones. It seems to me that this expression serves nihilistic purposes just as well as Christian purposes,[33] and that this partly explains its success.

But is there nothing to be said for the arguments of those who contend that use of 'meaning of life' as an interpretative category necessarily leads to a misrepresentation of Christian belief? They are right, of course, that the expression is of much more recent origin that Christianity itself. But that does not show that the expression can have no use within an exposition of the Christian faith. To give a parallel example, although the term 'hedonism' is also of nineteenth-century origin,[34] in

---

32   Gerhardt, 'Sinn des Lebens,' 816.
33   It was used without reservations, for example, by orthodox Dutch protestants in J. Severijn et al., *De zin van het leven* (The Hague 1957), and by the authors of the Dutch Roman-Catholic catechism of the 1960s, (*De nieuwe katechismus* [Bussum 1966], 5).
34   On the 19th-century origin of this term, see Michael Erler, 'Epikur,' in: Hellmut Flashar (ed.), *Die hellenistische Philosophie* (Basel 1994), 155.

that case I have never seen it defended that therefore it is not applicable to, say, Aristippus of Cyrene.

What about the argument that meaning is intrinsically related to meaninglessness, so that meaning can only be given by human beings to something that in itself is meaningless? Though it is true that there are nowadays many who do not believe in any meaning that is bestowed (by God) on human beings, I do not see any reason to claim an intrinsic connection between meaning and meaninglessness. I have mentioned above that 'meaning' was used in connection with texts before it was used in connection with human life, and this other and older use still influences the ways in which we talk about the meaning of life.[35] But in the case of a text we discover meaning rather than create it, and there would be few who believe that before we discover the meaning of a text, it is meaningless. Similar positions have been defended in the debate about the meaning of life, and I do not see how one could make it plausible that the use of the term meaning in itself renders these positions less feasible.

The final objection to the use of the expression 'meaning of life' which I want to discuss here, is that we have good reason to doubt its meaningfulness. This objection may take several forms. In a weak form, the objection asserts that this expression tends to evoke nihilistic undertones or associations, and that this renders the expression less useful. In this form, the objection appears to be untenable, since there is no clear connection with nihilism at all. In its strongest form, the objection claims that the application of 'meaning' to life betrays a category mistake: words and phrases and texts have a meaning, but objects and persons and life are not the kinds of things which can have meaning. The proper use of meaning, then, is restricted to language. Sauter seems to come close to this position, when he has no problems with 'Sinn' as direction and as applied to texts, but doubts the possibility of clarifying the expression 'Sinn des Lebens.' And several of the analytical philosophers whom I have mentioned above as discussing the meaningfulness of the expression, discuss this objection as well, but they all reject it. Let me quote, by way of example, an analytical philosopher whom I have not yet mentioned, Yeager Hudson. Hudson replies to this objection:

> The primary sense of meaning is not the only one. If I come home to find my wife walking out of the door with suitcases in her hands, I may quite properly ask, 'What is the meaning of this?' It is a perfectly intelligible question that

---

35   Cf. my 'Sisyphus Revisited: Reflections on the Analogy between Linguistic Meaning and the Meaning of Life,' *Neue Zeitschrift für Systematische Theologie und Religionsphilosophie* 38 (1996), 219-231.

admits of several different answers. 'I've had enough of your taking me for granted. I'm leaving you,' she might say, and this tells me in no uncertain terms what her actions mean. Or she might explain that her sister has been hospitalized and that she is going to help out for a few days – another entirely intelligible explanation of what the packed suitcases mean.

We need not explore all the different kinds of meaning in order to recognize that not just words, phrases, sentences, and paragraphs, but also such things as actions (leaving home, pounding the table, ripping up a letter), objects (packed suitcases, a puddle of water on the floor), and events (an ambulance approaching one's house, the lights suddenly going out) can have meaning. ... All these are quite proper senses of 'meaning' – and so is the sense we intend when we speak of the meaning of life.[36]

But, someone might object, the meaning of life differs from the meaning of actions, objects and events, in that the meaning of actions, objects and events can be explained within a larger context, whereas if one asks what the meaning of life is for a specific person, there is no larger context within which the explanation can take place. An action or event can have meaning within a life, but within what context can I assess the meaning of my life? For me, there is no wider context! In response to this, I would like to point out that this is begging the question. Firstly, many people would suppose that there is a larger context within which to assess the meaning of my life. And secondly, it depends on the interpretation of meaning whether such a wider context is really needed. If one interprets 'meaning' as 'value,'[37] such a wider context can be dispensed with. For if we ask whether life has value-in-itself, and not for anything else, that is to say whether life is worth living, this question can certainly be answered without referring to a wider context.

The weakest form the objection against the meaningfulness of 'meaning of life' can take, is that this phrase is used in so many different ways, that anyone who chooses to use it should clarify the way in which (s)he intends it to be understood. In this form, I would wholeheartedly accept the objection.

I conclude, then, that we can use the expression 'meaning of life' without hesitation, though we should not use it without definition or further clarification. Moreover, though the expression 'meaning of life' is of relatively recent origin, the concept expressed by it is not, and we may apply it to (ancient) religions without necessarily distorting our understanding of these. But this still does not answer the question

---

36   Yeager Hudson, *The Philosophy of Religion* (London 1991), 320.
37   Cf. Hudson, *Philosophy of Religion*, 320, and Gerhardt, 'Sinn des Lebens,' 815-816.

posed above positively: is it one of the functions of religion to bestow meaning on life? In the following, I will by means of an analysis of the Christian ideal of *imitatio Christi* attempt to show that it is one of the main functions of Christianity to point to a (the?) way of finding meaning in life.

5 Religion and Meaning: A Case Study of the Ideal of Imitating Christ[38]

According to W.D. Joske, 'the question "What is the meaning of life?" is notoriously vague. (T)he vagueness grows out of the obscurity of the word "meaning."'[39] In the following, I will use 'meaningful' in the sense of 'worthwhile, worth living.'[40] I hope that this clarification takes away the vagueness. But, as Joske notes, 'In addition to being vague it ['the meaning of life' – MS] is ambiguous. The questioner may be seeking or doubting the significance of life in general, of human life or of his own particular life.'[41] Here, I would like to stipulate that I will use 'life' in 'the meaning of life' for the life of the individual. When I announce here that it is my intention in this section to study one of the ways in which religion provides life with a meaning, I mean by that that I will study one of the ways in which religion makes the life of the individual worthwhile.

According to a traditional humanist account of the meaning of life, a person's life is meaningful when that person has fully developed his capacities for the good. In the ancient Greeks, this idea is called *eudaimonia*; nowadays, we would rather speak of self-actualization or self-fulfilment. A helpful analogy might be that of a seed that has to become a plant, and then metaphors like 'flourishing' and 'blossoming' may be used.[42] There are many forms of eudemonism, differing in many ways. One of the main ways to distinguish these, is by the capacities which they take to be the human good. Some forms of eudemonism are Christian in that they determine what is the good for human beings by means of criteria provided by God's revelation in Christ.[43] In this way, certain character traits or talents might be recommended as worth developing, such as, e.g., being loving towards one's

---

38 This part of my paper is based on my *Het goede leven: Idealen van een goed leven in confrontatie met de tragiek van het bestaan* (Zoetermeer 1997), 115-123.

39 Joske, 'Philosophy and the Meaning of Life,' 248.

40 Cf. my *Het goede leven*, 20; Wolf, *Meaningful Lives*, 5-6, 9-10; Marquard, 'Diätetik,' 36: 'Sinn hat, was sich – gegebenenfalls absolut – lohnt (was wichtig ist, erfüllt, zufrieden, glücklich macht...'

41 Joske, 'Philosophy and the Meaning of Life,' 249.

42 On eudemonist views of the good or meaningful life, see my 'Happiness,' 8-10, en *Het goede leven*, 104-115.

43 Sarot, *Het goede leven*, 115-117.

neighbour. From a philosophical point of view much more interesting, however, is the form of Christian humanism which offers a role model for emulation. The saints – or, in protestantism, the reformers, may function as such role models. The most obvious case, however, is the imitation of Christ. This ideal, one might argue, is characteristic of the most radical form of Christian humanism.[44] Moreover, and that is not unimportant for our present purposes, imitating Christ is not just the hobby of a few Christian fanatics, but one of the main ways in which Christian spirituality has through the ages been conceived. So Mark McIntosh: 'The response to Jesus that the Spirit evokes ... is not a neutral acknowledgement but a willingness to follow Jesus.'[45]

The theological background of the ideal of the imitation of Christ is the following. Human beings are created in the image and after the likeness of God (Gen.1:26-27). This image and this likeness may not have been entirely lost because of human guilt, but they have been largely obscured (fall of man). God then decided to send God's own Son to the world, who was simultaneously God and perfectly human. In this way God reminded human beings again of what it would mean to be fully human, and thus to be in the image and after the likeness of God (cf. Rom. 8:29). By imitating Christ, human beings can actualize their ideal potentials. Thus human beings are called upon to model their lives on that of a fellow human being. Sometimes this modelling takes place in a very literal way, as the term 'imitation' already suggests. An example of this are the monastic vows of poverty, obedience and celibacy. Whoever makes these vows, intends to follow in the footsteps of Jesus:[46] to be without possessions as Jesus was without possession, to renounce one's own will in obedience to one's superior as Jesus did in obedience to the Father ('not my will, but thine, be done' – Luke 22:42), to remain unmarried as Jesus was unmarried. A very literal interpretation of the ideal of *imitatio Christi* was characteristic of St. Bernard of Clairvaux (1090-1153)[47] and St. Francis of Assisi (1182-1226), with their concentration on Jesus' earthly life. St. Francis went so far in his imitation of Christ, that he tried to reproduce in his own life certain events from the life of Jesus. His biographers have it, that he several times enacted the Last Supper,

---

44 For the following analysis of the ideal of *imitatio Christi* I am indebted to: E.J. Tinsley, 'Imitation of Christ,' in: Gordon S. Wakefield (ed.), *A Dictionary of Christian Spirituality* (London ³1986), 208-209.

45 Mark A. McIntosh, *Mystical Theology: The Integrity of Spirituality and Theology* (Oxford 1998), 151.

46 St. François d'Assise, *Documents: Écrits et Premières Biographies* (Paris ²1968), 45, 55. Cf. Bartholomy of Pisa, *De conformitate vitae Beati Francisci ad vitam Domini Iesu.*

47 R. Newton Flew, *The Idea of Perfection in Christian Theology* (Oxford 1934), esp. 219-221; Étienne Ledeur, 'Imitation du Christ II: Tradition Spirituelle,' in: M. Viller e.a. (eds.), *Dictionnaire de Spiritualité Ascétique et Mystique* VII (Paris 1971), 1571-1573.

and so staged the details of his own death and burial, that these also resembled the death and burial of Christ.[48] He identified above all with the suffering Christ; his whole life became one with the crucified Christ, a *compassio passionis Christi*, a participation in the suffering of Christ.[49]

A turning point in the reflection about the imitation of Christ came with Martin Luther, who firmly rejected the mimetic[50] imitation of Christ. In *The Liberty of a Christian Man*, for example, he decidedly rejects participation in the suffering of Christ and the imitation of His life as a way to salvation. He suspected that the background of this ideal of imitation was a doctrine of works and a denial of grace.[51] He also poses the question in which respects it is permitted to imitate Christ, and answers that Christ may only be imitated, when He has explicitly prescribed this by means of a commandment.[52] In this way, Luther introduces an important problem:[53] what are the criteria for imitation? In which respects should we imitate the life of Jesus, and in which respects not? Should we imitate His clothing, His diet, His haircut? The way in which He behaved towards His mother? His driving the money-changers and traders from the Temple? His poverty, His celibacy? His suffering? H.J. Cadbury claims in this connection that 'an imitation of Christ that imitates the first century ideas of history and nature is no more demanded than one that imitates a contemporary diet and clothing of Jesus,'[54] and thus implicitly rejects the way in which St. Francis imitated Jesus.

Luther's criterion for imitation – imitate Jesus only when He Himself issued instructions to that end – sounds attractive, but is difficult to apply. (1) It would be necessary to distinguish between commandments which Jesus gave to certain groups only, and commandments which He gave to all. Thus it is sometimes claimed that the commandment to imitate Jesus in His poverty was directed at the disciples only

---

48 Ephrem Longpré, *François d'Assise et Son Expérience Spirituelle* (Paris 1966), 37-42.

49 Longpré, *François*, 46; for the Latin quotation, Longpré refers to Thomas of Celano. On St. Francis, see also Ledeur, 'Imitation du Christ,' 1573-1577.

50 *Mimèsis* is the Greek term for copying or mimicry. 'Mimetic representation' is sometimes used as a philosophical term for that form of representation that attempts to be an accurate copy of the original. See, e.g., Ilse Bulhof & Ruud Welten (eds.), *Verloren presenties: Over de representatiecrisis in religie, kunst, media en politiek* (Kampen 1996), 8, 131-136.

51 WA 7, 58, 31ff. Cf. Dennis Ngien, *The Suffering of God according to Martin Luther's 'Theologia Crucis'* (Frankfurt aM 1995), 35-37; Tinsley, 'Imitation,' 208.

52 Tischreden 1, 775; in: Heinrich Fausel, *D. Martin Luther: Leben und Werk 2 – 1522 bis 1546* (München 1966), 79.

53 More about Luther's views – and his criticism of the ideal of *imitatio Christi* – in my *Het goede leven*, 123, and in Olavi Tarvainen, 'Der Gedanke der Conformitas Christi in Luthers Theologie,' *Zeitschrift für systematische Theologie* 22 (1953), 26-43.

54 Quoted by Tinsley, 'Imitation of Christ,' 208.

(Mat.10:9, Mark 6:8, Luke 9:3, 10:4; but cf. also Acts 2:44-45), and that consequently not all Christians are expected to live without possessions.[55] Thus Jesus says to the young man that for entering into eternal life, keeping the commandments suffices. The selling of his possessions and distributing the proceeds among the poor are explicitly connected with striving for perfection and becoming a disciple (Mat. 19:16-26; more radical: Mark 10:17-27, Luke 18:18-27). Consequently, it seems that we should distinguish between different forms or degrees of imitation.

(2) The next problem with Luther's criterion is, that it can plausibly be argued that certain aspects of Jesus' life should be imitated, even though Jesus does not explicitly command it. This goes, for example, for Jesus' attitude towards children. Jesus had a very open and loving attitude towards children (Mark 10:14 par.), but does not explicitly prescribe the same attitude to His followers. But can one imitate Christ without adopting a similar attitude?

(3) A third problem that is not solved by Luther's criterion, is *the way in which* we should imitate various aspects of Jesus' life. Let me give two examples. Acts 2:44 has: 'All that believed ... had all things common.' In this way the commandment of poverty is often interpreted by monastic orders: the individual members have no possessions, but the community has. In many cases, both now and in the past, these communities have grown to be quite wealthy, and their members live in relative prosperity. In the Netherlands, few monks and nuns live in a poverty comparable to that of an unmarried mother with children on social security. And even if they do – and that is to be admired – they do not live in the same fear of unexpected costs ('What can I do if my washing machine breaks down?' 'If I am a month behind on my rent, I could be expelled from my house'); in case of emergency, their order will look after them. This is not meant as a criticism; someone who does not live according to the commandment of poverty should not criticize those who try to do so. But it does show, how difficult it is to imitate even a small part of Jesus' life under very different circumstances. And it would not be difficult to mention other, similar examples. The admonition to take our cross upon us, for example (Mat. 10:38; cf. Luke 14:27, Mark 8:34), has been interpreted in many different ways, leading to different courses of action.[56] Thus, even if it would be clear which aspects of Jesus' life we should imitate, this does not mean that we also know how to imitate these aspects.

It is of course not possible to solve the problem of criteria for the imitation of Christ here. It seems clear to me, that Luther is right that Christians should not try

---

55   See, e.g., Emmanuel V. Severus, 'Nachfolge,' in: Christian Schütz (ed.), *Praktisches Lexikon der Spiritualität* (1988; rpt. Freiburg 1992), 914.

56   On 'Kreuzesnachfolge,' see Gemma Hinricher, 'Kreuz,' in: Schütz (ed.), *Lexikon der Spiritualität*, 731-734; Sarot, *Het goede leven*, 121.

literally to mimic the life of their Saviour: copying is neither feasible, nor desirable.[57] Imitation should not be taken in the sense of mimicry or copying, but in the sense of emulation: the way in which we can imitate Christ depends upon the person we are and the circumstances we live in. It might in some cases be desirable – contrary to the views of Luther – to imitate aspects of the life of Jesus which he did not command us to imitate. In this connection a distinction which Ilse Bulhof draws from aesthetical theories may be useful.[58] Bulhof starts from the presupposition that imitation is a form of representation. Whoever imitates Jesus, represents Him (cf. 'We are the hands and feet of Jesus'). Works of art can be represented in two ways. Firstly, in the way one renders a picture present: by copying it. And secondly, in the way one renders a musical composition or a play present: by performing it. Such a performance, however, is not a copy but a creative interpretation. A good performance of a musical composition not only does justice to the intentions of the composer, but also shows something of the personality and the ideas of those performing it. Now Bulhof claims that the imitation of a person should be like the performance of a play or a musical composition rather than like the copying of a painting. Imitation is a creative process[59] with two focuses: the model or person to be imitated, and the imitating person. In this way it would be possible to do justice to the individuality of each particular person.

6   Conclusions

I have provided a two-stage argument in favour of the view that it is a main function of religion to show the meaning of life. In the first stage, I have argued that, despite a number of arguments to the contrary, there is no *prima facie* reason to assume that the 19th-century phrase 'meaning of life' cannot be used to describe a main function of religion. In the second stage, I have provided a case study of the Christian ideal of the imitation of Christ. I have argued that it is exactly the function of this central Christian ideal to show what could make life worthwhile or meaningful. Thus, it in fact is one of the functions (in the sense of proper activities) of Christianity to hold an ideal of the meaningful life before us. Of course, this does not entail that is characteristic for *all* religions that they help us to discover meaning in life. It does,

---

57   See also Martin Honecker, *Einführung in die theologische Ethik: Grundlagen und Grundbegriffe* (Berlin 1990), 150.

58   Ilse N. Bulhof, 'Levenskunst,' in: Bulhof & Welten (eds.), *Verloren presenties*, 152-174.

59   Cf. also Ernst Wolf, *Peregrinatio II: Studien zur reformatorischen Theologie, zum Kirchenrecht und zur Sozialethik* (München 1965), 241, who – referring to Roman-Catholic moral theology – speaks of 'schöpferische Nachfolge.'

however, add to the initial plausibility of the claim that there are close connections between religion and the meaning of life. Moreover, my analysis of the ideal of *imitatio Christi* has laid bare a characteristic way in which religion can give meaning, and has also uncovered some of the problems which religion encounters in doing so.

6. Christianity and Evolution

A Case Study

Keith Ward (Oxford)

1 Introduction

Since the sixteenth century there has been an explosive expansion of human knowledge of the universe. It has been caused largely by commitment to an ideal of scientific knowledge, which was made possible by a combination of the invention of new means of controlled observation and the development of sophisticated mathematical techniques. The results have been spectacular and totally unforeseen, and have revolutionised human thought about the universe.

It may be said that Christian belief is not primarily about the nature of the physical universe. But the Bible does contain remarks about the creation of the universe, about the first human beings, about the origin of death, about the role of angels and demons in human life, about the probable course of human history, and about the end of the universe. Christianity makes the life of Jesus of central importance to its account of the whole of the created order. Its iconography gives human beings, especially in the persons of Jesus, Mary and the saints, a privileged place in heaven. Its creed apparently places a young human being, Jesus, as co-equal with the creator of heaven and earth. In other words, the Christian story seems to make humans central to the existence of the universe, and the life of Jesus is seen as a culminating event very near the end of that story.

It is this placing of the one human life at the culminating point of cosmic history which the modern scientific view of the universe has put in question. There was always a 'scandal of particularity' in Christianity. Why should God act in just this one human person, when there are so many other human cultures and histories? But that scandal fades to insignificance in the light of the vast universe which science has discovered.

The universe is fifteen thousand million years old. The earth is one tiny planet on the edge of one galaxy out of millions. This planet will probably continue to exist for five thousand million years, before the dying and expanding sun in its death throes renders it uninhabitable. Humans are the results of millions of years of the gradual evolution of life-forms, and humans will eventually evolve into something else, or die out without causing more than a ripple in the universe as a whole.

The stage on which the Christian story was first thought to be played out has expanded so amazingly that it has, for many, become imaginatively impossible to see this planet, let alone one human life, as of any particular importance in cosmic history. In the face of such a revolution in perception, the question of how far Christianity can adapt, while retaining its identity, is a real and pressing one.

The challenge of the cosmic perspective of science faces virtually all religions, most of which originated in pre-scientific times. I shall, however, confine my attention here to Christianity. I shall also select for consideration just one rather crucial aspect of the scientific theory of cosmic evolution, the Darwinian theory of the evolution of life-forms by natural selection. That is because the Darwinian theory generates in a particularly sharp form the opposition that can arise between religious and scientific views. It thus focuses particularly acutely the issue of how far religious beliefs can change in the light of new knowledge.

I shall take it for granted that new scientific knowledge renders some traditional Christian beliefs false – a literal interpretation of the story of Adam and Eve, for example. The interesting question is whether the new perspective can add depth to some fairly central beliefs, so that new interpretations may plausibly be seen as part of a coherent re-organisation of the whole belief-system, rather than as merely *ad hoc,* slightly desperate adjustments. I shall defend the view that the scientific vision of cosmic evolution forces a coherent and interconnected set of changes on traditional Christian beliefs. In the course of doing that, I hope to clarify one sense in which a set of religious beliefs may be revised and develop, while continuing to constitute one religious tradition.

2   *The Theory of Evolution and the Existence of God*

It is a fairly safe assumption that the writers of the New Testament documents had not come across the theory of evolution. That theory was not invented by Charles Darwin, but his book, *The Origin of Species,*[1] published in 1859, presented it in what may be called its classical form. Darwin did not have access to modern knowledge of genetics, but with its aid we can state his basic theory in four simple propositions. Organisms reproduce. In the course of such reproduction, various mutations occur, now often called 'mistakes' in the copying process whereby DNA replicates itself. Organisms compete for scarce resources, and many of them are eliminated by the environment or by their competitors. Some mutations are naturally

---

1   Charles Darwin, *The Origin of Species by Means of Natural Selection* (rpt. Harmondsworth 1985).

selected by this process, simply because they survive and reproduce more effective-ly than others. Given these four propositions, one is able to see the whole history of organic life on earth as a process of random mutation, in which natural forces con-tinually act to select some mutations in preference to others, and so different species evolve over thousands of years. Homo Sapiens is a species which has evolved by millions of tiny mutations over millions of generations, as our non-human ancestors proved able to survive the hazards of their environments, and continued to produce mutated forms which were favoured by natural selection.

The four basic propositions of the theory have been experimentally well estab-lished. There can be no doubt that DNA replicates and produces continual muta-tions, and the process of natural selection has been repeatedly observed in relatively isolated animal populations. A simple example is that fluffy mice are selected in cold winters in preference to short-haired mice, so that the weather in this case naturally selects fluffy mice, which originally mutated from short-haired mice. The theory of evolution is a generalisation from these truths, which claims that they provide the basis for a general understanding of why organic life on earth today takes the very varied forms it does.

There is much room for dispute about the adequacy and implications of such a generalisation. Stephen Jay Gould takes it to imply that the history of life on earth is a matter of pure chance, an immensely improbable series of accidents which could very easily have taken a very different course. For him, there is no reason why conscious beings should have evolved at all, and humans are an accidental growth at which we should be extremely surprised, but which is in no sense a result of some plan or purpose.[2]

For Richard Dawkins, however, mutations will almost inevitably give rise to conscious organisms at some stage, and once they exist they will quickly eliminate possible competitors. There is an inbuilt tendency to complexity and consciousness. But there is still no purpose or need for a designer, since the process accounts for itself quite adequately, and the introduction of a designer would only complicate matters unduly.[3]

It is difficult to adjudicate between these differing interpretations. To know whether the process of evolution is inevitable or not one would have to know what mutations were liable to occur, and what selective pressures might exist which could be guaranteed to keep the process going in the direction of complexity. It is hard to see how one could know such things. But there is one way in which one could guarantee an evolutionary movement towards complexity and consciousness. That

2   Stephen Jay Gould, *Wonderful Life: The Burgess Shale and the Nature of History* (London 1989).
3   Richard Dawkins, *The Blind Watchmaker* (1986; rpt. Harmondsworth 1991).

is if the system was planned so that mutations of the right kind would occur, and so that selective pressures would favour complex life-forms. Such a plan would require vast intelligence and power over the laws of nature. But it is clearly possible that an evolutionary process could be set up by such an intelligence which would inevitably result, after millions of generations, in human beings, or at least in conscious, rational moral agents very like human beings.

Since this is so, any claim that the theory of evolution does away with the necessity for God, or that it shows that humans evolved by pure chance, is quite unjustified. Gould's interpretation claims that human life could evolve by chance, but that it is extremely improbable that it ever would. Dawkins' interpretation claims that, given the system, something like human life is bound to evolve, but the system itself, with its complex and highly integrated process of relations between mutations and selective natural conditions, just exists by chance. It is obvious, however, that such a system could also be intelligently designed. And the hypothesis of intelligent design makes the existence of the process much more probable than the hypothesis of pure chance. Dawkins may say that the theory does not need God, but it remains true that God is a much better explanation of the process than is chance (which is in fact no explanation at all). In this sense, God may not be necessary to the theory of evolution. But the theory of evolution is much more plausible if there is a God – and that is what Charles Darwin himself thought.

This conclusion may come as a surprise to those who have been accustomed to regard the theory of evolution with suspicion, as somehow in conflict with biblical truth. But that is partly because the theory has sometimes been presented as though it requires the 'pure chance' interpretation, or as though it subordinates the providential acts of God to some sort of impersonal or random process. I have tried to suggest that is just not true.

3   *God and the Cosmic Process*

In some popular presentations, science and religion are portrayed as enemies which can never be reconciled. But such a view would be wildly inaccurate from a historical point of view. Just to take the most obvious example, Isaac Newton was a pious Christian (though it is true he did not accept what he took to be the orthodox doctrine of the Trinity), and he records that he was able to formulate the basic laws of mechanics by postulating that the universe was created by a wise and powerful God. He asked himself the question what general laws such a God would create, and decided that they would be the simplest, most elegant laws, capable of giving rise to complex sets of effects. He turned out to be right, as everyone knows, and so not only did he discover the basic laws of nature, he also vindicated his postulate of a wise creator God.

Perhaps one could pursue Newton's question a little further, in a different form, and ask why a wise creator God might set up a process of evolution by natural selection. Putting it in an even wider context, why would God create a universe which evolves, as a whole, from the primordial Big Bang, an ultimate simplicity of infinite density, without complexity or consciousness, through the emergence of elementary particles, the formation of galaxies and planetary systems, to the evolution of those very complex forms of organic life with central nervous systems and brains that generate awareness and autonomous action?

I suggest that, from a Christian viewpoint, the first clue to answering this question is to see the distinctive value of a process of creative and co-operative realisation and comprehension of new forms of truth, beauty and loving relationships, within a community of sentient moral agents. For Christians, the goal of human existence is the realisation of the 'kingdom of God,' a community in which goodness can be actualised in a society of truth, fidelity, justice and peace. That community is a finite image of the Creator, who is the final truth, the utterly faithful and just, the supremely beautiful and the loving source of all things.

This is a goal which is depicted in Christian revelation, but which is worthwhile in itself, and which could be chosen by an intelligent creator. It would involve the creation of moral agents who could interact with one another in seeking to realise many forms of goodness, to understand their world and shape it in accordance with their imaginative ideals. In other words, a worthwhile goal of creation would be the existence of a community of moral agents, united in the pursuit of goodness.

It may be thought that fifteen thousand million years of cosmic evolution is a very roundabout way to achieve such a goal, when God could presumably create it directly, as many Christians used to think God did. But perhaps the goal is not just the culmination of the process, but the whole process itself, which is one of generating from within a material cosmos the ability of that cosmos to understand and take control of its own being. Human beings are parts of the cosmic process at which one can see this understanding and control begin to exist.

They are not mature conscious agents without a history, who just begin to exist, with the whole material cosmos as an unnecessary backdrop to their activity. They are highly complex material structures, carrying within themselves the history of their development, integral parts of a wider material order. It is that order which they can understand and help to control, and human life should be seen as just one part of a wider process of creative development.

The process is one of creative emergence, as new forms of intelligibility and beauty successively come into existence out of earlier and simpler structures. From the explosive destruction of primordial undifferentiated energy emerge the elements of hydrogen and helium. From the interaction of those elements emerge the stars and galaxies, and the more complex formation of carbon atoms. From the complex organisation of carbon atoms emerge RNA and DNA, the primal structures making self-replication possible. From the recombinations of nucleotides emerge self-sustaining organic structures which produce central nervous systems and primitive brains. And from the elementary forms of perception and semi-automatic response to stimuli emerge the capacities for abstract understanding and free action which characterise human beings.

One can see this whole process as if it were a work of creative imagination, continually building complex structures out of simpler elements, and always moving towards the capacity of the process to know and shape itself. If it is such a work, the whole process will have a beauty, intelligibility and imaginative flair that will be of great value to the creative intelligence which creates it and continues to move it towards that final goal which has been implicit in it from the first. Humans are not, in other words, spiritual substances dropped into the material world as alien intruders. They are parts of a continuum of growing complexity in the material order, realising possibilities implicit in that order from the beginning.

God values the whole cosmic process for its imaginative beauty, its continual realisation of new actualities out of the indefinite array of possibilities which are implicit in its origin. The whole process is of value to God. It is in itself an expression of the imaginative and creative activity of God. But the process of creative emergence is one which generates from itself communities of beings who can know and shape its future. Such beings come to share in the delight and imaginative creativity of God. They can become fellow-workers with God, co-operating with the divine creative Spirit in the task of making the material world a sacrament of the divine Spirit, a world in which wisdom, creativity and friendship can be celebrated and enjoyed.

One might envisage three stages of such a created cosmic process. First is the stage of imaginative creativity, in which the creator shapes ever more complex emergent forms out of the primordial energy, the 'great deep' of potentiality. The Genesis picture of the creative Spirit moving over the waters of the great deep, the sea of primal chaos, expresses this stage well. Next is the stage at which consciousness emerges as a property of the cosmos, and begins to co-operate with God in shaping the cosmos to a form in which it can express the divine Spirit itself. Again the Genesis picture of humans being given dominion over the earth, with the responsibility of making it fruitful, is a very apt one. Third is the consummation of the cosmos, in which it becomes a sacrament of perfect beauty, without conflict or defect, fully expressive of the divine nature as love, shaped by communities of love which share in the expression of the divine love. The New Testament picture of a universe united in Christ depicts such a fulfilled universe.

In this way one can, I think, see why a creator God might originate an emergent, evolutionary cosmic process. It would be a process culminating in the goal of a sacramental community of love, but the process leading to that goal would be an important factor in the value of the goal itself. In that final consummation, the whole process could be summed up and seen as having from the first been directed towards a partly self-shaped conscious union with the creator.

4   The Theistic Hypothesis and the Consummation of the Cosmos

I have suggested that the hypothesis of God makes the emergence of moral life in the cosmos by the general mechanism of Darwinian evolution much more probable than the hypothesis that it occurs by pure chance. But for the God hypothesis to be fully satisfactory, it has to be true that the third stage, the emergence of a community which fully expresses the divine life, will be realised. From a scientific point of view, we do not know whether or not it will be. Scientific optimists do look for a continued increase in knowledge and sensitivity, which will result in a just and peaceful society, free of disease and even of death. Scientific pessimists point out that humans are liable to exterminate themselves at any moment, and that the universe will run down anyway in the end, eliminating any possibility of a final goal of evolution.

Scientific optimists hold that we will be able to control our genetic constitution, thus eliminating the elements of randomness in evolution, with its consequences of disease and death. We will, they say, be able to replace the struggle for survival by co-operation, when we have the technology to ensure abundance of goods for all. Scientific pessimists, however, point out that the people trying to exercise genetic control will themselves be in the grip of the passions of greed and hatred, and are likely to create genetic monstrosities which will probably get wholly out of control. And technology does not make for abundance. On the contrary, it uses up energy resources at an alarming rate, so human conflict over scarce resources is liable to become universally destructive.

Atheists do not have much reason for optimism. It is highly unlikely that blind processes of ruthless competition will issue in the existence of a stable moral community of justice and peace. On the theistic hypothesis, however, the mutational process is not blind or wholly indiscriminate. It involves elements of randomness, but is set up to move inevitably to greater complexity and integrated order. One theistic explanation for the existence of such randomness is that it provides a necessary physical basis for the later development of responsible freedom, which in turn is necessary for the existence of fully personal relationships of love.[4] This requires that the universe is not completely determined, and so, at pre-rational stages, must be partly random.

Nor, for a theist, is the evolutionary process one of ruthless competition. On the contrary, it essentially involves intricate co-operation to produce and maintain living organisms. If evolution is to take place, there must be a replacement of lower by higher forms, but once the stage of rational reflection has been reached, co-operation can increasingly take over from competition, as a driving force for further development.

It looks as though theists will be optimists, expecting evolution to produce responsibly free and co-operative agents, who can subordinate their non-rational and competitive dispositions to more reflective and altruistic intentions. But the story is slightly more complicated. Evolution has produced such agents, but the price of producing them and leaving them free is that they can fail to rise to reflective altruism, and may choose rather to oppress and destroy others than to encourage and sustain them. Theists have to take freely chosen selfishness into account, and that qualifies any over-easy optimism about the future.

In fact, since the earth will be swallowed up by the sun in about one billion years, and the whole universe will eventually run down, it is fairly clear that any ultimate goal for the cosmos must lie beyond this physical space-time. This leads to the conclusion that the third stage will probably be beyond the confines of this cosmos, though it must also be the consummation and recapitulation of this cosmic process. Thus theists are committed to being trans-cosmic optimists. They are committed to believing that there will exist a community of wisdom, joy and love, from which all evil and egoism is excluded. From that viewpoint, the history of this cosmos can be seen as the preparation of sentient beings for existence in the perfected community, though that history has its own distinctive value as the arena of the creative activity of God and the place where created souls can either prepare themselves to share in the life of God or fall into the destructive patterns of egoistic existence.

5   Evolution and the Moral Order

It follows that the theistic hypothesis is the best explanation of the evolutionary process as we see it (making the evolution of sentient beings from initial unconscious states more likely than any other hypothesis). But it does require that one

---

4   Cf. Vincent Brümmer, *Speaking of a Personal God* (Cambridge 1992), 139-145.

sees the process as not wholly morally indiscriminate (not morally random) and as not one solely of ruthless competition.

I think that one's evaluation of these matters will depend largely on personal judgments about the moral value of human life. I would say that the evolutionary process does not look blind to moral values – it does issue in the existence of moral agents, who can shape the world to good or evil by their own choices. But it necessitates much conflict and suffering, and thus seems, considered on its own, to suggest a God who wills to create goodness through suffering, and is thus far from being a wholly kind and gentle God. We might recall, however, that the biblical God is one who inspires terror, who destroys as well as heals, and whose goodness is more awe-inspiring than tender-hearted. It may be that some modern Christian ideas of God fail to preserve the sense of terror and awe of which the Bible is well aware, and which depict the creator as one who wounds and heals, kills and makes alive, but who in the end offers an overwhelming good to those who persevere.

I also think that Darwin's gloomy view of nature as a continual struggle for survival is unduly one-sided. There is a struggle for survival, but most of that struggle does not involve the suffering that characterises organisms with highly developed nervous systems. And the evolutionary process also requires co-operation and self-sacrifice, a creative striving after fuller life and experience, not just a desperate attempt to stay alive at any cost. It is more a 'striving for fuller life' than a ruthless 'struggle for survival.' The process is well-fitted to implant dispositions both to selfish and to altruistic behaviour in the higher conscious animals. Seeing how evolution implants both survival and sacrificial dispositions in complex organisms gives a helpful explanation of why humans should be tempted to evil, and yet obligated to goodness. As the early theologian Irenaeus said, primitive humans were placed between good and evil, so that they might grow to maturity, whether for good or ill, through the responsible choices they made.[5] In the course of evolution, there must have been a first moment of conscious moral choice. That is the point at which the 'Fall of humanity' began, and humans were estranged from that natural fellowship with God which should have been theirs.

It seems to me, then, that the theory of evolution does not require that the process is blindly random, morally indiscriminate, and one of a ruthless war of all against all. These are evaluations, not parts of the scientific theory. The process can be plausibly seen as probabilistic, yet ordered to the realisation of good, and as promoting co-operation and altruism as well as a selfish will to survive. As such, it is best explained by a God with the power to establish such a probabilistic order, and with the will to create morally autonomous conscious agents. Yet the theistic

---

5   See John Hick, *Evil and the God of Love* (1966; reissue London 1985).

hypothesis will only be fully confirmed if there comes to exist a community of souls born in this cosmos but finding their final goal in a trans-cosmic state of unity with God.

That is only to say what most Christians have always said, that the purpose of God will only be fully realised beyond this world. The gospel on which Christianity is founded is that there is such a realisation, and that it has received its confirmation in the resurrection of Jesus. Such confirmation is beyond the investigative techniques of science. It is a matter of faith, but not some sort of irrational leap in the dark. It is a faith based on present experience of a God who promises good, and on the apostolic testimony to Jesus' resurrection as the foreshadowing of the creation of a new heaven and earth.

No scientific theory claims any knowledge of the existence of God and of life after death. Christian revelation is a primary source in history for such claims. It is Jesus who teaches, and shows by his life, that God is a personal God of love, who offers that love endlessly to those who respond to it. One would not expect a scientific description of the physical universe to discover such things. Nevertheless, the scientific description must be consistent with these truths, and one might expect that it may, at least in an indirect way, point towards them.

Some proponents of the theory of evolution may speak of mutation as random, yet it is undeniable that the process has led to the existence of conscious, intentional, morally reflective agents. They may speak of a battle for the survival of the fittest, but it is only by co-operation and inter-dependence that anything survives at all, and the end-state of the process so far is one where consciousness of truth, beauty and friendship have become conscious goals of at least a great many living beings.

Such facts are consistent with the Christian belief that humans are free agents who have trapped themselves in self-will, but are still capable of turning to goodness when it appears to them. The facts of evolution plausibly suggest a universe which is ordered by a wise creator towards the realisation of freely chosen goodness, which has been deflected from that aim by its own misused freedom, and which may yet be open to a restoration of its primal aim by the reconciling action of the creator. If the postulate of a creator is the best explanation of the facts of evolution (making its actual history much more probable than chance), and if the myopic choice of self is the best explanation of much of the suffering on this planet, then one might reasonably hope for some effective action by the creator to make the original goal possible. It is in that way that the scientific description of the universe may actually point towards the possibility of a historical disclosure of the creator, which would reveal the way to the realisation of the creator's goal in an estranged world.

At this point the surprising consonance of Christian revelation with the theory of evolution is apparent. Biblical revelation leads us to see God as the creator of all things. It leads us to see the cosmos as created through Wisdom, which delights in the creative process (Proverbs 8). It sees the cosmos as developing from primal chaos to ordered creation (Genesis 1:2), through the creative activity of the Spirit, patterned on the archetypal Word of God. Human beings are not seen as disembodied souls inserted into alien matter, but as formed of matter (dust), which is shaped to become a finite image of God, to be self-aware and self-directing.

Moreover, the whole created cosmos moves towards a goal, not yet realised but foreshadowed in Christ – 'He has made known to us ... the mystery of his will ... to unite all things in him [Christ], things in heaven and things on earth' (Ephesians 1:9-10). The Christ in which the whole cosmos is to be united is the eternal Word of God, 'the image of the invisible God, the first-born of all creation,' and 'in him all things were created' (Colossians 1:15-16). That eternal Word assumed human nature and was manifest on earth as Jesus, but in itself the Word is infinitely greater than any human life. He is the pattern of all creation, and according to Paul he is the completion of creation, within whose reality all things will be united.

At that time, 'the creation itself will be set free from its bondage to decay and obtain the glorious liberty of the children of God' (Romans 8:21). The Christian hope is not for personal immortality. It is for the transformation of the whole creation into a perfect sacrament of God. The New Testament even holds that this will be an inclusion of creation 'in Christ,' an assumption of the creation into the life of God, a state that some early theologians called 'theosis,' a sharing, by grace, in God.

The biblical picture of the cosmos is thus from the first an evolutionary one, according to which primal matter, the chaos of the 'great deep' is shaped by the Spirit on the pattern of the eternal Wisdom or Word of God, until it becomes finally united in the being of the one who is the perfect image of God, until it becomes the body of Christ, and so, we are compelled to say, the body of God. The history of the cosmos is the history of a development from the inert chaos of primal matter to the fulfilment of its proper function as an embodiment and personal manifestation of the life of God.

The New Testament writers see this development as having been corrupted by the doomed attempt of sentient creatures to turn away from obedience to God. The created cosmos falls away from its intended goal, and becomes subject to futility and spiritual death. The wages of sin is death, existence in estrangement from God, the only source of life. Within this estranged world, the divine Word takes human nature in order to heal the sickness of self, manifest the divine love, and lead humanity back to its proper destiny. When the first Christians looked for the *parousia* of Christ, the manifest presence of the eternal Word, they were looking for a future in which all creation will be renewed in the divine Word, restored to its predestined goal.

They may never have heard of the theory of evolution. But that theory fills out the Christian revelation in an enriching and illuminating way. Some early Christians thought the end of the world would come in their own lifetime. They were unaware of the millions of years that had preceded them, and of the millions of galaxies that surrounded them. They did not realise that the end of life on earth would leave the vast spaces of the cosmos virtually untouched. They suffered from a cosmic myopia for which they could hardly be blamed, given the knowledge available to them.

At the same time, they already possessed the cure for their myopia, though they may not have fully recognised it. The good news of liberation from the bondage of self, and the gift of life-giving union with God, was meant for all humanity, not only for a few contemporary Jews. Prompted by Peter's visions and Paul's enthusiasm, a mission to all nations was initiated which implied that the end of all things was not yet. Since the sixteenth century, the remnants of such Christian myopia should have been thoroughly corrected, as the full extent of the vision of cosmic redemption which is so central to Paul's recorded teaching has become clear. Humans may or may not have a central role in the redemption of the whole cosmos, but at least it is obvious that the death of this planet will not be the end of creation by any means. Creation will have an end, but it will not co-incide with the destruction of the earth, as the New Testament writers almost certainly thought it would. Such knowledge of the vastness of the cosmos does not undermine Christian hope, or the decisiveness of the life of Jesus for the history of planet earth. Its central teaching remains that the ending of the history of the cosmos will be, not a whimpering descent into everlasting darkness, but a recreation of all things in the glorious presence of the divine Word.

This hope does not license a lazy optimism or a relaxation of striving for the good. Our own lives, or the life of the whole planet, may indeed end at any time in disaster. For that reason we must indeed stay alert, for we do not know when the end of human life on earth might come. Nevertheless, the vision of contemporary Christianity is a cosmic vision of the reconciliation and uniting of the whole cosmos into a unity in Christ. It is impossible to say how and when God will accomplish that goal, but it is clear that if the divine purpose is not brought to a premature conclusion by human evil, we are as yet a very long way from its realisation.

There can be no doubt that belief in cosmic evolution forces changes on Christian belief. These changes, however, are not as radical as they may seem at first. If it were established that evolution is really random and non-purposive, that would undermine any form of Christian belief which makes objective claims about the nature of the universe. It would force either a radical form of non-realism, or, more plausibly in my view, an abandonment of Christian belief. Despite the efforts of anti-religious neo-Darwinists, I do not think the non-purposive interpretation has been established, and I am prepared to risk the bet that it will not be.

In that case, one plausible interpretation of a Pauline/Johannine Christology transposes quite easily into an evolutionary context. Such an interpretation was, indeed, very like a set of options current in early forms of Christian thought, even though such options have sometimes been officially denied (as recently as the Roman Catholic Encyclical *Rerum Novarum*, which apparently made belief in Adam and Eve binding).

The New Testament shows that there existed an early belief that Jesus would return very soon in glory to save a selected group of humans from imminent Judgment, and found the kingdom of God. Apparently a surprising number of American Christians (a remarkable 48%) still believe this, despite the fact that they have to reinterpret the 'very soon' quite radically.

This belief, however, already received re-interpretation within the New Testament itself, and it was bound to do so as soon as there was time for reflection on the implications of the nature of the Messianic claim made for Jesus. For it was soon seen that Jesus was the universal Saviour, the incarnation of the eternal Word, and that God had a goal for creation and a global mission for the Church. These beliefs are all incompatible with a literal coming in glory to 'save' just a few Jewish disciples and put an end to history within just a few years.

Reflection on the theory of cosmic evolution does little more than continue this process of re-interpretation. It does so in five main ways. First, it leads one to stress that, while Jesus is the incarnation of the Word on this planet, there may be innumerable worlds and forms of non-human incarnation. So it leads to a less anthropocentric view of redemption and of the possible inhabitants of heaven.

Second, it leads one to emphasise that Jesus shows the universal love of God for every sentient being, and so to adopt a less exclusive attitude to non-Christians and a broader view of the universal mission of the Church.

Third, it leads one to reflect on the immensity of the divine goal for creation, and so to adopt a positively world-transforming attitude to the Christian life, rather than quietistically wait for the world to end (an attitude which Paul anyway condemned).

Fourth, it leads one to adopt a non-literal reading of much of Scripture, especially the narratives of creation and Final Judgment, and so encourages one to explore metaphor and symbol in a way which would have been familiar to Jewish commentators.

Fifth, and perhaps more controversially, it leads one to accept a great degree of chance in nature, and a great degree of relatively autonomous freedom in created beings. Thus it stands in some degree of opposition to accounts of a total divine determination of all things. That reverses the tradition of Augustinian interpretation which was broadly accepted in many Christian churches, but it has strong support in many biblical texts.

Strange and unexpected as it may at first seem, Darwin's discovery may be seen as a valuable extension of our knowledge of the nature of God's creation, putting Christian faith in a wider context in space and time. It can give a greater appreciation of the wisdom of God which is shown in the complexity and beauty of the evolutionary plan, in the disclosure of the true goal of the cosmic process, and in the hope for the whole universe that is foreshadowed in Jesus Christ.

None of this could have been envisaged in this form by the first generations of Christians. It moves Jesus from being the last major event in history to being a proleptic disclosure on earth of a million-year process towards a cosmic goal. This revision can be seen as a development, because its core beliefs of a revelation in Jesus of God as love, of the human goal as sharing in that love, and of the means to the goal as participating in the life of the Spirit, are preserved. The Christian religion remains the same, because it continues to trace its originative and canonical disclosure of the divine to the person of Jesus. It must continually change, because growing knowledge of the context of that disclosure must change its meaning and significance. The impact of evolutionary theory on Christian beliefs is one case which shows how large-scale interpretative changes can plausibly be seen as developments, not repudiations, of a set of canonical and authoritative beliefs.

7. The Implications of Darwinian Explanations

Michael Scott (Utrecht)

1 Introduction

Keith Ward focuses on the Darwinian theory of evolution as a test case for the kind of changes to Christian religious belief that are required by the development of successful scientific theories about the universe, and specifically those aspects of the universe about which Christians have traditionally had something to say. He aims to work out a Christian position on evolution which, while it may not be appealing to many Darwinian scientists, is nevertheless compatible with the theory of evolution and moreover, is informed by scientific discoveries about the mechanism of evolution. To this end, he proceeds first, by pointing out certain weaknesses in the presently available kind of guarantees that can be offered by Darwinian explanations of the current state of evolution of biological life. Second, he modifies Christian claims about the creation of the world so that they remain committed to certain general matters of principle about God's involvement in it, without maintaining any matter of fact that is inconsistent with the current state of scientific knowledge about evolution.

In the first part of this paper I will outline Ward's argument and a number of objections to it. In the second I will argue that he has underestimated the potential threat of Darwin's methodology to religious claims, and that adopting the kind of strategy he advocates to account for discoveries about evolution offers no security against – indeed, invites – ever more dramatic changes in Christian belief.

2 Ward's Argument

Keith Ward takes the theory of evolution to state that conscious life arises from the mindless natural processes of natural selection, genetic mutation, reproduction and competition between organisms. 'Homo Sapiens is a species which has evolved by millions of tiny mutations over millions of generations, as our non-human ancestors proved able to survive the hazards of their environments, and continued to produce mutated forms which were favoured by natural selection' (93). Ward goes on to allow that the occurrence of these processes which produce human life have been experimentally well established. However, as Ward points out, given that these processes occur there remains the question of whether they can account for why biological life has evolved as it has, rather than in some other way. Why is it, for instance, that these processes have given rise to conscious and moral agents? Here, Ward observes considerable disagreement among biologists. He reports Stephen Jay Gould as claiming that 'there is no reason why conscious beings should have evolved at all,' and that 'the history of life on earth is a matter of pure chance' (93), whereas Richard Dawkins takes the contrary view that 'mutations will almost inevitably give rise to conscious organisms at some stage.' Ward doubts whether we can ever know enough about genetic mutation and selective pressures to justify Dawkins' claim, but believes that on either Gould's or Dawkins' interpretations there remains a significant explanatory role to be played by the hypothesis that the world was set up by a powerful and intelligent designer, a being who could design evolutionary processes in such a way that they would give rise to human life. I will call this the theistic hypothesis.

The theistic hypothesis, Ward argues, is not only consistent with evolutionary theory, but also underpins it by guaranteeing that evolutionary processes result in conscious beings. If we believe, along with Gould, that it is highly improbable that human life would result from evolutionary processes, the hypothesis of intelligent designer offers a much better explanation for why human life has nevertheless occurred. Whereas if we believe, along with Dawkins, that evolutionary processes are likely to produce conscious life, the theistic hypothesis explains the existence of those processes and why it is that they take the form that they do. Thus, Ward contends, 'God may not be necessary to the theory of evolution. But the theory of evolution is much more plausible if there is a God' (94). Ward completes this argument by offering a number of considerations, largely to do with the inherent virtues of a gradual development or 'creative emergence' of life, in support of the idea that it is likely that God would create a universe with human beings using just the kind of evolutionary processes that have been found to occur by scientists.

One notable, if minor criticism of Ward's argument, is that the theory of evolution, as he defines and presents it, is just *adaptionism*. Adaptionists claim that the phenotypic characteristics of populations are mostly the result of natural selection. However, many evolutionary biologists are not adaptionists. Indeed, Gould is highly critical of adaptionism. Gould maintains that there are many other constraints on evolutionary development in addition to natural selection, and that natural selection plays only a secondary role in speciation. I take it that Ward could meet this point by loosening his definition of the theory of evolution; I will, however, for the sake of simplicity, follow him in taking natural selection as the principal mechanism of evolution. The particular mechanisms that are in place are not germane to the argument.

A more serious problem concerns Ward's claim that biologists are divided on the idea of whether the evolution of human life is a matter of pure chance or is inevitable. He takes the dispute to be about whether or not the evolution of human life is causally determined. Indeed, he supports the idea that there should be random elements in evolution, since he believes that indeterminism is a logical requirement for free will (97f.). There are well-known and formidable difficulties with this account of free will, one being in showing how an uncaused event could be one for which somebody is responsible. But a more immediate problem is that Ward's interpretation of the debate about evolution seems to involve a misunderstanding of what is meant by the terms 'accidental' or 'random' when used by biologists in this context. When a biologist claims that genetic mutation is random, the point that is usually being made is not that mutations are uncaused, but that genetic mutations do not arise because they would be of advantage to the organism or population in which they occur. That is, genetic mutation is often taken by biologists as one of the given mechanisms of evolution, and is not itself explained in evolutionary terms. This is quite consistent with the development of mutations being given a reliable explanation in a different scientific field, for instance, biochemistry. Similarly, when it is claimed that human life evolved largely as a matter of *accident*, the point is not – as Ward appears to take it to be – that the evolution of life is literally a matter of pure chance, or that there is *no* explanation for it, but rather that the explanation of life does not fall entirely within the bounds of evolutionary biology. Indeed, it would be very surprising if all the conditions required to bring about conscious life could be given in biology. Even Dawkins, while he may claim that evolutionary biology has shown that conscious life is bound to arise from natural selection, does not mean that evolutionary processes will give rise to life *whatever else happens*. Presumably he means only that *given* certain uninterrupted environmental circumstances, and *given* a sufficient period of time, and also several other conditions, the evolutionary mechanisms will produce conscious life. Evidently, evolutionary biology cannot account for all the factors that produce conscious life, since many of them are not biological; for instance, conscious life would not have evolved if the earth had collided with a sufficiently large object from space.

If there is a dispute, it is not over whether or not there is a scientific explanation for human life, but rather on the extent to which that explanation can be developed within evolutionary biology, as opposed to some other scientific field. Ward advances the theistic hypothesis on the basis that it explains aspects of evolution that even evolutionary biologists allow are unexplained, that is, in Gould's case, why conscious life has evolved, and in Dawkins' case, why the evolutionary processes are there at all. The theistic hypothesis, Ward claims, 'is one way in which one could guarantee an evolutionary movement towards complexity and consciousness' (93). But the biologist may surely respond that even if it is conceded that those aspects of evolution that Ward has identified (at least in the case of Dawkins) are not explicable in the terms of evolutionary biology, it does not follow that they are scientifically inexplicable. The explanation for these aspects of evolution is neither the theistic hypothesis nor evolutionary theory, but an account of the physical conditions of the world and our solar system that give rise to them. Analogously, the chemical explanation of the reaction produced by heating iron filings in a test tube does not account for the fact that had the laboratory in which the experiment occurred been destroyed in an earthquake, the reaction would not have taken place; but this shows that if a scientific explanation of the reaction is to take account of such factors it would need to draw on work in scientific fields other than chemistry. In so far as evolutionary biology does not explain why human life was bound to evolve, the evolutionary biologist could argue, what we require is an evolutionary model supplemented with explanations from other areas of biology and physics. Ward expresses his doubts as to whether we could ever find these scientific explanations. This, however, is a purely epistemological worry, and since Ward does not address the obvious epistemological questions regarding his own speculations about whether God's plan would involve evolutionary processes, it offers little support to the theistic hypothesis.

There is, of course, a familiar fallback position available to Ward, namely, that even if God is not specifically involved in evolution or its processes, he nevertheless sets up the laws of physics which eventually bring about evolution. This not only produces consistency between the theistic hypothesis and evolutionary theory, but also between the theistic hypothesis and any scientific theory about events that result from physical laws. However, the consistency is achieved only with the consequence that the theistic hypothesis no longer has particular relevance to evolutionary theory: evolution is no more guaranteed than anything else that results from the physical laws that God sets up. Since it appears to be the purpose of Ward's paper to establish some particular relevance of the theistic hypothesis to evolutionary theory, I take it he would not wish to adopt this fallback position. In this case, we need an account of the sense in which biology is unable to explain the results of evolution that consists in more than just the claim that biology cannot explain non-biological factors that influence evolution. We also require an account of the sense in which the theistic hypothesis can explain evolution that consists in more than just the claim that the hypothesis guarantees that every state of affairs should occur in just the way that it does.

Turning now to Ward's central argument, it can be seen that he makes three claims about the explanation of conscious life:

1. Evolutionary biologists, although they have advanced a number of successful hypotheses about the mechanics of evolution, are unable to explain why these pro-

cesses should have the outcome that they have had. That is, they do not supply an account from which we could reliably predict that human life would evolve.

2. The theory of evolution does not *guarantee* the evolution of conscious life, such guarantees being the standard of ideal scientific explanation.

3. The theist's hypothesis provides an explanation that guarantees the evolution of conscious life, and which makes the theory of evolution more plausible than the hypothesis that it occurs by pure chance. (93-94, 100)

I will describe a number of problems with each of these statements.

1. Ward's first claim seems highly puzzling and misdirected. This can be shown by clearly distinguishing between two types of explanation, which I will call historical and nomological.[1] A nomological explanation for X states how X predictably arises from some preceding state of affairs according to certain general laws. The kind of explanations given by Newtonian mechanics are generally nomological, e.g., the trajectory of a tennis ball that has been struck by a player across a court, can be explained in terms of its being struck by a racket with certain properties at such and such velocity and at such and such angle, where the ball has certain properties, etc. in accordance with general laws. A historical explanation for X gives the state of affairs that most likely resulted in X. That this state of affairs occurred is inferred from the assumption that certain processes are in operation in nature, and the fact that X occurred. For example, the astronomer may determine the likely properties of a star, such as its density and temperature, by inferring that these properties would account for its appearance. But it need not follow that a star with these properties would invariably have this appearance. The astronomer may, of course, use general laws in making the inference; but general laws could not be used to predict the properties of the star without an enormous amount of additional information which we do not – and probably never will – possess. The explanations offered in astronomy and in most so-called 'soft sciences' are often, though by no means exclusively, historical rather than nomological. In some sciences, such as biology, chemistry and the more rigorous behavioural sciences, both kinds of explanation are found, and the kind of explanation will often distinguish a particular stage of an investigation, or characterise a distinct research programme. But it is not only the amount of information that we have, or the scientific research programme that we are engaged in that will determine which type of explanation is appropriate; it is also the complexity of the state of affairs being explained. Nomological explanation will

---

1   Here I follow Elliott Sober, *Philosophy of Biology* (Oxford 1993), ch. 1.

only tell us that if, say, a theoretical object with such and such properties occurs in such and such circumstances then it will behave in a certain way. Thus, a nomological explanation can only offer accurate predictions about a real object, when the number of factors influencing the object's behaviour can be sufficiently specified. It is sometimes possible to apply laws to reliably predict the behaviour of the tennis ball because it is possible to state the important influences on its movement. In cases where this is not possible, historical explanations may well be more useful, for they account for particular states of affairs without requiring that they fall under some generally statable law.

The aim of the evolutionary biologists that we have been considering is to describe those evolutionary processes at work in nature and show how life has evolved from these processes. Their aim, in terms of the distinction I have stated, is to provide historical explanations for evolved life. Ward criticises evolutionary biology on the grounds that it cannot predict that conscious life would evolve from natural selection. But it is hardly surprising that evolutionary biologists should not be in a position to explain why human life had to evolve, since this is not the objective of their research. The predictions that Ward expects should ideally be provided by evolutionary biologists would require a nomological explanation for human life. There are, of course, biologists who are engaged in the construction of models from which, given certain assumptions about a population, it is possible to predict, according to fairly rigorously stated principles, how a population with particular characteristics will evolve. An early case of this is a model constructed by R. Fisher which shows how, given a small number of assumptions about a population, it is possible to predict that its sex ratio will evolve to 1-1 and remain at that proportion.[2] This kind of research is generally fairly technical, and usually becomes more so as the model assumptions become more realistic; it is also a comparatively unexciting area of evolutionary biology, and for the most part has received little attention in most recent populist accounts of evolutionary theory. Since Ward advances the theistic hypothesis on the argument that biologists have not shown that human life can predictably arise from evolutionary processes, it seems incumbent on Ward to consider the adequacy of nomological explanations given by modern biology, rather than the largely historical explanations offered by Dawkins and Gould, to which his argument is irrelevant.

2. These objections also apply to the second claim made by Ward, that evolutionary theory does not guarantee that conscious life would result. Since the biologists under consideration are offering mostly historical explanations for why life has evolved, Ward's claim that these explanations do not guarantee that life would

---

2   R. Fisher, *The Genetical Theory of Natural Selection* (1930; New York 1957)

have evolved is evidently true, but not to the point. Providing nomological evolutionary explanations for human life and constructing historical explanations for human life, are the objectives of different research programmes in biology. However, Ward also implies in his paper that the *best* explanation for the evolution of conscious life, is one that guarantees that conscious life will be the result of evolutionary processes. On one reading of this, Ward means that a nomological explanation of the evolution of conscious life is in principle better than a historical explanation (or some other kind of explanation). Unfortunately he provides no argument in support of this claim, which is also eminently deniable. As I have indicated, the kind of scientific explanation put forward for an event will be determined by such matters as the information that we have about it, or the goal and methodology of the research programme we are engaged in. But even putting this aside, it seems quite possible that there should be certain types of event, perhaps with very complicated causal circumstances, which are such that the best generalisations that could be drawn about their behaviour are too complicated to allow us to conveniently formulate any predictions about them. The events do fall under laws, but the laws are too cumbersome and the events too complicated for us to calculate interesting facts about them. In this case, the best explanation for these events will not be nomological; indeed, searching for the laws that govern these events would be a waste of research time. The claim that scientific explanation should be nomological, therefore, stands in need of further justification. Since Ward suggests that God may have set down the laws of nature, I take it that he would both argue that any events do in principle fall under fairly simple natural laws, and also support a necessitarian theory of natural laws (i.e. that laws do not merely describe what occurs but express what must occur in certain circumstances) as opposed to the regularity theory (that laws just describe what invariably happens in certain circumstances) defended by, among others, Hume. But no arguments for or against the truth or plausibility of either of these theories about natural laws are given.

It is possible that Ward is not advocating nomological explanations over historical explanations. For what he claims is that explanations which guarantee results are better than those that do not, and what he means by the crucial term 'guarantee' is not stated. We are not told exactly what it is for an explanation to guarantee what it explains. The theistic hypothesis is the only example given of an explanation that guarantees a result. Even in this case it is unclear what it is that Ward takes the theistic hypothesis to guarantee. Ward suggests that given the truth of the theistic hypothesis, evolution would 'inevitably' result in conscious life, which might suggest that the guarantee offered by the theistic hypothesis is one of logical necessity. But he goes on to say, seemingly inconsistently, that the hypothesis makes it 'much more probable' that there would be a process that produces human life than the hypothesis that the process emerges by pure chance. He then undermines this latter claim by stating that the pure chance hypothesis 'is in fact no explanation at all.' It seems that Ward is making two distinct claims about the explanatory role of the theistic hypothesis. First, that if there are evolutionary processes the theistic hypothesis makes it inevitable, or guarantees (in some unspecified sense), that conscious life would eventually evolve from them. Second, that the theistic hypothesis makes it more probable that the evolutionary processes would exist at all than the hypothesis that they emerged by pure chance. While these claims are consistent, Ward does not appear to defend them consistently. Indeed, he seems to move between them, depending on whether he is addressing Gould or Dawkins. He defends the first against Gould, but seems then to concede the first and defend the second when arguing against Dawkins. So even if a satisfactory account of the notion of 'guarantee' could be given, it is unclear which claim about the explanatory role of the theistic hypothesis he believes to be true.

3. This leads to the third claim made by Ward, that the theistic hypothesis is an explanation of evolution that guarantees that human life will be the result, and makes the theory of evolution more plausible. I will say no more about the first part of this claim other than that in whatever sense it is that the theistic hypothesis is supposed to guarantee, and whatever it guarantees, it is clearly not a nomological explanation, since it involves no generalisation from which anything can be predicted. Regarding the second part, in what sense does the theistic hypothesis make the theory of evolution more plausible? I will describe four problems with this claim. First, Ward gives no argument to show that the theistic hypothesis makes the theory of evolution plausible, but only that it makes it more plausible than the hypothesis that evolution occurs by pure chance. Since Ward believes that the latter hypothesis offers 'no explanation at all,' the theistic hypothesis would presumably need to be only *an* explanation for it to be superior to the hypothesis of pure chance. It is consistent with Ward's argument that the theistic hypothesis makes the theory of evolution only barely plausible. Second, even if it is allowed that evolution is more likely to have been brought about by God than to have occurred by pure chance, it does not follow that the theistic hypothesis is the best explanation of evolution. At one point in his paper, Ward appears to adopt this much stronger position, since he asserts that 'the theistic hypothesis is the best explanation of the evolutionary process as we see it.' But to defend such a position would require, at the very least, an evaluation of rival hypotheses, such as the possibility, mentioned earlier, of a physical explanation for how the evolutionary conditions on the planet were set up and maintained. Such a theory, even if it were only loosely formulated, could give us reason to suppose that evolution would occur, and possibly lend more support to the theory of evolution than the theistic hypothesis.

Third, Ward offers a number of reasons for thinking that God would want not only to create conscious life but do so by means of evolutionary processes, and he claims that we can see the evolution of life as 'an expression of the imaginative and creative activity of God.' It is very difficult to evaluate such considerations. The fact that one can describe a plausible sounding story about the way in which God would want to create the world, lends only marginal support to the belief that this is the way in which it would happen. For there are a great many other plausible sounding stories about the way in which God created the world, and in many of these evolution does not occur at all. There certainly seems to be no basis for Ward's surprising claim that 'The facts of evolution plausibly suggest a universe which is ordered by a wise creator'(100), which would appear to represent the evidence of evolution as an argument for the existence of God. Even if we allow that God would have used evolutionary processes, it seems that any evolutionary process could be seen as an expression of imaginative creative activity, even if the processes involved were very different, or they resulted in life forms very different from our own. Thus on the assumption that the theistic hypothesis is true and supports the belief that some kind of evolution would occur, there is little reason to suppose that evolutionary processes or their results would take the form that they have done.

Fourth, Ward only establishes – at best – the conclusion that *if* the theistic hypothesis is true then it is more likely that the evolution of human life should occur than on the assumption that it occurred by pure chance. That is, Ward's argument shows only that if the theistic hypothesis is true then there is some likelihood that evolution will occur. He has not shown that the theistic hypothesis is at all probable. This, of course, falls significantly short of showing that the theistic hypothesis is a good hypothesis. The evolutionary biologist can still reject the theistic hypothesis as inferior to the hypothesis of pure chance (or some other hypothesis), even if it is the case that assuming the truth of the former would make the theory of evolution more likely than assuming the truth of the latter. This is because there are an arbitrarily large number of hypotheses the truth of any one of which, if assumed, would make the theory of evolution likely; more likely even than the theistic hypothesis. We could hypothesise a collection of circumstances which, however bizarre and improbable would, if they were assumed to obtain, make it very likely that the evolution of conscious life would occur. To take a different example, if I want to explain why somebody has fallen over, I may suppose that it is likely that the person would have fallen over if the ground they were walking on were slippery. But it is more likely that the person would have fallen over if deliberately tripped up by an invisible pixie. In other words, that fact that a hypothesis, if assumed to be true, would make a certain result likely, is no reflection of the probability of the hypothesis. So the argument that the theory of evolution is more plausible if theism is true than if it occurs by pure chance, does not establish an interesting conclusion unless it can also be shown that theism is probable.

Central to Ward's paper is the claim that in so far as there is a real point of dispute between Christianity and Darwinism, it lies not in the properly conducted scientific investigation into the origin of life, nor in the results of that investigation, but in the interpretation of the significance and the implications of its findings. For instance, it is often claimed that Darwinian investigations have shown that evolution is a blind process of ruthless competition, or that it is nothing more than a struggle for survival. But these interpretations, Ward argues, are not proven by any scientific discoveries, but are a reflection of independently held metaphysical beliefs and attitudes held by, among others, certain scientists. Provided that Christian tradition can accommodate the scientific evidence of evolutionary processes at work in nature, therefore, Ward believes that Christians can put forward and defend their own account of the meaning of evolution. I take Ward's general point to be that the only kind of change to the Christian belief structure that is demanded by scientific developments is on matters of fact that scientists have established to be the case; it should be possible to assimilate these matters of fact, once stripped of any metaphysical connotations such as materialism or naturalism, into the Christian viewpoint without any changes to fundamental theological principles. Thus Ward maintains that 'Darwin's discovery may be seen as a valuable extension of our knowledge of the nature of God's creation, putting Christian faith in a wider context in space and time.'

Given its importance to his argument, it is surprising that Ward does not say more about the distinction between scientific facts and theories and interpretations of them. It is not, of course, uncommon for philosophers to make a distinction of this type. Wittgenstein, for instance, wished to separate mathematical theorems, techniques and proofs from the interpretations of them put forward by mathematicians and philosophers, these interpretations being a legitimate target for philosophical criticism. But there are problems in drawing this type of distinction in any rigorous way in science. Ward believes that scientific discoveries render false much of the biblical creation story. But is it a fact that we are descended from apes, or is it only an interpretation of a large amount of scientific evidence? Similarly, has the claim (made by some creationists) that God created humans with the appearance of having evolved by natural selection been falsified, or is it a legitimate rival interpretation of the scientific evidence put forward for evolution? However, even if facts and interpretations could be satisfactorily distinguished in these cases, Ward's analysis of those elements of evolutionary theory that should be respected by Christians and may lead to changes in Christian belief, overlooks the significant role played by the scientific methodology that informs – what I shall call – *Darwinian explanations.*

A Darwinian explanation proceeds by showing how an object with certain features that have the appearance of design is the product of certain processes, such as natural selection, operating over a period of time on a collection of objects which do not possess the apparently designed features. In a Darwinian explanation facts about design features are accounted for in terms of facts about less complex features and physical processes. They are, in this sense, 'reductionist.' I suggest that the evident success of reductionist Darwinian explanations is more likely to undermine Christian beliefs and make Christian concepts redundant than either the discovery of facts about the process of evolution, or the anti-religious interpretations of evolutionary biology to which Ward objects.

One strength of Darwinian explanation is that it recognises that there are many features of the world that *have been designed*. However, rather than postulating a designer with a purpose, Darwinists explain how gradual mindless adaptive changes over a long period of time can produce features that fit their environment. Another strength of the Darwinian method is that it provides a strategy for explaining design that is not restricted to biology but may be applied to virtually any field of scientific investigation. Organised complexity of any kind may be subject to Darwinian explanations. So while it may be possible to achieve some measure of consistency between Christianity and Darwinism given the current state of scientific knowledge, the Darwinian method of explanation will always tend towards a godless explanation of the world.

The Christian, Ward argues, can accommodate – indeed wholeheartedly endorse – the discoveries made about the processes of biological evolution without breaking with Christian tradition; but, as I have indicated, it seems that the agreement between the Christian and Darwinian can only be superficial and only extend to particular matters of fact. The Darwinian strategy of explanation, by virtue of its reductionism, remains profoundly antipathetic to religious accounts of the world. For the same reason, Darwinian explanations will tend to support relatively minimal metaphysical theories such as naturalism, rather than Christianity. This is a point clearly made by Richard Dawkins, commenting on the hypothesis that God may have set up the original machinery of replication and replicator power:

Organized complexity is the thing we are having difficulty explaining. Once we are allowed simply to *postulate* organized complexity, if only the organized complexity of the DNA/protein replicating engine, it is relatively easy to invoke it as a generator of yet more organized complexity ... But of course any God capable of intelligently designing something as complex as the DNA/protein replicating machine must have been at least as complex and organized as the machine itself.[3]

In the light of this, to point out – as Ward does – that scientists often themselves have religious convictions, seems little more than hand waving. It is not the case, of course, that scientists with religious convictions have always reflected in any thorough-going way on the consistency between the views that they hold. Nor is it the case, as is more to the point, that the presence of religious scientists offers any security against the possibility that Darwinian investigations will proceed in such a way that Christians will be able to accept them without changing belief in a much more dramatic way.

Having said this, Christian belief can be modified on the lines that Ward suggests, so that it is not inconsistent with the current state of Darwinian investigations. If we address only the Darwinian explanations of the evolution of biological life on this planet, and if the doctrine of Creation is drawn up in a way that God does not interfere in any scientifically detectable way with any of the evolutionary processes discovered by biologists, then Christianity and Darwinism are certain to be consistent. But there seems little overall advantage in establishing this kind of consistency. The Christian has merely shifted ground to give room for the claims of the Darwinist, leaving Darwinists entirely free to go on to claim further territory. If the changes to Christian belief that Ward suggests do not seem like 'slightly desperate adjustments,' that is perhaps because he has taken into consideration only a narrow range of Darwinian explanations. Darwinian explanations have been put forward in recent years to account not only for the emergence and development of life, but also language, ethics, consciousness and culture. It has even been argued that the world, or the physical constants of the universe could be the product of evolutionary processes.

Ward claims that 'Despite the efforts of anti-religious neo-Darwinists, I do not think the non-purposive interpretation has been established, and I am prepared to risk the bet that it will not be' (p. 103). This seems a risky bet, not only because it seems to rest on a Canute-like confidence in limits to scientific progress, but also because, as I have argued, the success of Darwinian explanations is capable of undermining Christian concepts, even if they do not constitute a demonstration of the falsity of Christian beliefs, or conclusively establish the non-purposive nature of the universe. For these reasons, I do not believe that Ward's attempts to accommodate religious belief about creation with evolutionary theory offers a desirable long term strategy for the Christian.

---

3   Richard Dawkins, *The Blind Watchmaker* (London 1986), 141.

Is there an alternative? Ward states that if it were established that evolution is random and non-purposive, that would undermine objective Christian claims about the nature of the universe and require 'a radical form of non-realism, or, more plausibly in my view, an abandonment of Christian belief' (102f.). Notably, Ward himself moves towards non-realism, beginning with a non-literal interpretation of the creation story, as a way of accommodating the findings of evolutionary biology. However, I think that Ward is right to express the problem in terms of the question of realism, although it is not clear why religious non-realism should be the consequence of scientific developments. I suspect that Ward places undue importance on one account of realism, that there can be only one true description of the world. On this basis, and assuming that the description will be scientific, one can see the motivation for attempting to reintroduce religious ideas into a scientific picture from which they have long since been expelled. But the religious realist can safely drop the one-true-description account without undermining typically realist positions on other central issues, for example, whether religious discourse supports a robust notion of truth.[4] A case can be made for religious realism, just as it can be made for realism in mathematics, ethics or folk psychology, that does not require our applying to these discourses standards that are appropriate for scientific investigation. Such a case would consider the role of religious explanations and the nature of truth and representation in religion, but need not assume that a contribution to scientific descriptions and theories must be secured.[5] Once this assumption is challenged, the prospects for religious realism in the light of scientific developments look healthier.

---

4   For a recent discussion cf. Crispin Wright, *Truth and Objectivity* (Harvard 1992). Wright describes various realism-relevant features that may be possessed by a discourse, none of which require it to have a role in one true description of the world.
5   For an indication of what this case would look like cf. Michael Scott, 'The Varieties of Religious Realism,' forthcoming.

8. Does the Authority of a Tradition Exclude the Possibility of Change?

Paul Helm (London)

1 Introduction

There is an ambiguity in the expression 'the authority of a tradition' which we need to note before doing anything else. 'The authority of a tradition' may mean the authority that the tradition itself possesses; or it may mean the authority which authorises and constitutes a tradition. In this paper I shall endeavour to discuss certain aspects of the authority of a tradition in the first sense. I shall assume, and not discuss further, that in the case of the Christian tradition the authority which authorises and constitutes this tradition is God himself. Which is simply to say that the Christian religion is a revealed religion.

The nature of the authority of a tradition is bound up with the nature of its identity. Let us then begin by distinguishing different ways in which the identity of a tradition through time might be understood. Throughout this paper I shall assume that the Christian tradition is composed of at least two features; a propositional tradition, and a tradition of rites, practices and prescriptions. I shall also assume that there is an important connection between these; the rites, practices and prescriptions are intended to be enactments of, or ways of behaving rationally in the light of, the propositional element of the tradition. The propositional element makes the other elements intelligible; prayers, ordinances and moral prescriptions are warranted by the propositional element. Even if the ethic is naturalistic, or partly so, nevertheless the constitutive propositions of the tradition authorise and endorse it; they authorise, by example if not by precept, the use of natural human reason in ethics and in other areas of human enquiry. The propositional element is thus basic. So I shall from now on assume that this is roughly how it is with the Christian tradition or traditions; a complex of propositional and non-propositional elements, with logical priority accorded to the propositional.

It is important to stress that this is an assumption. To see the significance of this one may draw interesting analogies between theories of the identity of a tradition, and theories of personal identity. What I have just stated as the assumption of what is to follow is analogous to what might be called the Reidian or Swinburnian account of personal identity. The enduring propositional content of the tradition that I have just identified would then correspond to the enduring soul or self of the

Swinburnian or Reidian view; though it would not be metaphysically simple, as the Reidian or Swinburnian soul is simple. But just as on this view of personal identity it is a necessary and sufficient condition of being the same person at t_1 as one was at t_2 that one is the same soul, so I am assuming that it is a necessary and sufficient condition of being in the same tradition from time to time that one has the same core propositional beliefs through that time.

Locke argued, in general about identity through time, and particularly about personal identity, that A and B are the same thing if and only if they are spatio-temporally continuous and the same kind of thing. Roughly A and B are the same apple tree if A is an apple tree and B is an apple tree and there is a spatio-temporal continuity between A and B. No enduring metaphysical tree-soul is required. And similarly with personal identity, with memory carrying the epistemological burden. There are approaches to the identity of tradition like this, approaches which stress not a propositional core but overlapping beliefs and practices of a certain kind; it is not necessary for such a view of tradition that numerically the same belief is held over time, simply recognisably continuous beliefs.

To the Humean account of personal identity there corresponds what I shall call a *de facto* account of tradition. A *de facto* tradition is just what, as a matter of fact, follows on from what has gone before. I want to say a little more about this *de facto* concept of a tradition, and to contrast it with the *de jure*. A *de facto* tradition is what is believed or done over time; what makes it a tradition is that the same thing (or same sort of thing) is believed or done over time. Thus a person or a family may have a tradition of going to Clacton for their holidays, or playing golf on Sunday afternoons. This is a *de facto* tradition; nothing requires them to maintain or carry it on. The point can be brought out by noting the ambiguity of the English expression 'as a rule'; they go on holiday to Clacton as a rule, but they do not hold a rule to the effect that they must or should go to Clacton; the rule in question is simply the rule formed from their past regularity of behaviour, and is not a prescription requiring them to take their holidays in a particular place. The purely *de facto* does not license a counter-factual; *if I were to choose the place for a holiday, then I would choose Clacton*. The *de jure* sense of 'as a rule' does; because if I have a rule to the effect that I always go to Clacton for my holidays, then it is true that if I were to choose to go on holiday, Clacton would be the place that I would choose.

I shall at this stage assume that the Christian tradition is more like a *de jure* than a *de facto* understanding of tradition. This is how I shall understand the idea of tradition in what follows; for this is how I understand the Christian tradition to operate, and this understanding has at least the immediate advantage of making the issues somewhat more meaty than they would otherwise be. For the question of the authority of a *de facto* tradition is easily answered; such an account does not exclude the possibility of change, because being merely *de facto* the tradition has no grounds for any such exclusion; having as a matter of fact visited Clacton for my holidays for many years, and therefore having had the tradition of visiting that resort, I might perfectly properly choose Cleethorpes next year.

What of the *de jure* sense of tradition? It is only in this sense of tradition that it makes sense to make a mistake in practice or an error in belief. But there is an obvious sense in which, even on such a view of what tradition is, the possibility of change is not excluded; namely, where the tradition itself authorises a change; think of the way in which Jesus fulfilled the law; because of what he did, that element of the tradition which requires the people of God to keep certain dietary laws no longer applies. As Augustine puts it:

> By this law (the most righteous law of God) the moral customs of different regions and periods were adapted to their places and times, while that law itself remains unaltered everywhere and always. It is not one thing at one place or time, another thing at another.[1]

But this also is an uninteresting answer from a philosophical point of view. It raises no problems; at least no problems about tradition. And in any case (as with any law) one needs to distinguish between what a tradition requires, and what it permits. There can well be changes in the area of what the tradition permits even if none in what it requires. This distinction is very relevant in the history of Christianity if one thinks of the conflict between those who believe it is permissible in the course of Christian worship to do what the Bible does not forbid and those who believe that it is permissible to do only what the Bible commands. If a change occurs in the area of what a tradition permits, then there is a straightforward sense in which the tradition has not excluded the possibility of change; but there may also be a change in what the tradition requires, as Augustine says.

I shall also assume that it is perfectly possible for a tradition to atrophy and decay and go off the rails; just as Jesus taught that the Scribes and the Pharisees made void the law, the tradition of law-keeping authorised by Moses, by their tradition (Mark 7:13). The implications of Jesus' teaching on this point were not lost on the Reformers who held that the Papacy had made void the Gospel through *its* tradition. But the fact that a tradition can become deformed, important though it has been in Christian history, does not as far as I can see raise any special philosophical questions.

A word about change. It is possible to distinguish two sorts of change, what Peter Geach has called real change and 'merely Cambridge' change; it is sufficient

---

1   Augustine, *Confessions* III 7,13 trans. Henry Chadwick, (Oxford 1992), 44.

for a 'merely Cambridge' change that what changes simply changes in respect of some truth about it; it is necessary for a real change that that change in truth is somehow grounded in the object in question. If I lose a tooth, I really change. If you merely come to believe that I have lost a tooth, then I undergo a 'merely Cambridge' change; I change by its being believed about me that I have lost a tooth, for something is now true of me that was not true before you believed this about me, but I have not really changed by losing one.[2]

This distinction is not easy to apply in the case of a change in a tradition. For one thing, a tradition is constituted partly by beliefs, at least the beliefs of adherents to that tradition. And so to come to believe something within the tradition that one forms a part of that was not believed before may be for the tradition to undergo both a 'merely Cambridge' change – for something that was not true of it before is now true – but also a real change – for what is now believed within the tradition – say, that it no longer requires of women that they wear hats while in church – is a real change in the tradition. Even if every woman continues to wear a hat, the fact that it came to be believed to be consistent with the tradition that a woman not wear a hat in church would constitute a change in the tradition, even though these beliefs were at the level of 'merely Cambridge' changes. The change in belief warrants a change in practice even though no change in practice ensues. I shall take it in what follows that our question concerns the possibility of real change. Does the authority of a tradition exclude the possibility of real change?

There is a further sense of change that is relevant: change as development. A person may change and still be the same person; indeed certain sorts of changes to a person may be necessary for her remaining the same person. Similarly in the Christian religious tradition; perhaps certain practices have to be updated, and new words used if old meanings are to be retained. What Edmund Burke said of the state, that 'a state without the means of some change is without the means of its conservation' may also apply to a tradition. A church *semper reformanda* is enjoying both continuity and change.

But does Christian doctrine, the propositional core of the tradition, change by developing? Newman and others have been fond of organic analogies to make plausible the idea that it does.[3] But there is danger here; we know from experience and from our knowledge of the principles of organic growth whether a change in a tree is a genuine growth or a malformation. But the Christian tradition is *sui generis*; who is to say whether change is not also malformation? It would seem to be necess-

---

2   Cf. Peter Geach, *God and the Soul* (London 1969), 70-72, 99.
3   John Henry Newman, *An Essay on the Development of Christian Doctrine* (London 1845).

ary to be able to refer back to the origins of the tradition in order to settle such a question.

So I shall take it that the issue of the relationships between authority, change and tradition ought to be read in something like the following way: given that the authority of a *de jure* tradition is recognised, can one make real changes not authorised by that authority (or refuse to make changes authorised by it) while still remaining under the jurisdiction of that *de jure* authority? And the answer to these questions seems to me to be obvious: to the extent that one makes real changes which the authority of the tradition does not endorse, including what it does not permit, one removes oneself from its *de jure* authority.

However, there are prior questions of a more genuinely philosophical kind about the possibility of a tradition the answers to which are less obvious, and I shall concentrate my attention on these questions in the remainder of this paper. It seems essential for the wholeness of a historical religious tradition such as that known in Christianity that there are occasions when the past may exercise authority on the present, authority such that there are circumstances in which we would be led to say that what we are believing or doing now is not authentic; even that it is not true.

To think of the Christian tradition as presently exercising *de jure* authority one needs to be able to argue for the idea of a *de jure* authority of something that existed two thousand years ago, the idea of the past exercising authority over the present. I shall try to defend the idea that the past may properly exercise such authority by offering objections to two arguments, or rather two types of argument which if cogent would undercut such a possibility; the argument from rule-following and the argument from testimony. One argument is from the nature of rule-following, the other from the nature of testimony. I am using these arguments to clarify and defend the legitimacy of an appeal to *de jure* tradition. Of course even if the objections to which these arguments are addressed can be overcome – and I shall argue that one can be overcome more successfully than the other – this does not amount to a conclusive argument for the legitimacy of *de jure* tradition. So the paper may be thought of as a contribution to answering the question, 'How is *de jure* tradition possible?' I shall argue that the argument from rule-following presents difficulties for the idea of a *de jure* Christian tradition, at least given certain obvious facts about the nature of Christendom, but that the argument from testimony is less troublesome.

2   The Argument from Rule-Following

The first argument we shall consider against the possibility of the *de jure* authority of a tradition is that from scepticism about rule following. The ability to follow a rule, and to know when one is and is not following it, is, I take it, a fundamental feature of being under the *de jure* authority of a tradition. For as we noted earlier, the tradition comprises propositional, cultic and prescriptive elements. Not every feature of a tradition is rule-following, but nevertheless it seems fundamental to a tradition such as the Christian tradition that in order to maintain it in other than an accidental sense participants in the tradition need to have good reason to believe whether what they mean and the significance of what they do is what others earlier in the tradition meant and did. For if one cannot decide what belief, or piece of behaviour, constitutes an endorsement of the tradition, and is therefore a case of following the rule of the tradition, then no sense can be given to the distinction between following the tradition and breaking with it. If any belief or behaviour counts as following the tradition then the tradition has effectively disappeared.

I shall argue that current agreement, what I shall call synchronic collectivism, while it is sufficient for the maintenance of some traditions, perhaps, does not meet the truth requirement of Christianity. And that diachronic collectivism, agreement over time, while sufficient for the maintenance of a tradition, is not, as a matter of empirical fact, what we find in Christendom. For it seems an obvious fact that at present there is no common, authoritative tradition in Christendom, though there could be, or could have been. One reason for this state of affairs is that no one group or church has exclusive use of the term 'Christian' and that as a matter of fact that term is widely and divergently employed.

Let us begin by considering Wittgenstein's well-known remarks about rule following:

'But am I not compelled, then to go the way I do in the chain of inferences?' – Compelled? After all I can presumably go as I choose! – Not at all, I call *this* 'accord' – 'Then you have changed the meaning of the word "accord" or the meaning of the rule' – No; – who says what 'change' and 'remaining the same' mean here?

However many rules you give me – I give a rule which justifies *my* employment of your rules.

'But you surely can't suddenly make a different application of the law now!' But if I simply reply: 'Different? – But this surely isn't different!' – what will you do? That is: somebody may reply like a rational person and yet not be playing our game.[4]

---

4   Ludwig Wittgenstein, *Philosophical Investigations* trans. G.E.M. Anscombe (Oxford 1953) I

I shall interpret these and similar remarks as Saul Kripke does in *Wittgenstein on Rules and Private Language*[5] as being evidence of a general scepticism about rule following. This interpretation of Kripke's is controversial,[6] but as I am here considering a type of argument rather than the text of Wittgenstein, this does not matter. If the text of the *Philosophical Investigations* turns out not to endorse this type of argument, well and good. What I am focusing on is a type of sceptical argument about rule-following which if sound, has negative consequences for the authority of a tradition; I shall argue, with Kripke, that this argument is not sound, but also that the suggestions that he makes about how Wittgenstein thought such scepticism should be met do not help us over the question of the viability of a tradition.

Kripke's reconstruction of the sceptical argument he finds in Wittgenstein goes like this. It is a fact about any rule that it has been followed only a finite number of times. How does one know that the rule of addition 68+57=125 (let us suppose that I have never performed this computation before) applies and not the rule (which Kripke calls 'quus') that 68+57=5? I have in the past only added a finite number of times, never added these two numbers, and never added numbers as great as 57.

The sceptic doubts whether any instructions I gave myself in the past compel (or justify) the answer '125' rather than '5.' He puts the challenge in terms of a sceptical hypothesis about a change in my usage. Perhaps when I used the term 'plus' in the *past*, I always mean quus: by hypothesis I never gave myself any explicit directions that were incompatible with such a supposition.[7]

This, as Kripke says, is no doubt crazy, but nevertheless it is logically possible that the rule of addition only applies for numbers less than 57. Just as the sceptic might raise the question about what counts as following a rule, so we might raise a parallel sceptical question about what counts as following a rule of the tradition. [8]

Kripke's response to such scepticism about rules about meaning, a response which he also thinks Wittgenstein endorses, is to reject other proposed solutions, notably one in terms of dispositions, in favour of a form of communitarianism. In its own terms the sceptic's arguments are unanswerable,[9] nevertheless the sort of

---

113-115.

5   Saul A. Kripke, *Wittgenstein on Rules and Private Language* (Oxford 1982).

6   For a review of some of the discussion raised by Kripke's interpretation of Wittgenstein, and of the positive view he imputes to him, see Paul Boghossian, 'The Rule-Following Considerations,' *Mind* 98 (1989), 507-549.

7   Kripke, *Wittgenstein*, 13.

8   Kripke, *Wittgenstein*, 13.

9   Kripke, *Wittgenstein*, 66.

justification that the sceptic seeks is not necessary. (Compare Hume on induction; the solution offered is not in terms of reason, but in terms of expectancy conditioned by awareness of past regularity.) So Wittgenstein (according to Kripke) does not offer a straight refutation of such scepticism, but an assertability-conditions account of meaning.

> All that is needed to legitimize assertions that someone means something is that there be roughly specifiable circumstances under which they are legitimately assertable, and that the game of asserting them under such conditions has a role in our lives.[10]

I shall, as I say, accept Kripke's account of Wittgenstein, and accept it as the correct account, even though Kripke himself has doubts. This is because what interests me is what follows from this for the idea of a tradition, and for authority within that tradition.

Let us suppose that this anti-sceptical argument of Kripke's is cogent, whether or not it is a fair interpretation of Wittgenstein. It can be applied to Christian belief and the Christian tradition in the following way. It is essential for the maintenance of that tradition that there are rules, rules of belief and rules of observance, and that those rules are followed in new circumstances, as the tradition unfolds. What Kripke's anti-sceptical argument about rule-following does, assuming its cogency, is to maintain that meaning, and hence truth, is communitarian in character. When Jesus said 'Do this, as often as ye drink it, in remembrance of me' that command looks indefinite. Although there has only been a finite number of rememberings, we take it to be unrestricted. But how do we know that eating bread and drinking wine is what following that rule requires *now*? For we have, so far, only had a finite number of rememberings. Perhaps we have now entered new circumstances in which the rule does not apply, or is to be differently interpreted.

How do we know that Kripke's sceptical account of rule-following does not apply to religious tradition, and particularly to the Christian tradition? I don't think that it will do to say that in discussing scepticism about rules of counting in arithmetic Kripke is discussing a human activity that is basic in a way that the Christian religion is not basic. For the point is a general one about rule following; counting in arithmetic is simply a vivid example of this. Exactly the same point can be made about language, the rules involved in learning the use of a word or a sentence. For the same reason I do not think that one can evade the force of the scepticism by pointing out that there is more to the Christian tradition than rules like the rule of

---

10   Kripke, *Wittgenstein*, 77-78.

addition; there are propositional elements, and explicit commands. For the point about rule-following is a perfectly general one, embracing the rules of language, and hence the interpretation of the language, the propositions and explicit commands which lie at the heart of the Christian tradition.

Kripke interprets Wittgenstein's response to such rule scepticism as similar to Hume's scepticism about memory, or causation or induction. Hume claimed that the sceptic's arguments are unanswerable but that our ordinary practice is justified because the sceptic does not *need* to be answered to justify it. So Hume resorts to what without too much exaggeration might be called a communitarian response to, say, scepticism about induction. It is custom (a kind of tradition) that justifies the practice of induction. We cannot know that the future will be like the past; we simply together expect that it will be. No event can be known to produce another event; all that we can say is that certain event types produce in us a propensity to expect other event types.

As Hume accepts the argument of the sceptic, but salvages what he can in communitarian fashion, so (according to Kripke) Wittgenstein accepts scepticism about rule-following; there is no head-on refutation of the sceptical argument. Instead Wittgenstein focuses upon warranted assertability, and upon the role of the practice, say, of arithmetical addition in our lives, the lives of the community of language-users.[11]

Such a communitarian response to scepticism about meaning seems to involve invoking a tradition, and this may encourage us to think that a communitarian approach neatly combines a satisfactory anti-scepticism with invoking the centrality of the idea of a tradition. For it is in virtue of the tradition of the practice of counting that one can talk about mistakes.

> Now, what do I mean when I say that the teacher judges that, for certain cases, the pupil must give the 'right' answer? I mean that the teacher judges that the child has given the same answer that he himself would give.[12]

This might incline us to take the following view of Christian tradition. How do I know whether my belief, or practice, is the true belief or the correct practice? Answer: because it is the belief that present authorised teachers in the tradition have, or the practice that they themselves follow. To see why this type of answer will not do in the case of the Christian tradition, let us return to the distinction between synchronic and diachronic communitarianism that I mentioned earlier. Synchronic

---

11   Kripke, *Wittgenstein*, 72-73.
12   Kripke, *Wittgenstein*, 90.

agreement is current agreement. It is certainly necessary for the maintenance of the tradition at a time, and of its authority, that there is synchronic agreement among those who regard themselves as Christians. But it cannot be sufficient, for the agreement has to reach back. That we may each today agree on what the Christian tradition consists in, what it requires of us by way of belief and behaviour, does not mean that we are continuing the tradition. So it is certainly necessary for the maintenance of the tradition that besides synchronic agreement, there is also diachronic agreement among those who regard themselves as Christians. But though synchronic and diachronic communitarianism are each necessary, they are still not together sufficient; for the Christian tradition does not consist only in rules, but makes appeal to facts and the interpretations of facts; and it is possible that there should be communal agreement, both diachronic and synchronic, and yet for that agreement to be erroneous, making an agreed appeal to what is in fact false. Though one might argue that the fact of such communitarian agreement, if it existed, would count in favour of the truth of the beliefs embodied in the tradition. Nevertheless, the reforming role of a Luther is perfectly intelligible; although the emperor cannot have no clothes, his dress may nevertheless be pretty threadbare. And if, say, the bones of Jesus were found in Palestine – a logical possibility – or further letters of the Apostle Paul were discovered containing teaching widely at variance with the present canonical letters, then the tradition would face a fundamental epistemological crisis about its authority.

But the problem is that in the case of 'the Christian tradition' there is not as a matter of fact the sort of agreement that we have in arithmetic or in the meaning of the words of a language, though perhaps there could have been. Rather there are rival, incompatible traditions and sub-traditions, rival schools of interpretation. It is this that upsets Richard Swinburne's appeal to the church as the authoriser of certain books as being revelatory of God.[13] As Eleonore Stump remarks, we need to know, among so many rival claimants, which church is the true authorising church.[14] In the face of a certain sort of scepticism, communitarian accounts of meaning and truth may be necessary for the maintenance of the authority of a tradition, but they cannot be sufficient.

So much for the argument from rule-following.

---

13   Richard Swinburne, *Revelation: From Analogy to Metaphor* (Oxford 1992).
14   Review of *Revelation: From Analogy to Metaphor*, *Philosophical Review*, October 1994.

3 *The Argument about Testimony*

A tradition is by definition about the past, or necessarily involves reference to the past. In order for the tradition to exercise the sort of *de jure* authority that we have been trying to clarify, therefore, we must be pretty sure that we can identify and interpret the tradition clearly. We need to be able to discover, without too much trouble, what the tradition is authorising, and what not. This involves having beliefs about the past; in the case of the Christian tradition, beliefs about the fairly remote past. The concept of a viable *de jure* tradition stretching back a couple of millennia requires that one can gain fairly ready access to its inception, otherwise it is hard to see how the *de jure* can avoid lapsing into the merely *de facto*. Here I do not have in mind general sceptical arguments about the past, though of course the idea of a *de jure* tradition requires that such arguments can be answered; rather what concerns me are arguments about whether the past can have *de jure* authority. So this is not a question of whether the tradition ought to exercise, or ought to continue to exercise, *de jure* authority, over those who are within it, but whether it can.

There is a fundamental philosophical divide, one which separates some of the formative figures in modern western philosophy, figures such as Descartes and Hume, from others. This division concerns the place and value of testimony in human knowledge. No one can sensibly deny the important place that testimony plays in human affairs, in, for example, the authority of the expert scientist or the historian. The fundamental divide that I am referring to comes between those for whom human testimony is a convenient shorthand for what each of us may, with sufficient time and energy, find out for ourselves, and those who discern a more principled distinction between what we can know for ourselves and what we know only on the say-so of others.

Hume, for example, recognises the importance of human testimony, but for him such testimony, at least in so far as it is reliable testimony, must be evaluated or assessed by his own present beliefs. He writes:

> There is no species of reasoning more common, more useful, and even necessary to human life, than that which is derived from the testimony of men, and the reports of eye-witnesses and spectators. ... (O)ur assurance in any argument of this kind is derived from no other principle than our observation of the veracity of human testimony, and of the usual conformity of facts to the reports of witnesses... (A)nd as the evidence, derived from witnesses and human testimony, is founded on past experience, so it varies with the experience, and is regarded as a proof or a probability, according as the conjunction between any kind of object has been found to be constant or variable... The ultimate

standard, by which we determine all disputes, that may arise concerning them, is always derived from experience and observation.[15]

Hume here applies probability to testimony, asking if it is likely, with respect to any piece of testimony, whether what is testified to is true or not. And the evidence on which such a judgement of probability is to be based is to be derived from the experience we have of human testimony in general.

It will be sufficient to observe that our assurance in any argument of this kind is derived from no other principle than our observation of the veracity of human testimony, and of the usual conformity of facts to the reports of witnesses.[16]

Evidence of the veracity of testimony is derived from witnesses and human testimony founded on past experience. But the question is, whose past experience? In effect, Hume argues, credence is only to be placed upon the testimony of other people in so far as it is reasonable to believe that one could, with one's present stock of attitudes and beliefs, directly witness what is testified to.

The reason why we place any credit in witnesses and historians, is not derived from any *connexion*, which we perceive a priori, between testimony and reality, but because we are accustomed to find a conformity between them.[17]

And so we can at best only give the weakest assent to testimony of what is unusual.

But when the fact attested to is such a one as has seldom fallen under our observation, here is a contest of two opposite experiences; of which the one destroys the other, as far as its force goes, and the superior can only operate on the mind by the force, which remains.[18]

This raises two questions; what if we experience what is unusual? And why, if as Hume claims, the credit to be given to historians is not *a priori*, might there not be an *a posteriori* connection between testimony and the unusual?

---

15 Richard Wollheim (ed.), *Hume on Religion* (London 1963), 207-208. All the quotations from Hume are from the Section on Miracles in the *Enquiry*. Page numbers refer to *Hume on Religion*.
16 Hume, 207.
17 Hume, 209.
18 Hume, 209.

Hume applies these principles in his famous discussion of miracles, and he bases his critique of reports of miracles on his (and our) present experience of natural and other uniformities. Because our present experience is one of uniformity of nature, testimony to miracles is very weakly credible but not, it is important to note, totally incredible. In effect he says, had you or I, with our experience of natural uniformity, been present when the alleged miracle took place, and believed that it was a miracle, we would have been deceived. (Here Hume helps himself to a counterfactual that is surely disputable; namely that had I witnessed what is alleged, I would have had my present stock of beliefs, including those arising from my experience of natural uniformity, and so must conclude that I was being deceived; but why should not my witnessing what is unusual *change* my beliefs?)

On Hume's view, historical testimony is shorthand, and must be evaluated by the present. Indeed, everything about the past must be evaluated by the present. Let us call this the *reductionist view* of testimony. (Hume then reverses the argument: since this testimony is uniformly against the occurrence of miracles, one ought not, given that testimony, to believe the evidence of one's own senses that a miracle has occurred, since it is overwhelmingly likely that one's senses are deceiving or deceived.)

But this view seems hard, if not logically impossible, to maintain consistently. To start with, Hume himself needs to rely upon testimony to set up his argument:

> Some events are found, in all countries and all ages, to have been constantly conjoined together: others are found to have been more variable, and sometimes to disappoint our expectations; so that, in our reasonings concerning matter of fact, there are all imaginable degrees of assurance, from the highest certainty to the lowest species of moral evidence.[19]

How does Hume know all this, how does he know what is found in all countries and ages, but from testimony?

Hume's criterion seems readily applicable in those cases where we receive testimony directly from others, and where we are able directly, for ourselves, to check their credentials. But there are very few cases like that. More common are cases where we cannot check, and where this inability is not a contingent but a necessary one; it is not due to the fact that we do not have time or opportunity to check, but because, in our present circumstances, we cannot check, since we cannot now check what has happened in the past.

---

19   Hume, 206.

So what Hume cannot evade, it seems to me, is the conclusion that all evaluation of what has taken place in the past itself partly but necessarily depends on evidence from the past, viz. from testimony of those who lived earlier than ourselves. Because acceptance of testimony is necessary for any human intellectual activity, the sort of judgement involved over whether a particular report of a miraculous event is reliable or not essentially involves a judgement not (as Hume would have it) between the present and the past, but between different testimonies.

But does not Hume have a good argument for his modernism? Is it not reasonable that we should judge the past by the present? Indeed, how else can we judge the past? Of course, 'we must judge the past by the present' is true, if that simply means, *we must judge the past*. The fact that we do not (if we do not) witness the occurrence of miracles nowadays does not prevent us making a reasonable judgement, on the basis of the reliability and veracity of testimony, that miracles have occurred in the past. But Hume means more than this. He means that we must judge the past while holding the belief that the present is non-miraculous, and that the past conforms to the present, and he further holds that these beliefs are each the product of experience formed without any necessary assistance from testimony, and this seems doubtful.

For suppose that there are historical testimonies to miracles (as there are). How are we to handle these on Hume's *a posteriori* principles?

> In the foregoing reasoning we have supposed, that the testimony, upon which a miracle is founded, may possibly amount to an entire proof, and that the falsehood of that testimony would be a real prodigy.[20]

That is, a person's testimony to a miracle might be so credible as to overthrow our experience of natural uniformity. I ought to reject the greater miracle, and there is nothing *in Hume's argument so far* that prevents the greater miracle that I reject being my belief in natural uniformity. Certainly if Hume is to be faithful to his *a posteriori* approach, there cannot be any *a priori* reason why not. This is the conclusion of Part I of Section X of the *Enquiry*. However, Hume opens Part II by claiming that

> it is easy to shew, that we have been a great deal too liberal in our concession, and that there never was a miraculous event established on so full an evidence.[21]

---

20   Hume, 212.
21   Hume, 212.

Hume still endeavours to keep up his *a posteriori* approach; 'never was a miraculous event established on so full an evidence'; not, never *could* be.

My chief point here is not to offer an argument against Hume on miracles, but to show that his argument against miracles depends, whether he likes it or not, on an *a priori* appeal to the veracity of testimony, an appeal that in Hume's case is filtered by his modernist assumption that in these enlightened ages the past must be judged by the present, or by a certain sort of account of the present. Hume attempts to show that the conclusion that he has reached by the end of Part I is too liberal by appealing to certain historical facts for the knowledge of which he must, of course, rely upon testimony. However, such testimony does not in fact show that no one has ever borne testimony to a miracle because that is plainly false; Hume has to describe such as have borne testimony to miracles as lacking in good-sense, education or learning, or as lacking in integrity, or as in some other way being deficient in epistemological *bona fides*.

> There is not to be found, in all history, any miracle attested by a sufficient number of men, of such unquestioned good sense, education, and learning, as to secure us against all delusion in themselves; of such undoubted integrity ... of such credit and reputation.[22]

The dilemma that Hume is in is that he must depend upon testimony, in his argument against miracles and yet he wishes, as we all do, to distinguish between credible and incredible testimony. The way in which he does this is to make his appeal to testimony definitional; his appeal is an instance of what that admirer of Hume, Antony Flew, refers to as the 'no true Scotsman...' appeal.[23] No man of good sense, education and learning, of integrity, credit and reputation, can be found who bears testimony to a miracle. No one man or group of men, with such exalted characters, have in fact testified to a miracle; and if they have, then this shows that they did not possess such exalted characters after all.

Having collected this evidence from testimony, Hume then returns to the principle of subtraction

> It is experience only, which gives authority to human testimony; and it is the same experience, which assures us of the laws of nature. When therefore, these two kinds of experience are contrary, we have nothing to do but subtract[24] the

---

22   Hume, 212.
23   Antony Flew, *Thinking about Thinking* (London 1975), 47.
24   The edition of Hume that I use, has sub*s*tract(ion).

one from the other, and embrace an opinion, either on one side or the other, with that assurance which arises from the remainder. But according to the principle here explained, this subtraction, with regard to all popular religions, amounts to an entire annihilation; and therefore we may establish it as a maxim, that no human testimony can have such force as to prove a miracle, and make it a just foundation for any such system of religion. [25]

This appeal to testimony is inevitable, but in Hume's hands it is reductionist, and therefore question-begging. If it is experience which gives authority to human testimony, which experience does that? Hume's reductionism is essentially modernist in its thrust. It is an epistemological rather than moral modernism; the past must necessarily be interpreted by the present. But not only that; we must interpret the past by a particular view of the present. No miracles occur today, in what Hume called 'the enlightened ages'; anyone who claims otherwise cannot be a person of good sense.

Such a view is not only a reductionist view of the epistemological worth of human testimony, it also may be a reductionist account of divine testimony. If one takes the view that miracles do not occur today (as Hume notoriously did), and one is a Humean reductionist, then one will take the view that miracles did not occur in any period. Hence any supposed divine testimony to miracles will either have to be rejected or at best re-interpreted. The miracle stories are then perhaps held to be vivid fictions of presenting abiding moral truths.

The consequences of such a view for the Christian tradition are radical. If one comes to adopt this view of human testimony, as Hume came to adopt it, then one's understanding of the tradition, and therefore of its authority or possible authority, perforce changes.

I have argued that Hume's appeal to experience cannot be carried through consistently, but that he must rely on testimony; such reliance is not a contingent feature of his argument, as having a diary is a contingent aspect of having and using one's memory, but a necessary feature. Secondly (though here less importantly) I have argued that such reliance in Hume's case is partial, being based upon a definition of creditworthiness that we need not accept. The use of testimony is essential for most matters of fact, but this fact does not require that we accept Hume's reductionist account of the nature of testimony. Hume's view that the past must always be judged by the present, and can never correct the present, is thus question-begging. But even if I am mistaken about this, Hume's is not the only view of testimony, and so we are not obliged to accept it.

---

25   Hume, 222-223.

For others argue that it is only so far as I have confidence in the testimony of others that I can gain knowledge of anything, particularly knowledge of the past. Such credence is, so to speak, a primitive feature of the human cognitive situation, one that is not reducible to any other, and certainly not a shorthand or shortcut for one's own cognitive endeavours. Of course I must evaluate the claims that various 'authorities' make, but it is a fallacy to suppose that I can do this in such a way as not to rely on any authority in doing so.

Thus Augustine, for example, says:

> I considered the innumerable things I believed which I had not seen, events which occurred when I was not present, such as many incidents in the history of the nations, many facts concerning places and cities which I had never seen, many things accepted on the word of friends, many from physicians, many from other people. Unless we believed what we were told, we would do nothing at all in this life. Finally, I realized how unmoveably sure I was about the identity of my parents from whom I came, which I could not know unless I believed what I had heard.[26]

Augustine says that such trust of another person is not something that one *could* gain from knowledge of empirical matters of fact, but is itself a pre-condition of much knowledge. I cannot gain the knowledge that X and Y are my parents from experience. It is an illusion that one might, even in principle, get down to a bed-rock of experience each item of which one had personally verified.

How might we express this second view of testimony more exactly? Perhaps as follows. That testimony as a source of knowledge is not inferential in character. Hume maintains, on the contrary, that it is; that any appeal to testimony depends upon the acceptance of a major premise about trustworthiness. Of course it is not in dispute that some cases of the evaluation of testimony depend upon inference, but not all, as a matter of logic, can do so.[27]

This does not mean that in the case of this stronger sense of testimony it is not possible to evaluate testimony. The stronger sense does not entail total credulity. Of course it is possible to evaluate testimony, and testimony ought to be evaluated when there is reason to do so. What it does mean is that one cannot, as a matter of logic, check every testimony. For what would one then check testimony against? Take language as an example: induction into a language is the paradigm case of accepting testimony. One might evaluate some aspect of the language; one might

---

26   Augustine, *Confessions* VI 5,7 (tr. Chadwick, 95).
27   Michael Dummett, 'Testimony and Memory,' in: id., *The Seas of Language* (Oxford 1993), 419.

believe with good reason that one had been taught a part of the language wrongly or idiosyncratically. But one could only carry out that evaluation using language.

Such an approach is sometimes said to be one that rests upon the principle of testimony, the principle that one ought to believe the testimony of others unless there is good reason not to do so. This is an extension of what Swinburne calls the principle of credulity. As Swinburne puts it:

> I suggest that it is a principle of rationality that (in the absence of special considerations) if it seems (epistemically) to a subject that x is present, then probably x is present; what one seems to perceive is probably so. How things seem to be is good grounds for a belief about how things are.[28]

The principle of testimony is the belief that

> other things being equal, we think that what others tell us that they perceived, probably happened.[29]

What we have seen is that according to Hume, with respect to testimony to miracles, other things never are and cannot be equal. But the principle of testimony may be a weaker version of the non-reductive account of testimony, depending upon whether the good reasons for overturning the testimony of others are themselves reasons which do not rest upon the principle of credulity. If they do not rest upon it, then we are back to something like Hume's position. If they do rest upon it, then the principle of credulity is hard to distinguish from a non-reductive understanding of human testimony.

A stronger principle, one approaching the view expressed by Augustine, is that there is no knowledge without testimony; not merely that all testimony is *prima facie* credible.

So I suggest that there is nothing in Hume's assumptions about the nature of testimony in his argument against miracles that prevents the past from exercising authority, and therefore from exercising *de jure* authority, over the present. Denying Hume's position does not, of course, require total credulity about the past. It cannot, since our beliefs about the past are often in conflict.

---

28   Richard Swinburne, *The Existence of God* (Oxford 1979), 254.
29   Swinburne, *Revelation*, 271.

4   Conclusion

So, in conclusion, in this paper I have been more concerned with the presuppositions and philosophical preliminaries to the question of the compatibility or otherwise of the existence of *de jure* authority and the fact of change. Certain kinds of change are compatible with the existence of such authority, but these are, for the most part, philosophically uncontentious. I have argued that there is nothing in principle that prevents the past from exercising authority over the present, and that this is a necessary condition for the existence of a tradition exercising *de jure* authority over us. What gets in the way of us seriously thinking of the Christian tradition as having such *de jure* authority over all who call themselves Christians is the empirical fact that Christendom is fragmented into many different – though no doubt overlapping – traditions, in at least some of which the idea of *de jure* authority has all but vanished. Hence I conclude that the obstacles to the idea of a *de jure* Christian tradition are not so much philosophical as empirical in character.[30]

---

30   I am grateful to René van Woudenberg for encouraging me to clarify the argument of the paper at various points.

9. Religious Tradition, Change and Authority

Luco J. van den Brom (Groningen)

1 Introduction

In June 1969 Pope Paul VI visited the World Council of Churches in Geneva and started his address with the confident words 'Our name is Peter.' The story goes that he embarrassed his host, Dr Eugene Carson Blake, general secretary of the WCC, by referring to his own status as Bishop of Rome holding the Apostolic See which represents a direct line of descent from the apostle Peter, the *primus inter pares* among the apostles. The words 'Our name is Peter' implied that Paul VI claimed highest authority over Christianity including the WCC leaders present. On that occasion the pope referred to the meaning of the name of Peter given by Christ: apostolic responsibility for Peter and his successors.[1] This apostolic authority is validated only by the recognition of the Roman pontiff, the successor of Peter. This authority is based upon the idea of the apostolic succession which claims that the bishops of the church are a college which stands in continuity with the apostolic college. By becoming member of this college the individual bishop shares in the apostolic succession.

Anglican, Eastern Orthodox, Protestant and Roman Catholic Christians now and then disputed each other's claim of being the (or a) valid continuation of the Christian tradition, that is to say a tradition which can rightfully claim to be in line with the apostolic tradition. But the problem is how we are to determine whose arguments are convincing. Is there a universal criterion to settle such disputes? Is Scripture such a sufficient criterion or merely a necessary one? Do creeds, ecumenical councils or synods provide a consensus in order to determine which Christian denominations can be called to be a valid continuation of the apostolic tradition? Is there only one such continuation or is diversification included? All these Christian denominations sometimes blame the others for having changed parts of the classical or apostolic tradition. However, who has the authority to judge a Christian denomination as a deviation from tradition? Pope Paul VI appeared to claim such an authority with his remark 'Our name is Peter.'

---

1   See Lukas Vischer, *Die eine ökumenische Bewegung* (Zürich 1969), 124ff.

In his paper 'Does the Authority of a Tradition Exclude the Possibility of Change?,'[2] Paul Helm deals with the notion of authority. He distinguishes two meanings in the expression 'the authority of a tradition': on the one hand it may mean 'the authority that the tradition itself possesses'; on the other hand 'the authority which authorises and constitutes a tradition.' The first meaning is to be understood as the authority that the past of a tradition exercises on the present: that means that the past somehow constitutes a criterion to determine whether the behaviour and beliefs of religious believers are authentically Christian or not. Helm assumes for the Christian tradition that 'authority' in the second sense is 'God himself' who authorizes and constitutes that tradition. However, an authority which authorizes in this way the validity of a tradition, is *external* to that tradition. Apart from that, because God's authorizing authority transcends all traditions, such a God's eye view cannot be available for human participants within a tradition in order to settle disputes on validity. It is for that reason that I want to raise the question whether there is another form of authority which is *internal* to a tradition but not merely the authority of the past over the present. In his paper, Helm restricts the discussion to authority in the first sense: authority of the past.

Helm identifies tradition by referring to its constitutive propositions and to its 'rites, practices and prescriptions.' These aspects of a tradition are related in such a way that the latter are expressions ('enactments') of the former. So the fundamental propositions of the Christian tradition authorize prayers, baptism, blessings, doxologies, holy communion and other rites and further prescriptions. Therefore Helm claims that the propositional element has logical priority over the non-propositional elements of the Christian tradition.

In this paper I deal with tradition and its authority in another way. Although we are used to understand 'tradition' as a set of practices or beliefs that a community has held for a long period of time, and consider it as something that belongs to the past, the idea of the Christian tradition refers to an *activity in the present*. In the light of this understanding of tradition I will discuss some aspects of authority within a religious tradition which is not simply the authority of the past over the present. In section 2 I will analyse some problems of authority within a propositional interpretation of tradition. In section 3 I will argue for the fruitfulness of distinguishing between *traditio activa* and *traditio passiva*. Section 4 deals with tradition as 'passing on' and tradition as an ongoing conversation and communication of salvation. In the final section I will make some remarks about the authority of Scripture.

---

2   In the present volume, 119-137.

2   Authority and Propositional Tradition

In order to be able to determine whether believers follow the tradition or break with it, one needs a standard to decide whether there exists (some) continuity between present-day behaviour and beliefs of adherents of a tradition and that of their predecessors. What is the nature of this continuity between past and present of a tradition? Is this continuity a form of reproduction of activities, rituals, and expressions that correspond to practices of the past? Or is it more like a form of coherence between past and present practices? Does continuity imply literal reproduction or does it allow for the possibility of there being different forms of developing matters of content? Apart from this complex of conceptual questions we may raise the theologically important question about the extent to which continuity with the tradition includes or excludes the possibility of innovation and change within that tradition. Is the Reformation, for example, merely a break with or, rather, an (innovative) moment in the tradition of the Catholica, as Arnold A. van Ruler, my teacher in dogmatics, used to say?[3] In order to solve such questions we need an authoritative criterion.

It is clear that 'the authority that the tradition itself possesses' cannot solve questions about the continuity of a tradition, unless we were to conceive of tradition in the sense of an authority of the past. However, for its effectiveness, such an authority of the past depends on some form of recognition by present-day believers. These believers may raise the question of authority 'Where do we go to find out what is relevant to our faith?' They can refer to tradition to answer this question and by doing so they recognize its significance for their own faith. In our example, the effectiveness of the authority of the past also depends on how believers define their position within the tradition, and how they value the dichotomy of Reformation and Roman-Catholicism. This shows that the expressions 'to be an authority' and 'to have authority' are incomplete symbols. They refer to the importance of other people because their meaning is comparable to that of 'having a strong hold over someone else' or 'to have authority over someone else.' Therefore, if somebody is a great authority in a particular field of discourse, this suggests that she has a quality that induces other people to take notice of her statements at least in that area. Authority certainly is a *relational* concept.

Given this relational notion of authority we can distinguish between formal authority and personal authority. This distinction is important because it marks two different types of authority. We have formal authority if some institution officially

---

3   A.A. van Ruler, *Reformatorische opmerkingen in de ontmoeting met Rome* (Hilversum 1965), ch.1.

appoints us to exercise executive power.[4] For example, a synod may appoint you as president whereafter you are officially its leader and you could initiate new liturgical or doctrinal discussions. People have personal authority if their expertise in a certain area is recognized or acknowledged by others. A theologian, for example, might be an authority on Calvinist theology if she had a profound knowledge of the theology of Calvin and his successors and also had the capacity to explain their theological ideas with some flair and lucidity. The latter type of authority is not the result of an official appointment but of an unofficial and perhaps personal recognition of somebody's distinct capacities. In this way, we could state that Pilate's authority was formal while that of Jesus was personal. The personal recognition by other people is fundamental for a relational and intersubjective account of authority in the context of a tradition. This becomes clear from Paul Helm's analysis of tradition.

Helm makes a distinction between a *de jure* and a *de facto* understanding of a religious tradition – analogous to the one traditionally made between *de jure* and *de facto* uses of the word 'authority.'[5] A *de facto* understanding of a tradition is an account of the kinds of practices and beliefs a tradition actually has come up with over time. A *de facto* understanding does not claim that people maintain a tradition in the fashion in which they hold rules or prescriptions. We speak of a *de jure* understanding of a tradition when we want to emphasise its prescriptive character. For example, it is a *de jure* tradition that Christians are baptized, while it may be a *de facto* tradition that a christening robe is white. Helm argues that the Christian tradition should be understood as a *de jure* rather than a *de facto* tradition. He claims that only the propositional *de jure* sense of tradition makes sense of the notion of breaking with a tradition, which is the same as making mistakes in practice or errors in belief. In a *de facto* sense of tradition harbouring no regulative implications believers logically cannot make a mistake which contradicts that tradition. If, for example, the 'kiss of peace' and the 'holy kiss' are not gestures prescribed by the rules but merely habits, then a rejection of these gestures is no break with a *de jure* tradition. Sticking to his propositional account of tradition, Helm rightly claims that given the recognition of a *de jure* Christian tradition one cannot make real changes which are not endorsed or permitted by the authority of this tradition, without removing oneself from its *de jure* authority.[6]

---

4   See e.g. John V. Taylor, *The Christlike God* (London 1992), 19-21. Taylor distinguishes 'authority conferred' (i.e. official or formal) from 'authority discerned' (i.e. personal).
5   Cf. Paul Edwards (ed.), *The Encyclopedia of Philosophy* (London 1967), s.v. 'authority.'
6   The rest of Helm's paper discusses some philosophical questions about the possibility of a tradition. The first concerns the nature of rule-following whereby participants of a tradition have grounds to believe that what they mean or do is what others earlier in the tradition meant or did.

Now we may raise the question of whether a relational or intersubjective idea of authority is a *de jure* or a *de facto* account of authority. This is not an easy question to answer. Such a relational account of authority stresses the personal aspects of the authority relationship between people, especially the notion of recognition. We need to distinguish power and authority in this context because they are different concepts precisely on the issue of recognition. Someone can have power over other people in the sense that he can manipulate them as he likes. It does not matter whether people recognize this manipulative power, that is to say, their recognition will not make a difference to his influence over them in any way. A striking case in point is John Lucas's definition of power: A man, or a body of men, *has power* if it results from his saying, 'Let X happen' that X does happen.[7] There is no sign of other people's approval in this definition. Sometimes we use the term 'authority' as analogous to 'power' in the sense of 'formal authority,' for example, in expressions such as 'local authorities' or 'the competent authorities.'

Usually 'authority' does not imply coercion of unwilling people but, rather, recognition granted by one person to another, what we called above 'personal authority.' Again, Lucas proposes a helpful definition of authority: A man, or a body of men, *has authority* if it follows from his saying, 'Let X happen,' that X ought to happen. The important thing in this description is its prescriptive element 'ought' which distinguishes authority from power, because the relationship between the utterance and the event X is not causal but somehow regulative. However, Lucas's description seems to neglect the aspect of other people's approval or recognition of the moral character of the utterance 'Let X happen.' Unless the speaker is God who has or is absolute moral authority, we need to know the conditions under which a person may have this (moral) authority. John Taylor's description of the relationship of Jesus with his followers is a good example of this relational aspect of authority. 'Yet, with all this inherent authority, he left his hearers free to reach the true insight

---

Helm shows that agreement on what the tradition requires, does not mean that this agreement is a continuation of the tradition. Such an agreement might be erroneous because it is an interpretation of the tradition. The second question concerns the problem whether a tradition can exercise a *de jure* authority because of its testimony of past events which are constitutive for that tradition. This is followed by an argument against Hume's judgement of the probability of the truth of the testimony of earlier witnesses. Helm's argumentation sticks to his propositional account of tradition and religion.

7   J.R. Lucas, *The Principles of Politics* (Oxford 1966), 16 (his italics). This is, however, a phenomenological description of power that does not refer to any boundary condition for the exercise of power. For example, Lucas's definition does not distinguish between the coincidence of 'Let X happen' and the happening of X and a causal/manipulative relation between the speaker and the happening of X.

by themselves, and his unique way with parables was designed to that end.'[8] In a similar way people can refer to Mahatma Gandhi as a moral authority. However, both Jesus and Gandhi had a *de facto* authority, because they were not entrusted with some official responsibility, i.e. a *de jure* authority.[9] *De jure* authority usually means the competence to act on behalf of someone else or of a certain institution within a set of rules. It implies power. It is just power that is absent in a case of authority in a *de facto* sense when someone willingly recognizes that another person is entitled to say what is to be done or what is the case.

We see the difference between *de jure* and *de facto* authority more precisely when we consider the opposite situation, that of non-compliance with an authority. In the case of non-compliance with a *de jure* authority we should be afraid of some sanction being imposed on this disobedience or mistake. However, non-compliance with a *de facto* authority – that is, in spite of our recognition that the other person is actually entitled to tell us what ought to be done – may be interpreted or seen as a moral failure or an unreasonable action. Recognition of a *de facto* authority commits us to moral action adequate to this recognition, while recognition of a *de jure* authority does not. In the light of this analysis we may conclude that a relational or intersubjective account of authority is primarily a description of a *de facto* authority because of the emphasis on personal commitment of those who acknowledge someone's authority.

When we apply this insight to the Christian tradition, the result appears to be the opposite of Helm's claim that this tradition is a *de jure* tradition. We can consider Christian doctrine as the propositional core of the tradition, as Helm does, and Christian practices as the enactments of this core. In this propositional interpretation of tradition it is possible, by means of logical reasoning, to interpret new practices and doctrinal statements as proper or just enactments and developments of the essence of Christian belief. When we know the boundary conditions of new situations, it might be possible to make a useful proposal that is in line with the propositional core or essence of the Christian tradition. We can imagine the *ideal* situation that someone who has a complete overview of the propositional core of Christian belief can judge a proposal on its merits by looking forward and backward along the lines of the doctrinal tradition. In this ideal situation that person can speak with a *de jure* authority about the development of a *de jure* tradition, given a strictly propositional perspective. It seems to me that this is really an imaginary situation because it is comparable with a God's eye view. How do we know which propositions do

---

8   Taylor, *Christlike God*, 90.
9   Within a framework of a 'christology from above,' however, we can also defend in *retrospect* the point that Christ has *de jure* authority too.

belong to the hard core of Christianity? How do we know that we have the complete set of propositions that should be contained by that core? We may claim that because we are in the office of a *magisterium* we need to answer these questions in the affirmative, but even then we are not infallible.

Therefore, we can conclude that a propositional account of tradition cannot cope with the problem of how to apply the *de jure* authority *within* the actual Christian tradition. Indeed, no theologian or church leader has access to the ideal situation of having a complete overview of the core of the Christian belief. The propositional account of tradition, however, is not the only one. In the next section I will continue the analysis of the concept of tradition before I will return to the role of authority within a tradition.

3   *'Traditio Passiva' and 'Traditio Activa'*

In a propositional account of tradition we pay attention to a doctrinal object as a changeless treasury. As a *depositum fidei* this object is passed on in space and time, from believers to converts and from generation to generation. This notion of doctrine as a body of information that is passed on implies that we can distinguish the bringer of the message, the message itself, and the receiver of it. In a propositional account of tradition we can also deal with the message *independently* from the whole process of passing it on. We find this idea in Tertullian in his argument for the apostolic succession:

> Since Jesus Christ sent out the Apostles to preach, no others are to be accepted ... The substance of their preaching – Christ's revelation to them – must be approved ... only through the testimony of those churches which the Apostles founded by preaching to them both *viva voce* and afterwards by their letters. If this is so, it is likewise clear that all doctrine which accords with these apostolic churches, the sources and origins of faith, must be reckoned as truth, since it maintains without doubt what the churches received from the Apostles, the Apostles from Christ, and Christ from God. ... We are in communion with the apostolic churches because *there is no difference of doctrine*. This is our *guarantee of truth*.[10]

In this way Tertullian has a yardstick to test heresies: there should be kinship between these teachings and those of the apostolic churches.[11] If new churches

---

10   Tertullian, *De Prescriptione Haereticorum*, 21; the italics are mine.
11   Those churches relate their succession of bishops to a first bishop who was appointed by one

hold the same faith, that is, the same doctrine, as the apostolic churches, then they are in communion and confident of the truth of their teaching. The criterion of truth, therefore, is coherence with the teaching passed on by the apostolic churches. According to Tertullian, these received it from the apostles who did not diverge from one another in doctrinal issues. By means of such a test the process of tradition as 'passing on' does not affect the deposit of faith which is treated as a fixed set of statements. By stating this rule, Tertullian appears to conceive of tradition as a process of saying and doing the same things as one's predecessors did, which guarantees historical continuity with the main source of that tradition. In this construction the apostolic churches function as authorities *de jure*. We see that the propositional account of tradition and authority has old credentials. This changeless collection of religious statements is called *traditio passiva*, that is, the essence of the message which is to be passed on.

In the quotation from Tertullian, however, the substance of the apostolic preaching is referred to as 'Christ's revelation to them.' Whereas the mainline of his argument concerns the propositional content of the doctrine, Tertullian does not describe the core of the apostolic preaching as a set of coherent propositions but as an experience of a relational character: Christ's revelation to them. It might be that he interpreted this revelation as if it was to be recapitulated in religious propositions. We may, however, interpret that expression in a relational way as an activity or a process of building a personal relation between Christ and the apostles. If that is a reasonable alternative interpretation of Tertullian's words, revelation does not refer to a message apart from the sender and the receiver but includes them. If something is revealed, it seems natural to suppose that there is someone to whom it has been revealed: revelation is person-relative;[12] and in our case it is also reasonable to suppose that this revelation was a kind of action of Christ towards his disciples.

We can interpret Tertullian's expression 'Christ's revelation to the Apostles' in at least three ways. Christ shows the apostles *either* (1) something new to them *or* (2) something in a new way by transforming them (e.g. by opening their eyes to see things in another way than they did before) *or* (3) Himself. We might interpret the first case as revelation of new propositions and the second case as revelation of a new understanding of propositions. In the last case 'Christ's revelation to the apostles' is rather different, because it means that Christ reveals Himself to them in such a way that He creates a personal relationship with his disciples by becoming personally known to them. By revealing Himself, Christ makes Himself (part of) the

---

of the apostles or a so-called apostolic man, who is immediately related to an apostle.

12   See George Mavrodes, *Revelation in Religious Belief* (Philadelphia 1988), 99. He calls this feature of revelation 'person-relativity.'

message while the message can only be revelatory if there is someone to whom the message is to be revealed, and who actually comes to know it. Therefore, while Christ giving Himself is (part of) the message, the disciples or apostles are also part of the whole event of revelation. On this understanding, 'Christ's revelation to the apostles' includes both, Christ and the apostles. For this reason we may say that, in the case of the apostles, 'the substance of their preaching' is self-referring too: it supposes their own experience of salvation in their relation to the person of Christ. The act of preaching this revelation of Christ to the apostles is the paradigmatic picture of tradition as 'passing on.' That is, preaching the revelation of Christ is aimed at sharing this salvific *experience* of the revelatory event with others.

We can find this notion of tradition as sharing the salvation of the Gospel with other people in Paul's remark to the Corinthians: 'I commend you for keeping me in mind, and maintaining the tradition I handed on to you.' Further on he explains that 'the tradition which I handed on to you came to me from the Lord' (1 Cor. 11:2 resp. 23). Hans Conzelmann points out that, on the one hand, Paul joins the chain of tradition by becoming himself a link of it, but, on the other hand, breaks that chain by claiming that on every occasion of handing on, the tradition which is handed on remains immediate to its source, i.e. the Lord.[13] Oscar Cullmann explains this as follows: the Lord is present behind every act of passing on in such a way that every future reception of the message that Christ revealed Himself to the disciples is equivalent to receiving that message immediately from Christ. In other words: in Paul's theology tradition as 'passing on' means the handing on of *salvation*.[14]

We may conclude that the picture of tradition as 'passing on' is the exact opposite of the propositional account of it. This view of tradition as a process of communicating salvation experiences to other people or new generations is called *traditio activa*. This process of communication which creates personal relationships also involves the recipients and may evoke new practices as their responses in a new context or in a new period. These responses may be new because practices are partly determined by local culture which differs from time to time and from place to place. Thus we should not expect that authentic responses to salvific experiences like being grasped by the apostolic message would always be exactly the same. These responses may result in a diversity of rituals and liturgies as seen in the various denominations of Christianity. And as far as theologians reflect on these Christian practices they may produce creeds to express their faith in the language of their own

13   Hans Conzelmann, *Der erste Brief an die Korinther* (KEK) (Göttingen ²1981), 238f, 222f.
14   Oscar Cullmann, *Die Tradition als exegetisches, historisches und theologisches Problem* (Zürich 1954), 8ff.

time. So we can imagine that these processes of communicating salvation evoke new creeds as reflective responses which are characteristic of their context. Apart from that, communication within the perspectives of a new cultural setting can even result in new insights into what was handed on as the revelation to the apostles. Therefore we may expect changes in religious practices and theologies as signs of the ongoing process of tradition. These changes belong to another category as the changes in a propositional interpretation of tradition. In the latter, changes are just logical developments from prior propositions, while in an activity account of tradition there may be both changes with a contingent character and changes because of logical developments.

The distinction between *traditio activa* and *traditio passiva* is analogous to the doctrinal distinction between *fides qua creditur* and the *fides quae creditur*. The *fides qua* is the act and attitude of putting one's trust in God, being grasped and fascinated by what is experienced as ultimate trust in God. Such faith or *fiducia* means that the believer is confident that she can rely on God. We may say that faith in this sense is a response to what can be said to be the experience of a revelation of God as Ultimate Reality, or as Luther says in his *Large Catechism* in a comment on the First Commandment: 'faith and God have inevitable connections. Now, I say, whatever your heart clings to and confides in, that is really your God.'[15] From the viewpoint of faith this implies that God and faith cannot be separate issues. The *fides quae creditur* is often interpreted as the content of faith, that is the set of beliefs of the Christian faith. One of these beliefs is believing that God exists. From this viewpoint religious belief is faith detached from its relation to God and as such it can be the object of theological research. Theological questions then get a propositional character like, for example: 'What is believed in the Christian faith?' and they can be answered, for example, with 'It is believed that God exists' or 'God is the cause of the world.' These answers concern presuppositions of the Christian faith, at least in the eye of the non-believer. In the case of *fides qua creditur* theological questions do concern the meaning of being a Christian, for example, questions like 'What are religious believers doing when they put their trust in God?' or 'What are the appropriate responses for a Christian?' The answers to such questions are not true or false, but correct or incorrect, or they are appropriate or inappropriate. A tradition as 'passing on' intends to evoke the response of the *fides qua* because of the personal character of both the process of tradition and the answer of faith. Now we may raise the question: Are all responses appropriate? In which way can we answer the question of which responses and practices are appropriate and which are not? Is there any criterion or authority?

---

15   Martin Luther, *Der große Katechismus* ed. Wolfgang Metzger (Stuttgart ²1977), 22f.

4 Tradition and Authority

It can be convenient for authorities to teach their citizens the virtue of submission. They can make use of history to underpin existing political and social structures. Plato, for example, suggests that authorities make use of tradition in order to circulate fables or myths about a primordial situation which justify the claim that present established positions are beyond discussion. Such a fable might entail a deterministic course of history. In this way Plato devised his Great Lie about a fictional past, which is actually a deliberately designed history with which citizens of the ideal Republic had to be indoctrinated in order to further the acceptance of present relationships.[16] It is not completely evident whether in Plato's story of the Great Lie the political authorities have come under an ironical form of criticism, but nevertheless, he has a low opinion of the role of tradition as authority in political affairs. Although Plato himself is not always an accepted authority in religious questions, his warning is clear: tradition cannot in all cases justify practices and beliefs because it might be a deliberately designed history.

Is a Christian tradition designed in the same way in order to justify its religious practices and beliefs? Can we design a founding story for every practice? Are there some criteria? A propositional account might look for logical criteria for the coherence and consistency of the doctrinal propositions which are being handed on. In an activity account of tradition it is rather difficult to determine what the appropriate responses to the tradition have to be. It is claimed that tradition as a process of communication of the Gospel of God's revelation in Christ puts present-day believers immediately in touch with God. And this implies the further claim that there is not only human agency but also simultaneously a divine involvement in the handing on of the tradition. Therefore, the tradition puts the reality of our daily life in a new perspective by revealing a dimension or quality different from the visible and the audible aspects of the world. It does so by utilising these audible and visible aspects. In the theological understanding of this type of tradition one should refer to God the Holy Spirit who acts through history and tradition in order to get in touch with human beings.

On the one hand, the Spirit acts through the generations of believers by structuring and styling their lives in the covenant of grace, which is understood to be the new order in which the divine agency especially deals with them. The tradition hands on a form of life which is visible and audible and qualified by the presence

---

16 Plato, *Republica* III 389b, 415d; Karl Popper has blamed Plato for these lines and failed to see any irony in this part of Plato's writings, see his *The Open Society and Its Enemies*, part I, *The Spell of Plato* (London 1945).

of the apostolic preaching. On the other hand, the aim of the tradition as handing on is a renewal of the orientation of the believer: regeneration is the final touch of the tradition and this is more than believing a set of pious propositions.

What does authority mean in such a process of tradition as handing on? There is no standard or objective criterion for renewal or regeneration. How to determine from an external perspective that someone's life is restyled and structured in such a way that we can say that she is regenerated? The point is that this restyling activity of the tradition is self-authenticating because being touched, fascinated, grasped, impressed and inspired concern the individual person. She needs no external criterion that informs her that this is just a case of being touched or fascinated etc., because she knows it for herself. From her point of view, therefore, the authority of tradition is self-authenticating as well. In this context authority is interpreted as relational: it is the believer who recognizes the authority of the tradition, and it is logically impossible that anyone else could do that for her. In this way the authority of tradition as 'passing on' is *de facto* self-authenticating. To ask for an external authority to justify this self-authenticating authority would be to miss the religious point at stake. This can easily be discerned in our analysis of Lucas's description of authority. There the prescriptive element in an utterance of one authority depends upon the approval of other people and not upon another authority. Because in the latter case it would be precisely other people's acknowledgement of the authority$_2$ that is approved in the recognition of the prescriptive element in the utterance of the authority$_1$. The approval is based upon the ultimate experience of the audience whom the authoritative speaker is convincing. This ultimate experience is a relatively autonomous affair and creates its own sphere of life which needs no ground common to believer and external authority in order to be defended. So we may conclude that in this type of tradition the problem of authority has disappeared behind the individual or personal experiences. At the same time it seems as if the possibility of a discussion about the appropriateness of the response has disappeared. The question now arises to what extent this result really differs from the so-called post-modern view that all perspectives are correct on their own terms. Does this mean that religion disappears behind a whole set of individually shaped screens? Is this the end of all religious authority? I do not think so.

I want to emphasize that this type of tradition can in pneumatological terms be described as 'passing on.' We need to emphasize the mediate character of the work of the Holy Spirit. He works through history and tradition and especially through the generations in order to get in touch with believers of this time and place. New believers do not have the experience of being grasped and fascinated in isolation from other people but through others and even in communication with them. Religion is not an individual affair. The experience of being grasped and fascinated takes place in the context of a community of believers. And it is precisely this context that is the medium of the Spirit: the context in which communication takes place. There-fore, although the religious experience is self-authenticating and autonomous, the response to that experience is not. At least the members of the community of believers are in the position to recognize the appropriateness of the response. And precisely the community of believers can help new believers by offering them language which enables them to respond in a way that is recognizably adequate and meaningful to that religious community. The responses of new believers must be not too unlike the kind of communication to which the religious community is used. That does not mean that they need to imitate that community slavishly but that they should not say things that make the community say, 'We do not know what to make of it.' While learning the new language that enables them to make sense of their experiences, new believers may discover new possibilities that were unknown to the other participants of the tradition.[17] So the ongoing practice of communication, including the form of life of the religious community, is primarily authoritative because it constitutes the context of further communication. This does not imply that the practice of communication of the community is finally authoritative, but any final authority manifests itself through this communicative process in the commun-ity.

The community of believers does not start from scratch but is itself involved in an ongoing process of communication. That is to say, these believers themselves have been involved in a religious communication with, for example, their prede-cessors. They have acquired their command of religious language through com-municating with these predecessors who also belonged to a community of believers and learnt their religious language etc. So we get the picture of an ongoing com-munication between people throughout the ages, that is, a tradition of learning from 'the earlier links in the chain' to grasp the meaning of Christ's revelation to the apostles. In this ongoing process of communication the predecessors are masters or teachers who are in a sense recognised authorities in religious belief. Just because the catechumens trust their teachers and accept their authority in the form of life of the Christian faith, they learn how to be involved in the Christian practice. That is

---

17 This is an application of Polanyi's remark: 'To learn by example is to submit to authority. You follow your master because you trust his manner of doing things even when you cannot analyse and account in detail for its effectiveness. By watching the master and emulating his efforts in the presence of his example, the apprentice unconsciously pick up the rules of the art, including those which are not known explicitly to the master himself [!]. These hidden rules can be assimilated only by a person who surrenders himself to that extent uncritically to the imitation of another.' Michael Polanyi, *Personal Knowledge* (London 1958/62), 53. A theological conse-quence of this insight may be that the church as community of believers may have deeper insight in the revelation of Christ to the apostles than the apostles themselves had or even than Jesus of Nazareth had.

to say, the catechumens learn the 'skill' – to use Polanyian terminology – of how to cope with human life in the light of Christ's revelation to the apostles. Faith is among other things a skill. This skill is expressed in the words of Keith W. Clements:

> The unceasing exploration of God's goodness and graciousness is faith's real business: new experiments of trust, new ventures of commitment, new areas of understanding. To be realistic, much of the impulse towards such exploration stems from the stern challenges and questions that faith has to face.[18]

This skill can be acquired to a certain extent just by imitating the example of a religious authority. However, these authorized examples to which we submit as we learn are no goal in themselves but should bring us in contact with the reality of Christ's revelation to the apostles.

This idea of tradition as an ongoing communication, as a process of continuously learning and teaching, is opposed to an understanding of tradition as merely static or backward looking. When we understand tradition as ongoing communication, in passing it on we look to the past to learn from its efforts and mistakes, but also to the present, because that is the context of the present-day conversation with its current challenges. Thus we can describe tradition as an ongoing conversation, both diachronic and synchronic, in the very diverse contexts of its history. As ongoing conversation tradition does extend to the future because it also deals with the communication of Christ's revelation to the apostles in new circumstances with their specific challenges.

This argument is largely in agreement with Alasdair MacIntyre's description of a tradition:

> A tradition is an argument extended through time in which certain fundamental agreements are defined and redefined in terms of two kinds of conflict: those with critics and enemies external to the tradition who reject all or at least key parts of those fundamental agreements, and those internal, interpretative debates through which the meaning and rationale of the fundamental agreements come to be expressed and by whose progress a tradition is constituted.[19]

The difference between MacIntyre's description and mine consists in the fundamental role MacIntyre attributes to the conflict between rival opinions, as if tradition is

---

18   Keith W. Clements, *Faith* (London 1981), 121.
19   Alasdair MacIntyre, *Whose Justice? Which Rationality?* (London 1988), 12.

equivalent to war. Primarily, I would say that even when participants of a religious tradition try to interpret the substance of the apostolic preaching in new circumstances and translate it in such a way that it can be grasped by others, an *extension* of the tradition takes place which may establish itself. Debates and conflicts about the right interpretation of basic insights may be, of course, stronger tests of the viability of a tradition than an exercise in translating it to contemporaries. Sometimes these debates are more exciting than a conversation. But a conversation about the communication of the message of salvation need not end in a conflict but may also lead to mutual enrichment of the insights of the participants.

When we raise the question of authority in the Christian tradition, we need to keep in mind that it concerns authority in an ongoing conversation, both diachronic and synchronic, in very diverse contexts. We are now asking for what is seen to be constitutive for this Christian conversation. The easiest solution is that of Vincent of Lerins' *Commonitorium* (434), perhaps the most influential text in the debate on authority in the early church. According to Vincent the tradition of the Catholic Church is necessary because 'all do not accept it [i.e. Holy Scripture] in one and the same sense, but one interprets its words in one way, another in another; so it seems to be capable of as many interpretations as there are interpreters.' Therefore, to avoid a complete relativism in which 'anything goes,' he proposed the well known definition of authentic Catholic faith as a standard for interpretation of biblical texts so that Scripture 'secundum ecclesiastici catholici sensus normam dirigatur': every interpreter should accept 'quod ubique, quod semper, quod ab omnibus creditum est.'[20] This principle of consensus presupposes a propositional account of faith and tradition, but it raises its own problem: it is not self-evident because its own legitimacy and validity cannot be argued for by referring to the same principle. Apart from that, because of emphasis on the 'ubique,' 'semper' and 'ab omnibus' there is a kind of 'all-quantor' in the definition which reduces this consensus to a highest common factor that might become irrelevant or even unrecognizable for most of the participants later on in the tradition.[21]

Vincent of Lerins' criterion for authority in the Christian tradition points to a kind of central and uniform authority which decides what counts as really Christian faith. The trouble with this type of authority is its formal character because it is a *de jure* authority. In the case of non-compliance with this authoritarian rule people

---

20 Vincent of Lerins, *Commonitorium*, 2,2 and 2,3. He admits the possibility of growth of faith within the limitations of one and the same *doctrina*, in *eodem sensu eademque sententia*; ibid., 23. Cf. Christoph Schwöbel's contribution to the present volume, 179f.

21 The remark attributed to pope Pius IX 'I am the tradition' could be interpreted as an authoritarian claim but also – in a more generous way – as a humble expression of being only a link in the great chain of the process of tradition as 'handing on' the message of salvation.

will be excluded from the conversation of the Christian community, i.e. excommunicated. This solution cannot cope with a critical discussion of its own validity because it excludes new interpretations of biblical texts on *a priori* grounds. It is also vulnerable because it is not clear how it can deal with the challenges to *quod ubique, quod semper, quod ab omnibus creditum est*. This principle of consensus can be used as a fixed criterion in the hands of ecclesiastical authorities, which means that it will be an instrument of power. We can reject any form of authority as Bertrand Russell did: 'The triumphs of science are due to the substitution of observation and inference for authority. Every attempt to revive authority in intellectual matters is a retrograde step.'[22] Viewed in this light, a reinforcement of Vincent's criterion would certainly count as a retrograde step. Russell's own positivistic view, however, is not very helpful either. The substitution of observation and inference for authority might provide us with an objective criterion; but then the question becomes: why and on whose authority ought we to accept this new criterion?[23] When we accept this challenge to science, another question arises. Is there any alternative to Vincent's authoritarian principle that is not retrograde?

By defending the notion of tradition as 'passing on' which is described as an ongoing conversation and communication of Christ's revelation to the apostles, we accept that within the community of believers there is an agreement about the constitutive meaning of Christ's revelation for the Christian community. This agreement can be seen in the fact that believers communicate their faith by showing in one way or another the significance of Christ's revelation for their daily life. By doing so their way of communication depends, at least partly, upon the examples of predecessors they have seen but also upon the debates they hold with other believers on their understanding of the Christian faith in order to grasp the meaning of Christ's revelation to the apostles for present-day life. In the history of these debates the church reached decisions as to what is constitutive for the Christian community, especially in the creeds and dogmas. It is important to know the status of these ecclesiastical decisions: they form an authority within the community of believers, but is this authority a 'competent' or a 'supreme' authority – in Polanyian terminology?[24] This community of believers may accept the creeds and dogmas of the

---

22 Bertrand Russell, *The Impact of Science on Society* (London 1952), 110f.

23 Polanyi has criticised Russell's view for neglecting the role of authority in science itself, because the acceptance of the claims of science is a form of commitment to these claims the justification of which must go beyond the evidence; see Michael Polanyi, *Knowing and Being* (London 1969), 94.

24 Polanyi, *Personal Knowledge*, 164: 'I accept the existing scientific opinion as a *competent* authority, but not as a *supreme* authority, for identifying the subject matter called "science."' In an analogous way present-day believers may raise the question whether the creeds and dogmas of the Christian tradition are 'competent' or 'supreme' authorities.

Christian tradition as competent authorities and not as supreme authorities because they are the fallible result of debates among human beings. Therefore, these creeds and dogmas are open to revision. They function as a primary introduction to the ongoing debate on the message of salvation, but not as supreme or absolute authorities. Their material content is limited due to the fact that they were developed to counter particular opinions that were considered to be heretic. New circumstances may give rise to new questions, and new answers to these questions may attempt to show the significance of Christ's revelation to the apostles in these new circumstances. This dependence of confessions upon circumstances and contingent, false or confused opinions is responsible for the temporal, local and material limitations of these authorities. There is always the possibility that in new contexts there will be the need for revision if they cannot cope with the problems of those new contexts. This means that there cannot be an actual central authority[25] in a religious tradition because any human authority is temporal, local, historically contingent, and fallible. All human authorities, like creeds, dogmas, or decisions of councils, are recognised in so far as they lead to grasp the significance of Christ's revelation to the apostles in new contexts. We know about this revelation because of Scripture. This brings us to the question of the authority of Scripture to which I shall devote the final part of this paper.

5   *The Authority of Scripture*

What is the appropriate religious authority in the Christian tradition understood as 'passing on' by conversation? On this issue Protestants and Roman-Catholics disagree. Protestants claim that Scripture is the only source of authority in religious affairs, whereas Roman-Catholics recognize two sources, viz. Scripture and Tradition. It is not my intention to settle this dispute, but I want to point out that even the Protestant *sola scriptura*-principle, though certainly being of utmost importance, is not a sufficient criterion for deciding what is the appropriate response to the apostolic preaching or kerugma.

Constitutive for the Christian conversation is the apostolic preaching, as we have seen. The formal criterion in the tradition-as-communication is whether the good of the kerugma is present in the communication. We can interpret the New Testament as a commentary in which Christ's revelation to the apostles is understood in terms of the Old Testament. The implication of this interpretation is that the

---

25   Polanyi points out that within the scientific community there is no central authority that governs the research. The research of the individual scientist is coordinated by the adjustment of his efforts to 'the hitherto achieved results of the others'; see his *Knowing and Being*, 50.

New Testament recognizes the authority of the Old Testament, and by the same token that the recognition of the authority of the New Testament implies the recognition of the authority of the Old Testament.[26] If Scripture is the linguistic context for the communication of the apostolic preaching in the early church, then we can say that it is at least an authority for explaining the content of faith within the process of that conversation. But is 'Scripture alone' the final or supreme criterion in all Christian conversation?

The notion of 'Scripture alone' does not mean that Scripture has authority because it is authorized by the church. Rather, it means that because it has authority it has to be authorized by the church.[27] These remarks are really formal because the expression 'Scripture alone' is rather ambiguous. It is therefore far from clear what is meant by the authority of Scripture in the Christian tradition as 'handing on.' We can interpret the expression in a propositional way that might be in agreement with a propositional understanding of tradition. In that perspective, 'Scripture alone' means that it is the only source of religious truth claims. It is not difficult to see that this interpretation cannot justify itself because as such it would have to harbour self-referential implications. If Scripture were the only source of religious claims, then our expression could not itself be a religious truth claim, because 'Scripture alone' is not a claim of Scripture itself. In other words: the expression is either a non-religious claim or a meta-linguistic remark which belongs to the *grammar* of the Christian language without being part of it.

Another interpretation of 'Scripture alone' remains within a propositional point of view and may consist in a limitation of the range of the claims. In the theology of Protestant orthodoxy, for example, Scripture has authority primarily with respect to our knowledge of salvation. Scripture is not only necessary but also sufficient for that knowledge. This type of interpretation does not permit the same counter-argument as in our first interpretation. To know that Scripture is the only source for our knowledge of salvation is itself neither necessary nor sufficient for salvation nor for our knowledge of it. The source of salvation is Christ's revelation to the apostles and Scripture is the *testimony* to the apostolic kerugma of the Christ event, but not the kerugma itself. Therefore, this interpretation is inadequate.

A third interpretation of the expression under scrutiny describes it as the claim that Scripture is our only norm for religious claims. That is to say, Scripture is *norma normans* in order to *test* religious claims and prescriptions. That means that religious statements may be developed from other sources of knowledge than Scrip-

---

26 Cf. Gerhard von Rad, *Theologie des Alten Testaments* II (München 1960), 411: Both Testaments produce each other's authority.

27 It is debated by Roman-Catholic and Protestant theologians whether Scripture is a creation of the church (because of the process of forming the canon) or the church a creation of Scripture.

ture alone. We can argue against this interpretation that the canon of Scripture is established by the church and therefore, it cannot be *norma normans*. It is merely *norma normata*. This counter-argument depends on the way in which we interpret the history of the canonization of Scripture: we might also say that the Scriptures have established the faith of the church by showing that Jesus is the Christ of Scripture (i.e. in Old Testament perspective). Another argument against the *norma normans* role of Scripture is that there is no agreement among Christians as to how Scripture is to be interpreted. If that is the case, what remains of its normative character? This is a valid counter-argument in a propositional account of tradition and authority. But in an activity account of tradition we may claim that we are touched or fascinated or inspired by the message of Scripture. Under these circumstances it will be rather difficult to argue against it, because now the debate is not about a correct interpretation but about inspiration which is a self-authenticating experience. But even in an activity interpretation of tradition as handing on we cannot neglect the issue of the correct interpretation of Scripture. We may be worried about whether the inspiration through Scripture can happen without its interpretation. How do we know that we are inspired in the right way for the right type of action?

In a fourth interpretation of 'Scripture alone' Scripture is a source apart from and above other sources of knowledge, and/or a norm apart from and above other norms. That means that we may have various sources of religious knowledge but Scripture is the final one. A very generous interpretation of this approach would be to see Scripture as the central testimony of the Christ event which plays a role in the communication of the kerugma. That is to say, Scripture is authoritative in so far as it contributes to the communication of the kerugma. Whether it does so, depends on the reception. Scripture's authority is not an inherent property of it but part of a personal experience, viz. that it gets authority in the interaction between the members of the community of believers and between them and new believers. The authority of Scripture can be explained with reference to the activity of the Holy Spirit who uses it as a means for creating a salvific relationship with believers. Scripture gets its authority at the moment that believers understand that the Spirit acts through it. 'Authority is a communicative action.'[28] That is to say, the authority of Scripture is a relational and not an inherent property. In Reformed theology this relational character of authority is understood in terms of the *testimonium Spiritus Sancti internum*.

---

28   Kurt Schori, *Das Problem der Tradition* (Stuttgart 1992), 225-255.

10. Rationality, Tradition and Theology

Six Theses

Christoph Schwöbel (Kiel)

1 *Introduction*

The topic of this contribution appears at first sight straightforward enough. It seems to call for a comparative inquiry into the way theology functions in different religious traditions. If such a task is given to a systematic theologian the expectation would seem to be that he or she deals with it both descriptively and prescriptively, thus offering an outline of the different ways the relationship between theology and religious traditions is construed and proposing what he or she sees as the most appropriate ways in which the role of theology can be exercised. This seems clear enough and could be embarked on without much ado.

On closer inspection this clear picture becomes uncomfortably opaque and, henceforth, the task of the paper more complicated. The problems concern the two leading concepts of the topic, 'theology' and 'tradition.' Although the term 'theology' has its roots some time before the advent of Christianity on the stage of history in the philosophical critique of the images of the deities offered by the classical poets of Ancient Greece, its present meaning is almost exclusively shaped by its history in Christianity. From this particular context of application the concept is then transferred to cover other religions. Yet, it is by no means obvious that such a transfer can successfully be made. Even in the case of the two religions that are historically Christianity's closest relatives, Judaism and Islam, the adequacy of the concept of theology to characterize the way in which these religions engage human rationality has been severely challenged.

Writing on Jewish theology in a well-known dictionary of religions the Jewish historian of religion R.J.Z. Werblowsky states that, because there is no authoritative *magisterium* in Judaism, Jewish thought developed in exegetical, homiletical or even philosophical frameworks rather than in one that is comparable to Christian dogmatic or systematic theology. Werblowsky writes: 'The "theologies" of Judaism ... are mostly attempts to collect religious doctrines from the rabbinical sources and to force them in a systematized form into the straight-jacket of a Christian model. That applies even in those cases where such works were authored by Jews...' He quotes the ironic comment in a review of a book on the systematic theology of the

synagogue: 'First of all, there is no synagogue (that is, the term is a Christian invention in order to find an expression that corresponds to the term 'church'), and even
if there were one, it would not have a theology (in the Christian sense), and if it had
one, it would not be systematic.'[1]

In the same dictionary the Islamic historian A.Th. Khoury writes that an Islamic
theology would have to be construed from the results and methods of different disciplines, like the study of the confirmation of the oneness of God, the *kalam*, i. e. the
study of the word (or proof) that has an apologetic function, and the tracts on the
foundations of the study of law. On the *kalam*, often referred to as being analogous
to Christian theology, he remarks that it has its origin in defending the teachings of
Islam over against Hellenistic philosophy so that 'theological reflection' became a
kind of defensive apologetics and was less concerned with illumining the contents
of faith. As a result, it did not exercise a determinative influence on the life of the
congregation, the expression of its religious beliefs and the shaping of its life. From
Khoury's discussion it becomes clear that if one speak of an Islamic 'theology' it
is notably different from what one understands as theology in a Christian context,
and it has different functions in the life of the Islamic community.[2]

The situation does not seem to become much easier when we turn to the concept of tradition. I take it that the term 'tradition' in our topic is employed rather
loosely to designate religions as religious traditions. I leave the question aside
whether it is indeed entirely fitting 'to single out traditionality as the most basic
characteristic of a religion.'[3] However, if we look at the history of the concept it
also seems that it has been decisively shaped by its use within Christianity. The
concept may originally have been employed in legal terminology to signify the legal
transfer of something to a new owner. In early Christian authors we find from the
second century a metaphorical use of the concept so that the term could be specified
by adjectives referring either to the process of transmitting something from one
generation to the next or to the content that is in this way transmitted, as in the
expressions *traditio evangelica, traditio apostolorum* or *traditio catholica*. This
metaphorical extension of meaning makes *traditio* an equivalent of the Greek *para-
dosis* which was already established in philosophical language. The modern usage
of 'tradition' depends on this extension of meaning that occurred early on in the
Christian tradition. It is presupposed in the Enlightenment's criticism of tradition

1   R.J.Z. Werblowsky, 'Theologie II: Jüdisch,' in: Hans Waldenfels (ed.), *Lexikon der Religionen*
    (Freiburg ²1988), 645-646, 646.
2   Cf. A.Th. Khoury, 'Theologie IV: Islamisch,' in: Waldenfels (ed.), *Lexikon*, 648-649.
3   Paul Valliere, 'Tradition,' in: Mircea Eliade (ed.), *The Encyclopedia of Religion* (New York
    1987) vol. 15, 1-16, 2.

and the counter-criticism of writers like Edmund Burke of rational endeavours that claim to be independent of tradition.

These brief observations should make us careful in dealing with the topic of the role of theology in religious traditions. I therefore propose to start with a general discussion of the place of rational expression and rational reflection in the religions (§2). Following that I will make some general remarks on the phenomenon of tradition in religion (§3) and its interrelationship with the forms of rationality in religions (§4). Against this backdrop I shall then look at an account of the specific characteristic of rationality in the context of Christianity (§5) and the specific problems associated with the notion of tradition in Christianity (§6) in order to make some suggestions about how to approach the question of the role of theology in the Christian tradition (§7).

2   Rational Expression and Reflection in the Religions

In all religions the disclosure experience of a divine reality provokes forms of expression which include forms of rational expression in religious symbols, myths, doctrines and dogmas. They are means of re-identifying the divine reality so that it can be the foundation of a particular view of reality grounded in the foundational disclosure experience of a religion. In every religion this rational element is interrelated in specific ways with the experiential, ritual and social dimension of that religion. Both the specific forms of expression of the rational element in religion and the patterns of interrelation with other dimensions are shaped by the foundational disclosure experience of a specific religion.

In his lecture series *Die Entstehung der christlichen Theologie und des kirchlichen Dogmas* Adolf von Harnack, the famous historian of dogma, characterized Christianity as a 'thinking religion.' He interpreted this characteristic as a distinctive feature of the Christian religion over against all other religions with which it came into contact in its early development. For Harnack none of the other religions in the Roman empire possessed a theology or a dogma or had successfully attempted to acquire them. Harnack makes some allowances for Alexandrian Judaism which, in his view, attempted to elevate the Jewish religion with the help of Greek philosophy to the level of a thinking religion by developing a particular mode of reflection about the law. However, this synthesis, impressively exemplified by Philo, did not last. Over against attempts by the Slavonic emperors to destroy Judaism, Harnack argues, Judaism discarded its Hellenistic elements in the interest of self-preservation.

In contrast to this view Carl Heinz Ratschow has argued in an important paper with the title 'Das Christentum als denkende Religion' that every religion is a 'thinking religion': 'Alle Religion ist denkende Religion.'[4] All of Harnack's criteria for a 'thinking religion' – theoretical reflection on cultic practice, the shaping of the entire life of believers through the fundamental insights of their religion and the attempt at forging relationships between religious practices and the intellectual endeavours in their environment, most notably philosophy – can be shown to be met singly and jointly in all religions. For Ratschow it is an intrinsic element of religion as religion that it provokes rational forms of expression. The difference between Christianity and other religions is therefore *not* that Christianity is a thinking religion and the others are not. Rather, the difference is to be found in the distinctive way in which Christianity is right from the beginning a reflective faith so that it develops a theology as its particular rational form of expression.

All religious experience is according to Ratschow characterized by an intrinsic tendency towards expression. This tendency also leads to rational forms of expression which Ratschow sees primarily exemplified in the ascending scale of religious symbols, myths, doctrines and dogmas.[5] In Ratschow's interpretation this rational element is not to be interpreted exclusively as rooted in the fact that humans are rational animals, but rather in the specific character of the foundational event of each religion. He sees the drive towards rational expression as intrinsic to the foundational event from which a religion develops. The disclosure experience of a divine reality which is experienced as the ground of life and salvation requires of necessity to be expressed in rational or theoretical forms. Once the disclosure experience is past it must be identified, signified and mediated in order to enable the re-identification and thus the recognition of the divine reality. The form in which it is identified and signified must be appropriate to the event itself.

Religious symbols are for Ratschow the most prominent rational expression of religions, because they are the most comprehensive. They make the divine disclosure experience communicable and as such they can retrieve its impact when it has passed. *Myths* are for Ratschow in the same way forms of rational expression of the divine reality. However, it would mean to miss the point of myths if they were interpreted as some kind of primitive science. The particular form of rationality of religious myths becomes apparent when we pay attention to their narrative form which, so to speak, compresses the divine reality in a narrated sequence of events

---

4   C.H. Ratschow, 'Das Christentum als denkende Religion,' in: *Neue Zeitschrift für Systematische Theologie und Religionsphilosophie* 5 (1963), 16-33, now in the first volume of the collection of Ratschow's papers *Von den Wandlungen Gottes: Beiträge zur Systematischen Theologie* (Berlin 1986), 3-23, 5.

5   Cf. Ratschow, *Von den Wandlungen Gottes*, 5ff.

in space and time. The universal ground of being and salvation can be represented in a particular story. This form of mediation between particularity and universality, one of the hallmarks of rationality, is most apparent in etiological myths which communicate a fact of universal significance by telling a particular story about how it all started. They point to a particular story in the past as the reason why things are as they are in the present. Furthermore, Ratschow follows Robert Redfield and Werner Jaeger in seeing a doctrinal element already in the coordination of particular myths and symbols which we find both in so-called primitive religions and, for instance, in Hesiod. While we may call this form of coordination an *implicit* form of doctrine, the rational expression of religion gains a new quality when it is *explicitly* expressed in doctrinal form. In this explicit form *doctrine* is propounded with a normative intention in the interest of offering reasons for particular religious practices. In many religions doctrines serve to explain the spatial coexistence or the temporal succession of different cults. Perhaps the most significant characteristic of doctrine is its use in the instruction of the acolytes to the priesthood. With the concept of *dogma* one can describe a stage where doctrine has become fixed in a process of development so that new insights are expressed in the interpretation of formulated dogmas.

The aim of Ratschow's description of all religions as 'thinking religions,' which he supports with many examples we cannot recount here, is to show that rational expression and reflection is constitutive for every religion, although it is not expressed in the same way. The rational expression of a religion is a function of its particular foundational disclosure experience. The differences between the forms of rational expression in different religions are therefore a function of the differences between their foundational disclosure-experiences. Since religious experience is universally characterized by the drive towards expression it has an inherent rational element which is necessary to enable the repetition, the 'calling back,' of the foundational disclosure experience. In order that this can happen the encounter with the divine reality must be in some forms identified and predicated. Ratschow uses the terms 'individuation' and 'objectivation' for these fundamental traits of rationality.[6] From these basic acts follow the other forms of rationality in religions: the synthesis of the particular and the universal, as in symbols and myths, and the narrative 'explanation' of a state that is experienced in the present by telling the story of how it came about as in etiological myths.

Ratschow's general thesis that all religions are 'thinking religions' in the sense that the elements of rationality are constitutive for them as religions is not offered as a general account of religion *an sich*. Ratschow strictly follows Schleiermacher's

---

6   Cf. Ratschow, *Von den Wandlungen Gottes*, 14.

rule that religion (singular) is only alive in the religions (plural). Therefore, if we want to characterize the specific rationality of a specific religion we can only attempt to describe the specific forms of rational expression which are provoked by the specific character of the foundational disclosure experience of a religion. If we want to inquire into the character of rational expression in different religions there is no other way than that of a comparative analysis of different religions.

We can supplement Ratschow's account of religions as thinking religions, which we have already expanded here for the purposes of our discussion, by taking two further aspects into consideration. The first is a view of religions as multi-dimensional phenomena which was introduced by Ninian Smart and Eric Sharpe.[7] On this view, religions are not to be viewed as phenomena which are accessible to one-dimensional interpretation, but as multi-dimensional phenomena which require a multi-dimensional description and interpretation. Smart distinguishes experiential, mythological, ritual, social and doctrinal dimensions in religions. In our context it is important to note that the rational element in religion is not only to be located in the doctrinal dimension, but in all dimensions of religion. The myths, ritual practices and social forms of community organisation are not devoid of rationality. The rational element belongs inherently to all dimensions, because they are all concerned with the identification and interpretation of the divine reality of a religion's foundational disclosure experience – albeit in experiential, mythological, ritual or social form. The particular patterns in which these different dimensions are ordered are distinctive for particular religions and are connected to the specific character of the divine disclosure experience.

The second further consideration is that in the doctrinal dimension the rational element implicit in all dimensions becomes explicit. We have already mentioned three aspects of religious doctrine: it has a normative intention, it is concerned with clarifying the relationship of particular religious experiences, myths, rituals and social practices with others, thereby reflecting on what can be included and what must be excluded from a particular set of religious practices and beliefs, and it is connected with the instruction of believers or particular groups among believers. In all three aspects the doctrinal dimension plays a regulative role with regard to other dimensions. Doctrine lays down rules for how religious experiences are to be interpreted, how myths are to be told, rituals to be performed and how the social life of a religion is to be organized. The doctrinal dimension therefore represents a second-order activity with regard to the first-order activities of religious practice. The distinction is not a rigid one. It is a distinction which concerns what somebody does

---

7   The most comprehensive discussion of this approach can be found in Ninian Smart, *The Phenomenon of Religion* (New York 1973).

in a particular context. Narrating a myth as part of a ritual is not the same as telling the same story as part of instructing people who are to be initiated into the practice of the ritual. In the doctrinal practice of religion as a second-order activity the rational element inherent in all dimensions of religion becomes the explicit focus. The forms of identification and interpretation of the divine reality practised in myths, rituals and social action become thematic by themselves.

The specific way in which the doctrinal dimension of religions relates to other dimensions is to focus on their relationship to the foundational disclosure experience and on their relationship to one another. Two of the criteria which are employed in doctrinal reflection can be expressed in the following questions: How can religious practices correspond to the foundational disclosure experience of a religion? And: How can religious practices in the different dimensions of a religion form a coherent whole? The first question concerns the relationship between religious forms of expression to that which provokes these religious expressions. The second question concerns the relationship of the different religious forms of expression. It presupposes the first question. If all forms of expression are ultimately grounded in one and the same disclosure experience they may not contradict one another. Otherwise they would obscure their relationship to the disclosure experience which is their shared origin.

It is no accident that these two criteria of religious doctrine closely resemble two criteria that are usually employed to characterize theories of truth: correspondence and coherence. It would be tempting to explore this relationship further. Perhaps it may suffice for the moment to say that in religions the question of the truth of doctrine is closely related to the correspondence of religious practices to that foundational disclosure experience from which they develop and to which they refer, and to the question of the coherence of religious practices.

3   *Tradition in Religion*

In all religions a foundational disclosure experience produces particular traditions in which its impact is handed on from one generation to the next. Since they are to be viewed as processes of communication, religious traditions are always social and semiotic in character. As religious traditions develop the process of communication is structured in specific ways. Institutional forms of the maintenance of tradition as an ordered system are developed which define the role of the bearers of tradition, the content of tradition and the methods of transmission. In this process many religions define a specialized concept of tradition which has a specific role in the wider process of tradition. Religious traditions provide a framework for the understanding of tradition as a constitutive element of human culture.

Let us start with the last point of our thesis. It has become customary to interpret tradition as a constitutive element of being human. In this sense it is interpreted as an anthropological constant. This implies that human being is neither exclusively interpreted as a product of biological evolution nor as a novel creation in each instance. Neither of us starts at the absolute beginning, and each of us is aware that the process of life does not finish with our personal end. The phenomenon of tradition deals with two fundamental facts about being human, our mortality and our sociality. Sociality includes here not only the synchronic relations to our contemporaries but also the diachronic relations to those who went before us and will come after us. The fundamental questions and tasks we face and the answers and strategies that are devised for approaching these tasks concern more than one generation. Without tradition every human being and every generation would have to start in every respect from the beginning only to see all that is acquired in terms of skills and experience etc. during a life-time extinguished at the moment of death. The historical character of human being is characterized by the fact that in addition to the biological transmission of information by our genes there are exogenetic mechanisms for transmitting cultural skills to the next generation.[8]

The most fundamental understanding of tradition is to see it as a process in which patterns of praxis (of the organisation and of the interpretation of the world) are handed on from one generation to the next.[9] Traditions are rooted in the fact that humans have a relatively open relationship to their natural and social environment which is not completely conditioned by a causal mechanism of stimulus and response. We have to bridge the gap between ourselves and the world by intentional action which involves the exercise of rational planning, of symbolic means of communication and of tools. Taken together with the fact that humans are finite beings existing in time, this has the result that our interaction with the environment and with one another cannot be reinvented from an absolute beginning at every instance. We establish patterns of action and interaction, customs, which form the raw-material of traditions. In order to make up for the deficiencies of our instinctual equipment these patterns of action help us to make interaction with the world of nature more successful. The openness for the world which lies at the heart of the necessity of forming traditions implies human openness for the future, the capacity to transcend any given moment and to prepare for future situations by anticipation. Traditions form a horizon of expectation in which temporal beings can act. As a public and social phenomenon tradition corresponds to the phenomenon of experi-

8   Cf. Max Seckler, 'Tradition und Fortschritt,' in: Franz Böckle e.a. (eds.), *Christlicher Glaube in moderner Gesellschaft* Bd. 23 (Freiburg 1982), 7-53.
9   The discussion on the interpretation of tradition is best portrayed and analyzed in Edward Shils, *Tradition* (London 1981).

ence for the individual person. According to Aristotle's classic definition experience is remembered praxis, and in this way tradition can be described as the public and social process of remembering past praxis for the shaping of the present in the horizon of the future. Tradition can therefore be seen as an essential expression of the fact that human beings are by nature cultural beings.

The primary form of tradition as the handing on of patterns of praxis is a personal relationship of an asymmetrical structure. The most basic form of this asymmetry is temporal where the older partners in a relationship hand on experiences to the younger partners: parents teaching their children, handing on skills of life to the next generation, teachers handing on skills to their pupils, craftsmen to their apprentices. These relationships, however, have a very peculiar dynamic. They start from a situation in which the older partner plays exclusively an active part directing the activity of the child or the pupil, whereas the younger partner has a passive part, following the guidance of the instructor. The relationship is completed when the younger partners can take over the active part in becoming themselves parents, master craftsmen and teachers, able to exercise their acquired skill in the absence of their instructors. The dynamic process of tradition leads from receptivity to spontaneity, from dependence to independence. The process is completed when the personal relationship is no longer necessary for the exercise of the acquired skill so that children can survive in the absence of their parents, craftsmen exercise their skills in the absence of their master.

This dynamic has a variety of implications. The first is that the process of tradition nearly always involves *change* in the mediation of patterns of practice from one person to another, from one generation to the next, from one context of application to another. This element of change is implied in the personal mediation of practice in the process of tradition.

The second implication is that this process always involves *interpretation* on both sides of the relationship. The pattern of practice exercised by the teacher has to be interpreted for the pupil in order to enable the transition from dependence to independence. This involves a particular order in which patterns of practice are handed on. Elementary practices, elementary skills come first so that they can form the basis for further, more sophisticated forms of practice. This introduces an order of significance into the process of tradition where a distinction between fundamental aspects and aspects of secondary, i.e. derived importance is introduced. The pupils are also involved in a process of interpretation in applying what is received as the patterns of practice from their teachers to their own situation as its new context of application. Interpretation usually involves some form of linguistic mediation and of rational reflection. There are limits to the extent to which traditions can develop on the basis of strict imitation.

The third characteristic is that this dynamic process involves *personal appropriation*. The path from dependence to independence will only reach its goal if the pattern of praxis is personally appropriated by the pupil so that it remains no longer external as the example of the teacher but becomes an inherent characteristic of the pupil's praxis. Appropriation involves a negative and a positive element. The negative element is the denial of the necessity of the presence of the teacher for the competent exercise of the skill in question. This is the presupposition for the positive affirmation of the pattern in the pupil's independent practice. The elaborate rituals of leave-taking and initiation which in all cultures accompany the process of tradition are effective illustrations of the dynamic of appropriation. This brings us to an important insight. Where the process of tradition is concerned, appropriation is the dominant paradigm. Identical repetition is the exception and not the rule. Handing on patterns of practice by means of identical repetition requires a controlled environment, a controlled context of application in which the personal dynamics of this process which we have characterized as change, interpretation and appropriation can be excluded.

The process of tradition itself requires an element of rebellion against tradition. Leszek Kolakowski has captured the dialectics of tradition very well when he pointed out that we would still live in caves if the new generations of the past had not continuously rebelled against the inherited traditions. On the other hand, we would return to the caves if the rebellion against tradition would at one stage become universal.[10] Because the process of tradition is such that it requires that the older partner in the relationship becomes redundant in order to give space to the independent practice of the younger partner who can then, in turn, become the older partner in a new process of mediation, the content which is mediated in this process acquires a relative independence over against the process itself. It then becomes possible to speak of tradition not only as the *process* of handing on patterns of practice, but also as the *content* which is handed on in this process. Observing the process over three or more generations enables the observer to make a distinction between invariant elements of the tradition and variable elements of the appropriation of tradition in a new context of application. The point is that the invariant content of the process of tradition is not that which remains unaffected by the elements of change, interpretation and appropriation, but that which *in* the processes of change, interpretation and appropriation remains continuous over against discontinuous elements which change from generation to generation and do not become part of the content of tradition.

---

10   Leszek Kolakowski, 'Der Anspruch auf selbstverschuldete Unmündigkeit,' in: Leonhard Reinisch (ed.), *Vom Sinn der Tradition* (München 1970), 1-16, 1.

When we leave the relatively simple social cosmos of personal relationship and move to the world of pluriform and complex social relationships in a differentiated culture, we can see that two developments are likely to occur. First of all, there is likely to be a transition from 'natural' social relationships to culturally organized social relationships. This usually involves an institutionalization of the process of tradition. These institutions give a formal structure to the process of tradition over many generations. Secondly, there is likely to be a codification or canonization of the content of tradition which attempts to formulate the invariant elements in the process of tradition. It is here that the problem of authority arises in a decisive way.[11] As long as the process of tradition is not institutionalized and the content of tradition is not codified, authority is an implication of the asymmetrical relationship between the older and the younger partner in the process of tradition. The place of authority in this relationship is derived from the structure of the relationship so that there is a change in the position of authority in every transition from one generation to the next. Once the process of tradition is institutionalised authority resides no longer exclusively in the relationship, but transcends this relationship so that both master and pupil have to conform to this authority in their respective roles.

A similar process happens when the content which is handed on in the process of tradition is codified. Formerly, the invariant element of the content of tradition is the result of the process of tradition. Now the invariant element is explicitly defined. Whereas in the non-institutional form of the process of tradition the 'definition' of the invariant content is the outcome of the process itself, it now becomes a presupposition of the process of tradition which defines the role of the teacher as well as the role of the pupil in their relationship to this content. This imposes boundary conditions on the process of tradition. The new question which arises is this: Whose authority regulates the process of tradition and whose authority defines the content of tradition and its application in the context of tradition? The answer to this question requires an explicit justification of authority which regulates both the investment with authority and the recognition of authority. It is at this point that we encounter definitions of the bearers of tradition, of the content of tradition and of the prescribed processes of tradition.

All the elements we have enumerated so far also apply to religious traditions. However, religious traditions have a specific point. We noted at the beginning of this section that traditions have a special anthropological significance because nobody starts at the beginning and nobody can identify his or her end with the end of everything. Religious traditions are concerned with beginnings and endings. They present us with images of an absolute beginning and a notion of an absolute end.

---

11   Cf. the contributions of Paul Helm and Luco van den Brom to the present volume.

'(T)he sacred traditions of all religions offer access to beginnings and insight into endings that personal experience and unaided reason cannot supply,'[12] writes Paul Valliere. Although they are transmitted in historical processes of tradition religious traditions offer a framework for all traditions in referring to an absolute beginning and an absolute end. Religious traditions thereby envelop our personal story and the story of our community and relate it to the all-encompassing story which connects the primordial beginning with the ultimate end. Religious traditions therefore explicitly address the issue of human mortality which is one of the background factors giving tradition its anthropological significance and in this way offer a framework which comprehends but also relativizes the claims of other traditions.

In all religions traditions develop from a particular disclosure experience which has foundational significance for this particular religion. It is important to note that the relationship between the foundational disclosure experience and the traditions which develop from it is a two-way relationship. Traditions develop from the foundational disclosure-experience, but they also reflect back on this disclosure experience. As the significance of the foundational experience is developed in the process of tradition, this process retroactively shapes the foundational experience of a religion.[13] This two-way process of tradition developing from the foundational disclosure experience and of tradition retroactively shaping the foundational disclosure experience raises the question of authenticity in religion.

Although religious traditions develop from a particular foundational disclosure experience this does not mean that this disclosure experience is an absolute beginning. In many religions the disclosure experience does not only elicit traditions, it also presupposes traditions. The complex relationship between Judaism and Christianity can illustrate this point. A disclosure experience can be regarded as foundational if it does not only shape the traditions succeeding it but also the traditions preceding it. The antecedent traditions may still provide the context for the disclosure experience but their significance changes fundamentally through the fact that they are now to be interpreted in the light of the disclosure experience. The way in which the messianic expectations in the Hebrew Scriptures provide one context for the Christ-event, but are now also interpreted from the perspective that they have been fulfilled by the Christ-event gives an example of this relationship. In this sense the disclosure experience of the Christ-event is for Christianity both the reason for the reception and preservation of the canon of the Hebrew Bible and for the production of the writings of the New Testament and their canonization.

---

12   Valliere, 'Tradition,' 1.
13   Cf. Gershom Scholem, 'Offenbarung und Tradition als religiöse Kategorien im Judentum,' in: id., *Über einige Grundbegriffe des Judentums* (Frankfurt a.M. 1970), 90-120.

In many religions we find not only a complex interplay between oral and written tradition, but also a specialized elaborate concept of tradition in which a particular mode of tradition is defined with regard to its processes and with regard to its content. Such an elaborate concept of tradition is usually the product of particular doctrinal attempts to clarify the processes of tradition of a particular religion by ordering them in a particular normative way. Although a specialized concept of tradition is the result of doctrinal reflection and debate, it also provides one of the reference-points of doctrinal argument. It is here that we encounter a specific relationship between the rational element of a religion and its traditions. This relationship derives its specific character from the disclosure-experience which is seen as foundational for the way in which religious experience engages human rationality and for the way in which it shapes the processes of tradition.

4   Tradition and Forms of Rationality in Religions

In all religions the element of rationality and the element of traditionality are closely intertwined. On the one hand, that which cannot be rationally expressed cannot be handed on in the process of tradition. Tradition depends on rationality. On the other hand, the exercise of rationality in religion requires tradition, since the rational forms of expression are themselves transmitted in the process of tradition, both with regard to the rational skills they presuppose and with regard to the content they embody. Rationality depends on tradition. Although it is a relationship of mutual dependence, it is also dynamic and, at least potentially, full of tension. Since tradition constantly changes through being transmitted in time and space and since rationality, because it is dependent on tradition, is also subject to change the need for regulating the processes of religious tradition (and of religious rationality) arises. In many religions doctrinal instruction, the second-order activity of rational reflection in religion, responds to this need by developing an elaborate normative concept of tradition which defines the process of tradition with regard to its contents, bearers and processes of transmission. Although it is the product of doctrinal reflection it also becomes a fixed reference point for doctrinal reflection, once it is accepted in the process of tradition.

When one surveys the interrelationship between the rational elements of a religion which make it a 'thinking religion' and the traditional elements which make it possible to speak of religious traditions, one observes a relationship of mutual dependence. The rational elements of religion are necessary for the process of tradition. They are required by a process of communication which is based on such rational skills as identification and interpretation. Therefore these rational elements need not be added to a process of tradition, they are already present whenever such a process occurs. Conversely, tradition is required for rationality to function within the context of a religion. It is through tradition that the rational skills are mediated that are required in the exercise of a 'thinking religion.' One could even make this point stronger by saying that rationality is a set of acquired skills and not a complex of innate capacities. If the skills of rationality are neither genetically inherited nor autonomously created in each new instance, they must be learnt. That means that rationality is of necessity dependent on tradition, since only in the dynamic of learning the skills of rationality we acquire the independence to exercise them ourselves.

In a religious tradition the skills of rationality are not handed on apart from a particular content, but only together with that content. This is not surprising since the rational elements of a religion cannot be detached from the 'content' of that religion which is rooted in its foundational disclosure experience. It follows that the content of rational inquiry is neither invented nor discovered afresh in each instance but handed on in a tradition going back to the foundational disclosure experience of a religion. The material of rational inquiry is presented in the form of *indirect knowledge*, it is received and not spontaneously produced. The productivity of reason is exercised within the boundaries of what is received through a process of tradition. This implies that rationality is in religious traditions never a set of purely formal capacities but inextricably bound up with the material in which and through which the rational elements are communicated.

If tradition and rationality are mutually dependent in religions, this also implies that what affects the one also affects the other. As we have shown above, change is a constitutive element in traditions, because the process of tradition itself involves change, interpretation and personal appropriation. Since religious rationality and religious tradition exist in mutual dependence, the changes in the process of tradition also concern the modes of religious rationality. There is a dilemma here. Without change tradition is not possible. If, however, the variations exceeded the invariant elements we would no longer have changes within a tradition, but a change from one tradition to another, a *metabasis eis allo genos*. The fundamental condition for the maintenance of tradition is therefore the management of change. This management has a twofold aim: to consolidate the changes that are a condition for tradition and to prevent those changes which would destroy the tradition. This requires to define the relationship between invariant elements and variable elements in the process of tradition.

Maintaining the tradition through the management of change is the task of doctrinal reflection and instruction as a second-order activity of rationality in the religions. We have already indicated that in all religions there is a second-order activity of doctrinal instruction in which the rational elements implicit in religious practice become the explicit focus of attention. How is the second-order activity of doctrinal reflection and instruction related to tradition? We have already suggested that it plays a regulative role with regard to religious practices. Can it also play such a regulative role with regard to religious traditions? In order to do so doctrinal instruction must focus on those elements in the process of tradition where the problem of the relationship between invariant elements and variable elements arises. The three elements which we have singled out as involved in every process of tradition are change, interpretation and personal appropriation. If one surveys the field of doctrinal reflection and instruction in religions it seems that they are all concerned with laying down rules for these three issues. In doing so it seeks to answer the following question: Which changes are allowed, indeed, required by the process of tradition and which changes would disrupt the process of tradition? Which interpretations on the part of the bearers of tradition and on the part of the recipients of tradition are required for the process of tradition and which interpretations would endanger the process of tradition? And what are the boundaries within which personal appropriation can be exercised without deviating from the continuity of tradition?

The answers to questions such as these lead to an elaborate concept of tradition as we find it in many religions where a specific form and content of tradition is claimed to have a normative function in the process of tradition. It seems possible to show that such a normative concept of tradition is the outcome of second-order reflection on the process of tradition, although it later defines the boundaries not only for the rational elements in first-order religious practices but also for the second-order activity of doctrinal reflection and instruction. We can see that the attempt at maintaining a tradition through the management of change by means of doctrinal instruction leads to an elaborate concept of tradition. This concept of tradition then defines the invariant elements of the tradition and so indirectly defines the realm where variations are allowed. The formulation of dogma is an interesting example of such a definition of tradition. It implies that once a dogma is formulated and recognized as such it belongs to the invariant elements of tradition. Variations are now no longer permitted with regard to the actual form and content of the formulated dogma. They now must take the form of *interpretations* of the dogma. Every attempt at fixing the invariant elements of a tradition also defines the range and status of possible variations that are required to maintain the process of tradition.

In developing a definition of tradition which then serves as a fixed reference point for doctrinal reflection, the character of doctrinal reflection itself changes. It must secure the continued transmission of the defined tradition and it must develop rules for the interpretation of tradition. In effect, doctrinal instruction and reflection must be organized in such a way that the capacities for the maintenance of tradition become themselves the object of processes of tradition. Forms of structured interaction must be established for the maintenance of tradition. The development of a defined concept of tradition leads in this way to the establishment of schools for doctrinal reflection and instruction.

We have mentioned time and again that rationality and tradition in religions are dependent on the specific disclosure experiences which are foundational for a religion. Both the specific forms of rationality and the specific forms of tradition can only adequately be described in the context of a particular religion because they are ultimately rooted in the disclosure-experience from which this religion developed. In order to say something more specific about the role of theology in religious traditions we have to turn to that religion which claims the term 'theology' and the activity signified by it for itself: Christianity.

5   Christianity and Rationality

In Christianity the rational forms of religious expression are shaped by the characteristic features of the Christ-event as the foundational disclosure experience of Christianity. The specific form of rationality that finds expression in Christian theology is motivated by the task of bearing witness to the world of God's salvation in Christ in forms appropriate to the recipients of that message. It is determined by the emphasis on the spatio-temporal character of its foundational disclosure experience which points to the eschaton as the full disclosure of God. It is focused on the existential question of faith how the salvation that is experienced in Christ can be maintained in the face of evil and suffering in a world that is believed to be God's creation. These determinative features give the form of rationality in Christianity its specific profile.

In attempting to characterize the specific way in which the rational elements in Christianity are shaped in a specific way by its foundational disclosure experience we can return to Carl Heinz Ratschow's description of Christianity as a thinking religion.[14] While he maintains that all religions are thinking religions he nevertheless claims that Christianity has a very specific profile as a thinking religion. In these specific features we can see the reason why Christianity developed a particular kind of theology which cannot be found in the same way in other religions. Ratschow lists three distinctive features of rationality in Christianity.

First of all, the message that Christ is the salvation for the world directs the rational expressions of Christian faith not towards the re-identification of the disclosure of the divine reality as the repetition of the epiphany of Christianity's God,

---

14   Cf. Ratschow, *Von den Wandlungen Gottes*, 14-23.

but towards witness before the world. Rational reflection does not serve primarily the aim of calling back the foundational disclosure experience but it is undertaken with the purpose of making the Christian message rationally plausible to the world in its specific cultural contexts. The awareness of being sent into the world means that the rational forms of expression must be taken from the world into which Christians are sent. Becoming a Jew to the Jews and a Greek to the Greeks involves developing the Christian message in the specific forms of rationality that are characteristic for a Jewish or a Hellenistic context. The rationality of Christian theology is therefore always a form of contextual rationality. If Christian theology is to remain true to the identity of Christian faith as it is rooted in the Christ-event it must change when it moves from one cultural context with its particular forms of rationality to another. The criterion of the adequacy of the rational expressions of Christian faith is the intelligibility and credibility of the Christian message to its recipients. We have the paradoxical situation that Christian theology can only preserve the identity of the Christian message by initiating and supporting such changes in its rational forms of expression that make the Christian witness plausible to its recipients in their respective context.

The second feature that gives a distinctive character to the rationality of Christian theology is that it cannot transcend the spatio-temporal character of the foundational disclosure of God in Christ. Ratschow sees a thorough-going difference in the spatio-temporal character of the Christ-event with the epiphany of deities in space and time in other religions. While in other religions the epiphany of the deity in space and time is an exemplification of the timeless transcendence of God so that the spatio-temporal determinants do not invade the timeless transcendence of God, the situation is different in Christianity. Here the spatio-temporal character of God's disclosure in Christ belongs to the very essence of the being of God. The incarnation is a real 'inhistorization' of God as John Hick called it, following H.H. Farmer, in one of his earlier essays on Christology.[15] In history God cannot be encountered apart from God's historical incarnation in the timeless transcendence of the divine being. The immediate encounter with God is only expected in the eschaton. The eschatological tension which is in this way introduced into Christian faith also shapes the form of rationality of Christian theology. Its subject-matter is not the timeless being of God which transcends all history, it can only be the in-historized God in Christ who directs believers towards the eschaton as the full disclosure of the Godhead. The rationality of Christian theology is therefore not a

---

15 John Hick, 'Christ and Incarnation,' now in: John Hick, *God and the Universe of Faiths* (Glasgow 1977), 148-164, 152.

timeless rationality reflecting the eternal laws of God's mind, but a form of rationality that remains bound to the spatio-temporal determinants of the incarnation.

The third feature which determines the specific shape of rationality in Christian theology is for Ratschow the tension between the experience of salvation in Christ and the experience of evil and suffering in the world. The rational expressions of Christian theology cannot transcend the tension between God experienced in the salvific relationship of faith and the evil and suffering of the world in which God's love is not transparent. The tension between the disclosure of God's love in Christ and the hiddenness of God in the world cannot be rationally transcended. According to Ratschow the rationality of Christian theology is always confronted with the question of theodicy but it cannot offer a theoretical solution to it which could somehow 'explain away' the evil and suffering in the world. This element which preserves the existential character of Christian theology prevents it from becoming pure speculation uncontaminated by the experience of suffering.

Ratschow sees these three features as the features which distinguish Christianity as a 'thinking' religion from other 'thinking religions' and their specific forms of rationality. These characteristics have surprising implications for the role of theology in the tradition of Christianity. The first is that theology participates in the character of Christian faith as witness. The task of theology is therefore to translate the Christian message into the thought forms of a particular cultural context. If theology participates in the character of faith as witness its task is to achieve the *external communicability* of the Christian message. The theological task of demonstrating the internal coherence of Christian faith serves to secure its external communicability. Theology is therefore not primarily directed at maintaining the Christian tradition. Rather, the task of maintaining the Christian tradition is subordinate to spreading the Christian message. It is not an aim in itself. The dogmatic task of Christian theology serves its missionary task. The conceptual work of theology is therefore constantly engaged in a process of translation of the Christian message into the conceptualities of a foreign cultural context. The conceptual game of Christian theology consists in a series of 'away matches.' Conceptual change is therefore not an inevitability encountered in the dynamics of the process of tradition, it is positively demanded by the character of Christian faith. If Christian theology participates in the character of Christian faith as witness, a *theologia perennis* is forever out of its reach. While this can explain why Christian theology has found expression in a bewildering series of conceptualities in its journey from its Palestinian homeland in the first century to the pluralistic global village at the end of the 20th century, it also points to the seriousness with which the problem of identity is raised. Furthermore, the character of Christian faith as witness before the world can explain why Christianity is from the beginning a pluralistic phenomenon and why it must

176

be pluralistic with regard to its conceptual expressions. This nevertheless raises the question wherein the unity of Christian faith or of Christian theology can be found.

The second implication which must be mentioned here concerns the spatio-temporal character of the Christ-event as the foundational disclosure experience of Christianity. This explains why Christian theology is first and foremost interpretation of the biblical Scriptures. *Nostra theologia fere tota est grammatica* said Johann Gerhard in the 17th century. The biblical writings have this particular status in Christian theology because they present the paradigmatic witness to the Christ-event as the foundational disclosure experience of Christianity. They are not themselves the revelation of God, but the authentic witness to God's revelation. Their authority is an eccentric authority, it is external to the writings themselves and resides not in their testimony but in what they testify. However, what they testify is not accessible apart from these testimonies, it remains bound to the biblical writings. Therefore Christian proclamation has its specific character in the interpretation of the biblical witness and the Christian community is essentially a *community of interpretation*.

The irreducible spatio-temporal character of the foundational disclosure experience of Christianity has a wider significance. It underlines the historical character of Christian faith and Christian theology. This means that in order to recover its identity in the changes caused by the missionary character of Christian faith it must constantly refer back to its origin in the Christ-event and can only do so by means of the interpretation of the biblical witness. The historical character of the disclosure experience belongs to the essence of this disclosure experience. It cannot be transcended so that the historical could be interpreted as the exemplification of timeless truths. The spatio-temporal character of the incarnation implies that the historical, i.e. a series of contingent events, can become the medium of the disclosure of ultimate truth. This is in sharp contrast to the mainstream of philosophical opinion in Greek philosophy where the historical, the contingent and the empirical cannot be the basis of true knowledge since that is concerned with timeless truths which can only become accessible through pure reason. In contrast to this epistemic ideal Christian theology claims that the historical and the empirical is the medium for the disclosure of truth, so that its rationality is a historical and empirical rationality.

This emphasis on the historical and empirical in Christian theology is in sharp contrast to the universality of the truth claims based on the Christ-event. This introduces the tension that characterizes the whole enterprise of Christian theology. What has been disclosed in the particularity of a particular series of spatio-temporal events is nevertheless true, although it is not universally evident in history, but will only become universally evident in the eschaton. The particular form of rationality in Christian theology is characterized by the fact that it is grounded in spatio-temporal events in the past which can only be witnessed but cannot be repeated, and by the fact that it expects the universal verification of its truth claims in the eschaton which has not yet been realized. These two boundary conditions give Christian faith and Christian theology their particular character.

The third characteristic of Christian faith, the tension between the experience of salvation in Christ and the experience of suffering in the world, emphasizes the experiential character of Christian theology. When Luther stated *experientia facit theologum*, he referred to this tension between the unconditional promise of salvation and the daily encounter of an unredeemed world characterized by evil and suffering. This prevents Christian theology from becoming abstract speculation which could somehow leave the trials and tribulations of experience behind. This tension receives its sharpest expression where the contrast between the experience of redemption and the experience of the way things go in the world is understood in a strictly theological sense, i.e. in the horizon of faith in God. How can the God who is disclosed in Jesus Christ also be the one who created and rules this world in which evil is a painful reality for experience? The question which in the seventeenth century philosophical theism attempted to solve under the heading of theodicy belongs to the very core of Christian faith and hence to the most central questions of Christian theology. In not attempting to evade this question by escaping from the painful contrasts of experience into the realm of pure speculation where every antinomy can be resolved, and in seeking to deal with this question from the perspective of a faith that has at its centre the suffering and resurrection of the Righteous One, Christian theology has to remain faithful to its experiential character.

The three characteristics we have taken from Ratschow's account of Christianity as a thinking religion do not represent an exhaustive list of the features that characterize Christian theology as the particular form of rationality in Christianity. One could add to this list many features which rationality in Christianity shares with other religions as thinking religions, but these three can help to illustrate the most distinctive features of Christian theology.

6   *Notions of Tradition in Christianity*

In Christianity tradition is from very early on an essentially contested concept. On the one hand, Christianity is like no other religion dependent on tradition since the spatio-temporal character of its foundational disclosure experience prevents its cultic repetition or its sublation into a set of beliefs comprised of timeless truths. On the other hand, the message that is handed on through the processes of tradition contains at its core a distinctive emphasis on the liberation from tradition in various forms and a pervasive stress on eschatological novelty. The debate about the notion of tradition in Christianity therefore revolves around the question how the form of tradition can be in accordance to the message it claims to transmit.

Like all religions Christianity depends on tradition. However, it is perhaps the religion in which there is the liveliest debate about the role and interpretation of tradition. The gospel which witnesses to the Christ-event claims to be 'good news' and not ancient wisdom. Its point can be summarized in the message: 'Behold, I make all things new' (Rev. 21:5). Whenever the content of the Christian message is expressed there is a consistent stress on novelty in the proclamation of a new covenant, a new humanity and a new creation. In many aspects Christian faith claims to offer not tradition, but liberation from tradition, perhaps most succinctly in the Pauline dialectic of law and gospel. We become aware of this tension when we realize that this message of liberation has reached us through long chains of traditions. Does this mean that it has thereby lost its liberating capacity and is now securely chained by tradition? Is yesterday's good news today's ancient wisdom? Is yesterday's message of liberation today's bond of tradition? Can tradition be the means of a promise of liberation?

In the history of Christianity we can find three main models of tradition which are the result of a theological construal of tradition. The first is the model of tradition as a *continuous chain* of the original message. This model was introduced by Irenaeus of Lyon as a response to the challenge of gnostic sects in the church claiming to have a special privileged tradition which offered higher knowledge than the mere faith of ordinary believers.[16] Here the criterion is the authenticity of tradition which is guaranteed by an unbroken chain of bearers of the tradition from the apostles to the present. The warrant for this unbroken chain of tradition is the succession of bishops. It is not the office of the bishop which guarantees the authenticity of the tradition. Rather, apostolic succession is an expression of the unbroken chain of tradition linking the present to the apostolic origin. In Irenaeus' view it is the Spirit who enlivens the tradition and the church in which it is preserved so that it retains its youthful power. The strength of this model is that it sees tradition as a process the continuity of which guarantees the authenticity of the tradition.

The second model is the *consensus model* of catholicity which was expressed in its succinct form by Vincent of Lerins.[17] His question in the *Commonitorium* was how orthodoxy and heterodoxy can be distinguished. He first refers to Scripture which in its material sense is sufficient for orthodox doctrine. However since it is not in all aspects clear and needs for its interpretation the ecclesial sense it needs to be supplemented by tradition. Tradition becomes here the name for the interpreta-

16 Cf. E. Flesseman-van Leer, 'Tradition, Schrift und Kirche bei Irenaeus,' in: K.E. Skydsgaard & L. Vischer (eds.), *Schrift und Tradition* (Zürich 1963), 45-61.

17 Cf. J. Speigl, 'Das Traditionsprinzip des Vinzenz von Lerinum: Id teneamus quod ubique, semper ab omnibus creditum est,' in: G. Schwaiger (ed.), *Hundert Jahre nach dem I. Vatikanum* (Regensburg 1971), 131-150.

tion of faith in the church that follows Scripture. The task of the church is to preserve tradition in the sense of what has been believed *ubique, semper, ab omnibus*. The three criteria which are listed here can be employed successively and jointly. *'Ubique' (universitas)* points to the consensus of believers in the spatial extension of the church. If that criterion fails to distinguish orthodoxy from heterodoxy we can turn to the second indicated by the word *'semper,'* which refers to the *antiquitas* of a belief. The third criterion combines the two, *'ab omnibus,' consensio in vetustate*, probably intended to refer to the councils of the church and to specific sentences of the Fathers. The consensus model is the model of a *cumulative tradition* which brings together different types of traditions in one consensus of faith. Vincent was opposed to any change. The tradition is sufficient for all purposes of doctrine, because the history of the church has come to an end. It is characteristic of this cumulative understanding of tradition that it treats tradition not as a process, but as a static body of doctrine which comprises different layers of which the older layers are the more reliable. Development is only possible as growth in the knowledge of the given tradition.

The third model is the model of *return to the origin* of tradition which is expressed in the slogan *sola scriptura* of the Reformation. It is important to understand this slogan as implying a particular understanding of tradition developed in a situation where both the continuity model of Irenaeus and the cumulative model of Vincent of Lerins seemed to fail to provide the guideline for orthodoxy and orthopraxis in the church. The character of this model becomes clear if one sees it as a theological expression of the humanists' battle cry: *'ad fontes!'* In this model Scripture has the function of providing the sole rule and guideline for judging doctrine. Scripture is understood here as the authoritative witness to Christ as the subject-matter of Scripture. The gospel of Christ as it is witnessed in Scripture is understood as being clear in the sense that it is not in need of authoritative interpretation, but is its own interpreter. This reverses the roles of Scripture and tradition. It is not that tradition is needed for the interpretation of Scripture, rather Scripture is needed for the interpretation of tradition. According to this view tradition has its legitimacy as interpretation of scripture, but its authority is to be assessed in each case by reference to Scripture. Scripture is not the *interpretandum*, but tradition is the *interpretandum* that finds its *interpretatio* in Scripture. On the one hand, the *sola scriptura* principle as a guideline for understanding tradition offered liberation from tradition since it permitted to assess all tradition in the light of the Gospel as it is witnessed in Scripture. On the other hand, it reinstated tradition as the interpretation of Scripture which has a derived authority from Scripture which, in turn, only possesses derived authority from what it witnesses to, Christ as the Word of God. In this sense the true tradition is the tradition of the Gospel, the tradition of the proclamation of the good news of God's salvation in Christ.

It cannot be the purpose of the discussion here to examine the strengths and weaknesses of these different models of tradition which we could only sketch in their barest outlines. Not only are these models associated with different confessional traditions and different forms of ecclesial community organisation. They have also been subject to considerable changes and modifications in the history of their theological interpretation. What seems more important here is that each model focuses on one particular point, but in order to present a viable model of tradition in Christianity it must also in some way integrate the main emphases in the other models.

The three models are based on different notions of normativity. In the first model normativity of teaching is based on the *continuity of tradition*. The second model sees the *consensus* of all believers as the warrant for the normativity of teaching. It explicitly integrates the emphasis on continuity in its second criterion, but does no longer associate it with a particular line of tradition. The difficulties arise if no consensus in all places and at all times can be found so that a qualified consensus must be developed as it is suggested in the third criterion *(consensio a vetustate)*. If the consensus is not obvious this model needs to be supported by the notion of a qualified consensus which in effect is based on a *selection of authorities* in the past and present. It does not seem surprising that this model had to be supplemented by the *magisterium* offering an interpretation of the consensus of believers so that this qualified consensus can be regarded as normative. The third model addresses the situation where the line of tradition has been disrupted so that there is apparent discontinuity in the tradition of the church and where there is apparent dissensus in the church. This model has a notion of normativity that is based on the *return to the origin* of tradition which is seen as being external to tradition, so that tradition itself has a secondary status in interpreting this foundational experience. Nevertheless, this model also has to show how the return to the origin can help to reconstruct continuity of tradition and can offer a notion of consensus in tradition. The first is achieved, for instance, by replacing the succession of bishops with the succession of true believers *(successio fidelium)*, the second by developing a notion of consensus concerning the origin of tradition, so that there need not be consensus in all doctrines but consensus concerning what should underlie all forms of consensus in the church.

Viewed from this perspective we can see that a sufficient understanding of tradition in Christianity must comprise all three elements: continuity, consensus and return to the origin. The difference consists in where the normativity of a tradition is located so that different notions of normativity emerge. These considerations can show that a developed concept of tradition is a theological construction which is intended to regulate the process of tradition by stating what is to be regarded as normative in the process of tradition. However, once such a concept of tradition is developed it has repercussions for the way in which theology is to be practised.

7   The Role of Theology in the Christian Tradition

In Christianity the role of theology consists in 'managing' the relationship between identity and change in the Christian tradition. The role of theology must be exercised in three fields:

–   in proposing and testing such conceptual innovations that make the Christian witness before the world intelligible and credible in new situations and new contexts (systematic theology);

–   in relating the expressions of Christian faith to its origin in the disclosure experience of God in Christ as it is witnessed in Scripture and in the history of the Christian community, so as to safeguard its identity in the processes of change (historical theology);

–   in reflecting on the forms of the practice of Christian faith in which it becomes the basis for the development of personal and communal identity in the changes of personal and communal history (practical theology).

In all three fields the 'management' of the relationship between identity and change consists in:

–   attempting to recover and preserve the authenticity of the Christian message in its changing forms of expression;

–   opening up possibilities that lead from dissensus to consensus in the Christian communities;

–   reconstructing the continuity of tradition.

Christian theology is not a discipline that could autonomously determine its own tasks. It is a function of Christian faith and it reflects the characteristics of Christian faith. It is, on the one hand, part of the Christian tradition; on the other, it stands over against the Christian tradition by making it the subject-matter of reflection. The agenda of theology is therefore not chosen by itself, it is imposed on it by the dynamics of the Christian tradition. Theology is the way in which the Christian community attempts to clarify its situation and its tasks. In this thesis I have described the task of Christian theology as that of 'managing' the relationship of identity and change. I have chosen this rather technocratic expression to characterize a role which is not a special field of theological reflection but which theology has to play in all its different fields of activity. Webster's Dictionary gives two definitions of the verb 'to manage' which seem to be appropriate here: 'to oversee and make decisions about' and 'to treat with care: use to best advantage.'[18] It is important to note that theology is the way in which the Christian community *oversees and makes decisions about* the relationship of identity and change that it encounters in the processes of tradition. And it does so in order *to treat* the tradition *with care* so that it is *used to its best advantage,* that is in accordance with its task.

The task of managing the relationship between identity and change is approached by theology in three different but related fields of inquiry which are all rooted in specific characteristics of Christian faith. The first is the field of *systematic theology.* It is rooted in the character of Christian faith as witness to the truth of the Gospel of Christ before the world. We can describe one main aspect of its task with a term employed by Vincent Brümmer as that of 'conceptual innovation.'[19] Systematic theology seeks to devise conceptual means to communicate the truth of the Christian message in new situations and in new contexts where the concepts provided by the Christian tradition are no longer adequate or intelligible, so that new concepts must be found to express the Christian message. The primary criterion for conceptual innovation is that it makes the Christian message intelligible to those outside the Christian community in the context of the thought forms they employ. The proposals of systematic theology must therefore be externally communicable. External communicability presupposes internal coherence. That which is not internally coherent cannot be communicated to those outside. There are many examples in the history of theology for the way in which proposals for conceptual innovation developed in the interest of the external communicability of Christian faith confronted Christian theology with the task of reconstructing its internal coherence.

By proposing conceptual innovations systematic theology initiates changes in the Christian tradition. The conceptualities for expressing the truth claims of Christian faith change, sometimes dramatically, and this raises the question whether they are still in accordance with the Christian message. Change raises the question of identity. Here a problem arises. In most cases the new concepts proposed cannot be understood as 'translations' of a preceding conceptuality. The concepts of classical theism cannot be translated into the concepts of process theology, the metaphysics of substance cannot be translated into the categories of transcendental philosophy. This is only to be expected, since the need for conceptual innovation arises in the first place because an existing conceptuality is regarded as externally or internally inadequate for the task of presenting the truth claims of Christian faith in a new situation or a different context. But how can it be shown that the proposed concept-

---

18 *Webster's New Encyclopedic Dictionary* revised edition 1995, 607.
19 Vincent Brümmer, *Speaking of a Personal God: An Essay in Philosophical Theology* (Cambridge 1992), 20ff.

ual innovations are nevertheless expressions of the Christian message and do not preach a different gospel?

The way of dealing with this question in Christian theology is to test the conceptual proposals by comparing them with the authentic forms of the Christian message. Can the conceptual innovations be seen as expressions of the foundational disclosure experience of the Christ-event? This attempt at going back to the sources of the Christian movement is necessitated by the spatio-temporal character of the Christian disclosure experience. But how is this authentic form to be found? In Christian theology it is especially the task of *historical theology* to attempt to retrieve the authentic form of the Christian message from its earliest testimonies in the biblical writings. Questions of authenticity are exegetical questions in Christian theology. It would, however, be naive to suppose that one could simply by means of historical or exegetical inquiry find the authentic Christian message which would provide the theological yardstick by which to measure the degrees of authenticity in the conceptual proposals of theology. The oldest texts are themselves witnesses to an event that is external to them so that they are themselves an early stage in the history of reception of the Christ-event and not the event itself. And they are just as much conditioned by their particular cultural situation as we are by ours. This, however, does not mean that everything disappears in a kind of relativistic mist where the quest for authenticity must soon end in frustration. It must be taken into account that these texts have provoked a history of interpretation and application that connects the first century (and earlier centuries) with the end of the twentieth century. In this process the biblical texts have acquired a paradigmatic function for determining what is regarded as the authentic Christian message. The task of historical theology consists in this way in uncovering the foundational paradigm of Christian witness. This requires not only attempting to retrace the history of interpretation of the Christian message back to its beginning, but also to follow the history of interpretation and application, the *Wirkungsgeschichte,* of these texts through history. It seems that the paradigmatic character of the biblical texts can only be understood if their capacity to elicit new forms of interpretation and application is also taken into account. This cannot be restricted to texts in which the biblical texts are interpreted and applied, but also to the application of these texts in all dimensions of culture, in community organisation, art, architecture etc. We can call this aspect of the work of theology with Vincent Brümmer's term 'conceptual recollection.'[20]

In the theological interpretation of the process of tradition from the biblical writings to the present there is a consistent emphasis on the external authority of the biblical writings. They have authority in virtue of what they witness to, their author-

---

20   Brümmer, *Personal God*, 4ff.

ity is not an inherent authority which they possess as texts. They are not regarded as self-authenticating. The Reformers have attempted to clarify their particular character by the distinction between the *external word* of Christian proclamation, the biblical texts, the sacraments etc. and the *internal word* by means of which God the Spirit authenticates the message for individual persons and so creates faith. In this theological model two distinctions are brought together: the distinction between the human activity of witnessing and the divine activity of authenticating that witness to create the certainty of faith, and the distinction between the external word, i.e. public semiotic forms of communication and the internal word that creates certainty in the heart of the believer. This model has important implications for the reconstruction of the witness of the Christian gospel in the different stages of its history. What is open to historical investigation and conceptual reconstruction is the external word and its transformations in the history of Christianity. The internal word, the process by which certainty concerning the truth of the Gospel is created, is not open to investigation and reconstruction in the same sense. It can only be described by following the testimony of believers who use the external signs of Christian witness to describe the occurrence of the creation of certainty in the language of the confession of faith.

It is here that the *confessional traditions* of the Christian churches have their significance. In these confessional traditions, exemplified by the creeds of the ecumenical councils, we find the confession of faith that expresses that which is recognized as a valid expression of faith. The history of confessions documents the process in which the churches have expressed their faith as a response to the Christian message. Because they are recognized by many churches as an authentic and normative expression of faith and therefore have the status of authoritative traditions, they are significant in the process of testing the viability of conceptual proposals of theology. In comparison to the biblical witness they have a secondary significance with regard to the criterion of authenticity because they are forms of response to Christian proclamation and teaching based on the biblical witness. However, their significance is of a different character since they are expressions of the historical and communal character of Christian faith. For theology they also illustrate how conceptual innovations could be received in the church as expressions of the authentic character of faith. The *homoousios* agreed at the Councils of Nicaea and Constantinople is a classical example. In testing whether its conceptual innovations are in accordance with the confessional tradition of the church, theology can also make the process of theological reflection and its effects on the church transparent. In testing whether conceptual proposals can be seen as authentic expressions of the Christian message, biblical hermeneutics and confessional hermeneutics are complementary aspects of the history of interpretation in the Christian tradition.

In *practical theology* the conceptual proposals of systematic theology assessed by the findings of historical theology are put to the test as proposals for the praxis of the church. The connection with systematic and historical theology is of the utmost importance. The problems which systematic theology deals with are not self-generated problems. They occur first in the context of ecclesial praxis. It is in the praxis of Christian proclamation, education or pastoral care that the problems which create the need for conceptual innovation are experienced before they become problems of systematic theology. On the other hand, the conceptual innovations proposed by systematic theology are directly used to initiate and guide changes in the Christian tradition when they are applied in the practice of ecclesial life. Without this link to the life of the Christian communities which is made explicit in practical theology, systematic theology could be accused of solving problems that one would not have without it.

Practical theology is concerned with reflecting on the ecclesial practice of Christianity. It is in a direct sense theory for praxis. In offering theological training for those who have important functions in the life of ecclesial communities and in this way influence the whole life of those communities, it influences in a direct way the way in which the relationship between identity and change is shaped in the practice of the church.

It seems appropriate to see Christian worship as the primary institution of the life of the Christian tradition. In Christian worship the process of tradition is directly and actively cultivated so that the problem of identity and change is most apparent in this context. Every act of worship is a direct example of the management of identity and change in the Christian tradition. It is in the processes of communication in the life of the church that the relationship between identity and change permanently gains concrete expression. It is therefore necessary that the proposals that are made in systematic theology for conceptual innovations in the interpretation of the Christian tradition are assessed with regard to the *orientational capacity* they have for ecclesial practice. In this way theology can fulfil its role of 'managing' the relationship between identity and change in the Christian tradition with responsibility in the awareness of the effects its activity has for the life of the Christian tradition.

We have described the role of theology in the Christian tradition as that of 'managing' the dynamic of identity and change. *Webster's Dictionary* lists two senses of 'to manage' which do not apply to the activity of theology and which should be expressly excluded from any description of its role. These are 'to succeed in one's purpose' and 'to make and keep compliant.' The first cannot be guaranteed on the basis of theological effort, the second should not even be attempted. With regard to the 'management' of identity and change in the Christian tradition both should be respected by theology as a divine privilege.

186

11. A Plea for Inverting the Hermeneutical Relation

Gijsbert van den Brink (Utrecht)

1 Outline of Schwöbel's Argument

After having explored at some length the concepts of theology, religion and tradition in an illuminative way, at the heart of his rich and stimulating article in the present volume Christoph Schwöbel comes to what I take to be his central thesis: 'The fundamental condition for the maintenance of tradition is ... the management of change.'[1] On the one hand, without change tradition is not possible. In fact, a tradition is an ongoing process of mediation, interpretation and personal appropriation of patterns of practice, which always involves change as a constitutive element. On the other hand, however, 'if the variations exceeded the invariant elements we would no longer have changes *within* a tradition, but a change from one tradition to another ...' (172).

Schwöbel then goes on (after having discussed three features that mould the specific shape of rationality in Christian theology, 174-178) to point out different ways in which the invariant elements in a tradition may be determined. In this connection, he distinguishes between the continuity-model, the consensus-model and the back-to-the-origin-model. He suggests that in order to present a viable model of tradition, the main emphases of each of these models should be integrated (181). Nevertheless, the models are based on different notions of normativity (ibid.), and Schwöbel passes over the obvious question which notion might be the right one and why (or how the three notions should be integrated). Instead, he observes that the model of (normative) tradition that one adopts has repercussions for the way in which theology is to be practised – and this seems clear enough.

So it is here that the role of theology comes in. As to Christianity, this role consists in '"managing" the relationship between identity and change in the Christian tradition' (186). With 'managing' Schwöbel means in this connection: to oversee and make decisions about this relationship, and to treat the tradition with care so that it is used to its best advantage (182f.). Schwöbel ends up his paper with an outline of the distinctive contributions to these management tasks that may be

---

1   Christoph Schwöbel, 'Rationality, Tradition and Theology,' 172; subsequently, numbers between brackets in my text refer to page numbers of this article.

expected from the disciplines of systematic, historical and practical theology. Systematic theology has to keep the doctrinal tradition externally communicable and internally coherent, historical theology has to watch over its historical continuity, and practical theology should warrant the practical relevance of any change- (or, presumably, continuity-) proposals that are being made.

2   Some Further Considerations on Change

Now although I have one major problem with the way in which Schwöbel fleshes out his argument (I will come to this at the end of my contribution), it seems to me that his thesis as such stands, and that his use of the management-imagery in this connection is original and deserves to be explored and tested on its explanatory power. In a time which expects its salvation to a large extent from economic growth and efficiency, the choice of the management-imagery is in any case a fine instantiation of translating the message in the conceptualities of one's own cultural context. Thus, since I agree with most of Schwöbel's exposition, my response will not take the form of a counter-argument by means of which I try to refute him.

Instead, I will try to take up the ball at the place where Schwöbel has left it. Hopefully that is a fruitful approach, since Schwöbel's account is largely descriptive and of a fairly general level; it concludes not with some concrete illustrations of how his proposed management-strategy might work in practice, but with an encyclopedic survey of the tasks of different theological disciplines. So he does not put his own proposals to the test. As a result, the question arises whether these proposals do indeed enable us to make responsible decisions in the change/continuity issue in concrete instances. How should, e.g., the distinctive criteria which hang together with the three fields of theology be balanced and weighed in relation to one another? How do we know when a particular proposed change is to the advantage of the tradition, and when it is to its detriment, perhaps even to the extent that it 'would destroy the tradition' (172)?

Schwöbel gives us one clue when he notes that 'if the variations exceeded the invariant elements we would no longer have changes within a tradition, but ... a *metabasis eis allo genos*' (ibid.). This remark suggests a *numeric* criterion. It conjures up the image of a neat division of the doctrinal heritage of a tradition in separate units ('elements'), a majority of which should be left unaffected, and a minority of which may be changed. If I may caricature a bit: from every ten proposals to change the tradition, maximally four should be supported and at least six rejected, for otherwise the variant elements of a tradition will in due course exceed its invariant elements. But clearly, it is not as easy as that (and Schwöbel does not want to suggest it is). Further considerations are needed in order to see how changes in religious traditions come about in practice, and to what extent they affect the future of the tradition.

First of all, one may wonder whether this picture of a doctrinal tradition consisting of separate *elements* is correct. Especially if we have to do (as we may expect) with a to some extent consistent and internally coherent tradition, we should reckon with the fact that many elements are closely bound up with each other. As a result, if we change one element (let us say: one doctrine), this may have far reaching implications for the whole body of doctrinal beliefs. In important respects, this whole body of doctrinal beliefs resembles a house or a wall, in which you cannot replace a limited number of bricks without risking the collapse of the entire structure. If we look at the way in which religious communities have in fact changed their theologies, we may find this picture confirmed. For example, when a Christian community changes its doctrine of Scripture (especially when this change leads to the suggestion that Scripture is no longer the normative source for regulating faith and life), in the course of time many subsequent doctrines and beliefs turn out to be affected and changed as a result. Or, more likely perhaps, some of those other doctrines and beliefs had already changed, and this process inspired in due course a modified view on the nature of Scriptural authority. In this way, the Dutch *Gereformeerde Kerken* (accepting a modified view on the nature of Scriptural authority in 1981) are said to have been the most rapidly changing churches in the world from the sixties onwards (Hendrikus Berkhof).[2]

Secondly, if we grant for a moment that a doctrinal tradition does consist of separate elements, it is clear that not all of these are equally important. Theologically, the dogma of papal infallibility seems more important than that of the assumption of Mary, since the former in contrast to the latter has many possible future implications for all segments of theology (from the point of view of popular piety, Mary's assumption may be more important). And the doctrine of justification by faith, though not distinctively Calvinist, is much more important to Calvinism than the *extra-calvinisticum* (the specifically Calvinist doctrine that Christ's divine nature is also outside his human nature). Nevertheless, even if the 'less important' dogma's and doctrines would be replaced by others, one wonders what would follow from that. If the dogma of Mary's assumption would be relinquished, that would at least be indicative of a much more encompassing change in the theology of the Roman-Catholic *magisterium* (including e.g. a changed view on the retractability of dogma's, and possibly on the importance of marial piety as such).

---

2   Cf. on the history of doctrinal changes in the Reformed Churches in the Netherlands Hendrik Vroom's contribution to the present volume.

Thirdly, it is clear that the extent to which a tradition is affected by the change of some of its elements, also depends upon the nature of the newly introduced elements which replace the ones that were given up. It is of course not necessarily the case that these new elements are straightforwardly *opposite* to the old ones. On the contrary, in most situations that will not be the case. Usually, views change gradually, and so do the formulations by means of which they are expressed. It may e.g. be the case that a particular change does not take the form of a denial of the existing article of faith, but of a decision to accept alternatives next to it. Presumably, even if a radical departure of a traditional point of view has taken place, this will seldom be explicitly stated. More often formulations will be sought that link up as closely as possible with the traditional ones, in order to make the changes more palatable to the community of believers. It is possible, however, that underneath such formulations which have only slightly been adapted, more drastic changes in spirituality are hidden. In that case, the influence and practical relevance of a particular change may be much higher than the new formulations suggest.

In sum, it is clear that the 'management of change and continuity' which a tradition requires is not simply a matter of appointing enough invariant elements. Proposals to change (or not to change) the tradition at a particular point should be weighed in relation to what lies behind them spiritually, and tested upon their foreseeable effects, both in theology and in practice. Non-theological factors which may play a role, such as social and psychological processes, should be taken into account as well. Now given this complexity, is it possible to decide in a particular case whether change or continuity is 'to the advantage of the tradition'? Or more precisely: is it possible to make such a decision in a way which does not purely depend on one's own stance, but on more or less objective criteria? Let us test the criteria that Schwöbel proposes and our subsequent considerations by means of a case-study.

3   A Case-Study: Atonement in the Contemporary Dutch Debate

The doctrine of atonement has been a source of much upheaval in Dutch protestantism ever since the sixties. Almost every decade has had its own champion-theologian who openly and sometimes crudely rejected the classical view that Christ died for our sins (most well-known among them have become P. Smits and H.A. Wiersinga). Each of them roused a lot of rumour in church circles, but ultimately all kept their rights. In 1997, a new commotion concerning the doctrine of atonement was prompted by a publication of the New Testament scholar C.J. den Heyer on the topic.[3]

In this book Den Heyer argues that the New Testament contains many different and even incompatible interpretations of the death of Jesus. It is impossible to deduce a uniform doctrine of atonement from the fragmented and multifarious New Testament testimony, which sometimes strikes us as a 'cacophony of voices.' Paul's voice, articulating most clearly that Christ's death was a redemption from the consequences of sin, is only one among others. And even Paul employs such a surprising variety of metaphors that no well-defined doctrine of atonement can be derived from it. Jesus himself may perhaps have seen his death in line with the death of the suffering righteous, the martyrs for the noble cause of God. But he did not think of it in terms of substitutionary sacrifice or satisfaction. Nor, for that matter, did Paul or any of the Gospel writers have such interpretations in mind when they ascribed salvific meaning to the death of Christ. The clearest witness for the view that Christ's death should be interpreted as a sacrifice for the sins of the world is in the letter to the Hebrews and the (so-called) first letter of John – but their testimony should not be confused with that of Paul and John themselves.

Den Heyer concludes that, given this irreducible plurality in the New Testament, there is no need to stick to confessional apprehensions of the atoning character of Jesus' suffering and death, but there is room for other interpretations apart from the classical ones. In particular, it is enough to see Jesus' trust in God as an inspiring example, which stimulates us to strive after reconciliation in our own context. Those who find consolation in the traditional doctrine of atonement, however, should continue to believe just that. As to Den Heyer himself, he observes that the traditional doctrine can no longer move him, and he therefore opts for the alternative view.

4   Den Heyer's Case Tested

Let us now see what might happen if we try to evaluate Den Heyer's proposed conceptual innovation by means of Schwöbel's criteria. For the sake of brevity we shall just distinguish between Den Heyer's proposal (viz. to see Jesus' trust in God as an example which inspires us to strive after atonement ourselves), and what I will call the classical or traditional doctrine. We shall not take into account any further alternatives or nuances, and we shall use the designation 'classical' or 'traditional' doctrine as a catch label for all such theories that consider the Christ-event[4] as in

---

3   C.J. den Heyer, *Verzoening: Bijbelse notities bij een omstreden thema* (Kampen 1997).
4   Following Schwöbel, I shall use the term 'Christ-event' as an umbrella term for the incarnation,

some way or another *constitutive* for bringing about atonement between God and humankind.

First of all, what about the primary criterion of systematic theology: the external communicability of the innovation? Does Den Heyer's proposal 'make the Christian message intelligible to those outside the Christian community in the context of the thought forms they employ' (183)? That depends, of course, both upon what kind of people one has in mind and upon what one considers to be 'the Christian message.' As to the former, it cannot be taken for granted that in our postmodern times everyone employs the same thought forms. As to the latter, it seems that we are in a circle here; for what we understand by 'the Christian message' depends at least in part upon which doctrines we take to be invariable (and therefore not open to innovation).

Despite these difficulties, perhaps a case can be made for a positive answer. There are at least two reasons for thinking that Den Heyer's innovative proposal does indeed make the Christian message more intelligible for our times. First, as Vernon White has put it, there is a 'crisis of credibility' concerning the claim that the Christ-event does have universal saving significance.[5] The idea that the death of Christ was somehow *required* for making atonement between God and human beings does not square with the moral intuitions of many present-day people. 'We can't believe in a God who wants to see blood,' is the usual complaint. Apart from the fact that this crude rendering misrepresents the point of the traditional doctrine, it may be the case that the moral intuitions of those who utter the complaint are wrong. But if, as Schwöbel argues, the Christian message is in principle translatable in all different kinds of thought forms, it can only be welcomed if this message may be presented in a way which is not offensive to people who share these contemporary moral sensibilities.[6] And Den Heyer seems to achieve just that. Second, the

---

life, suffering, death and resurrection of Jesus, thus leaving aside the question where exactly the atoning significance is to be located.

5   Vernon White, *Atonement and Incarnation* (Cambridge 1991), 3.

6   There is, however, a strange incompatibility between the way in which contemporary moral sensibilities develop with regard to the presuppositions of atonement in human relationships and in the divine-human relationship. As to human relationships, we become increasingly aware of the fact that enormous *prices* have to be payed for realizing atonement, and that atonement should include rather than exclude *justice*. Look at Bosnia, or at the difficulties involved in atoning relationships which have been broken by incest. Usually, these difficulties are not at all the result of the fact that the victims are unduly revengeful; rather, forgiveness and atonement without justice being done is simply impossible. It is precisely this intuition which is captured by the traditional Anselmian idea of Christ paying the necessary price for atonement with his life, and doing justice to God in this way. Cf. on this point C. van der Kooi, 'Verzoening: De paradox rondom een thema,' *In de waagschaal* 25 (1997), 206-208.

fact that Den Heyer does not simply *replace* one doctrine by another but leaves us our own choice, fits neatly in the free market thinking which dominates our age. Den Heyer invites us to pick out for ourselves that interpretation of the death of Christ we feel best about, without bothering about the alternatives. Clearly, this way of treating the classical doctrine finely suits the thought forms of our liberalized postmodern society.

As to the second criterion of systematic theology, however, it is difficult to see how Den Heyer's proposal contributes to the internal coherence of the Christian message. On the contrary, it seems unavoidable that the element of choice and personal preference which he introduces into the debate on atonement theory, has a disintegrating effect on the Christian faith. In so far as we are interested in the *truth* of Christian doctrine, we cannot simultaneously accept divergent accounts[7] of atonement – since not all of them can be true. Perhaps, however, we should interpret Den Heyer's tolerance towards the classical doctrine as a matter of prudence, and take him as judging in fact that this doctrine should be dispensed with. In that case the question is whether the view that Christ's life, suffering and death only inspires us to make atonement with one another, is coherent with the larger body of Christian beliefs. *Prima facie* it is not clear why this could not be the case. Neither is it clear, however, why this view should be *more* coherent than the classical one. So the result of confronting Den Heyer's proposal with the second criterion of systematic theology is at worst negative and at best inconclusive.

Secondly, we come to the criteria of historical theology. Can Den Heyer's views 'be seen as authentic expressions of the Christian message' from the point of view of biblical hermeneutics and confessional hermeneutics? As to biblical hermeneutics, Den Heyer spends a lot of energy in trying to support his case. It is not the place here for a meticulous examination of his arguments. Not being a biblical scholar, I am not in a position to probe them adequately. Nevertheless, I observe that Den Heyer's biblical hermeneutics is heavily criticized by some of his colleagues. For example, A. Noordegraaf argues that Den Heyer leaves some important texts out of consideration, and is highly selective in the way in which he applies historical criticism. As a result of his biased approach, says Noordegraaf, Den Heyer interprets different shades and accents in the New Testament testimony as sheer contradictions. In fact, the rich plurality in the biblical witness concerning

---

7   The accounts are indeed divergent, rather than mutually exclusive; for clearly, there is nothing
     in the traditional doctrine which denies that Jesus' way of life is an example for us today in
     striving after atonement. In this sense, the traditional doctrine squares with Den Heyer's pro-
     posal. It is not compatible, however, with Den Heyer's plea for *reducing* the doctrine of atone-
     ment to this single aspect.

atonement does not alter the fact that the salvific meaning of the cross and resurrection of Christ is absolutely central for all New Testament writers.[8]

So clearly there is room for discussion here. Given the fact that this discussion has been conducted in one way or another ever since the time of Anselm and Abelard, the prospects for a final and unanimous resolution seem rather dim. Let us, however, give Den Heyer the benefit of the doubt, and concede for the sake of argument that his views are warranted by the biblical texts as belonging to 'the authentic Christian message' (184). Then, according to Schwöbel's criteriology, this is not in itself decisive for seeing them as 'expressions of the foundational disclosure experience of the Christ-event' (ibid.). For before jumping to such a conclusion we should also take into account the *confessional traditions* of the Church; given the fact that the confessional writings are recognized by many churches as authentic and normative expressions of the faith, 'they are significant in the process of testing the viability of conceptual proposals of theology' (185). On a strong reading, this may be taken to mean that innovation-proposals should be *in accordance with* the church's confessional tradition. On a weaker reading, it means that our proposals should at the very least be *confronted with* and presented as somehow *an interpretation of* this confessional tradition. It is not entirely clear which reading Schwöbel has in mind: there are some expressions which suggest the strong one, but the weaker one seems more in line with the gist of his argument.

Now how is this confessional hermeneutics functioning in Den Heyer's argument? The answer is: not at all. Den Heyer simply rejects what the creeds say about atonement, without in any way trying to link his own proposal to the credal texts or even to the religious motives lying behind them. Apparently, he is quite aware of the fact that his proposal cannot find support in the confessions of the church. So at this point, we can neither give him the benefit of the doubt nor grant anything for the sake of argument. His innovative proposal does not pass even the most minimal confessional test. Thus, the result of confronting Den Heyer's proposal with the criteria of historical theology is at best inconclusive with regard to biblical hermeneutics, and negative with regard to confessional hermeneutics.

Thirdly, then, let us compare Den Heyer's proposal to the exigencies of practical theology. For 'the conceptual innovations ... are directly used to initiate and guide changes in the Christian tradition when they are applied in the practice of ecclesial life' (186). Now which changes might be initiated and guided by Den

---

8   A. Noordegraaf, review in *Wapenveld* 47 (1997), 163. For a more extensive examination of the New Testament testimony in response to Den Heyer's book, resulting in similar conclusions as those of Noordegraaf, see H. Baarlink, *Het evangelie van de verzoening* (Kampen 1998). Baarlink especially emphasizes the substitutionary character attributed to the death of Jesus in the New Testament (9, 133 etc.).

Heyer's innovative proposal in relation to the doctrine of atonement, and how should we evaluate them? I can think of three possible effects for the practice of ecclesial life in this connection.

The first possible effect is, that the community of faith is stimulated to foster *plurality* in belief patterns in its life. Any believer is entitled to think as s/he wants on the significance of the suffering and death of Christ, and there is no reason why we should not fully accept those who don't see any salvific meaning in it at all. We may evaluate this effect either negatively or positively. Negatively, because this plurality disintegrates the sense of unity and community in faith which may be experienced in church. The church is no longer the community of those who celebrate their salvation by the atoning power of the blood of the Lamb; the church may now also consist of people who experience these very formulations as utterly repugnant. That makes things pretty complicated. Positively, however, the plurality which is stimulated may give room to more diverse people in the church, and prompts us to share fellowship and to have communion not only with those who think and believe more or less like we do, but also with people of rather different inclinations. On the other hand, doesn't real communion presuppose that you share with each other at least the most precious and important feelings as to what constitutes the communion?

The second possible effect (and now we interpret Den Heyer's proposal not as a plea for plurality but as a plea for a purely subjective doctrine of atonement) is that church members feel more directly inspired by the example of Jesus to strive after atonement and reconciliation in their own relationships with other people. Of course, the classical doctrine does not deny the importance of striving after reconciliation in human relationships, but its primary focus is on Jesus reconciling us with God by means of his sacrifice. So it may be the case that the classical doctrine leads us to contemplating on Jesus' love and power rather than to acting ourselves in reconciling ways. If it is an effect of the subjective doctrine of atonement to remedy this or at least to restore the balance, then it seems that we cannot but welcome Den Heyer's proposal as a positive contribution to the future of the Christian tradition. Perhaps sociologists of religion can devise some creative experiments to check whether those who advocate the classical doctrine are less inclined to realize atonement in their own environment than those who adhere to a subjective doctrine of atonement. I would not dare to predict the outcome.

The third possible effect of Den Heyer's proposal, however, is that the church becomes empty. J. van der Graaf, a leader of the confessional wing in the *Netherlands Reformed Church*, has warned that two generations of theology students educated by professors like Den Heyer will be enough to empty the church of its last members. Perhaps he was exaggerating, but basically he may be quite right about the secularizing effect of Den Heyer's proposal. If the point of the doctrine of atonement is that we develop a positive attitude towards striving after atonement and reconciliation in our own environment, and if the Christ-event is considered as just a psychological stimulus in his connection, then the Christ-event *itself* is no longer crucial. Commemorating it is purely instrumental to a higher goal, which presumably is not distinctively Christian, viz. the promotion of reconciliation, unselfish love, well-doing etc. in human relationships. It is not clear why other stimuli into this direction (e.g. the examples of Gandhi, Socrates, or Lady Diana) may not work as well or perhaps even better. But if our children discover that this is the way we think about it – i.e., that we foster religion only for the sake of human morality – they may easily (and for good reasons!) disconnect both domains, and stop going to church. Of course they may still consider themselves Christians, but *their* children possibly won't any longer.[9]

If this would be the effect of accepting Den Heyer's proposal,[10] from the point of view of Schwöbel's criteriology we must certainly come to a radically negative evaluation. For, as Schwöbel says, managing the relationship of identity and change entails 'to treat the tradition with care so that it is used to its best advantage, that is in accordance with its task' (183). However one wants to specify this task (Schwöbel formulates: spreading the Christian message, 176), it seems improbable that the Christian tradition can fulfil it when this tradition has come to an end! The Christian tradition just does not understand itself as the kind of institution which may discontinue itself because it has reached its goals; rather, it is clearly not to its best advantage when it is marginalized still further in our society. So from this perspective, we should decisively reject Den Heyer's proposal and opt for continuing the traditional doctrine rather than for changing it. Den Heyer's proposal fails the test of showing 'orientational capacity' (186) for ecclesial practice.

But what if Den Heyer is simply right and the traditional doctrine wrong? Should we in church theology for practical reasons stick to a doctrine when we are convinced that it is false, and deny an alternative theory which strikes us as true? Of course not. But note that this is a wrong way of putting things. For whether or not a (proposed) doctrine is true depends, in our context, precisely upon whether or not it meets the criteria we employed in evaluating it. If Den Heyer's proposal is not externally communicable or internally coherent, or if it is not an authentic expression of the foundational disclosure experience, or if it lacks orientational capacity for

---

9   Cf. the point made by Vincent Brümmer in his contribution to the present volume, that to be a Christian means to connect the meaning of life with (an interpretation of) the Christ-event.

10   In general it must be said that those churches and communities which have brought about many doctrinal and ethical adjustments during the past decades, hardly have become more attractive to 'those outside' by doing that. On the contrary, much more than communities that remained true to their tradition they suffer from decline in membership, decreasing church attendance etc.

ecclesial practice, then it cannot possibly be true. Even if it would fulfil all these demands but for one (e.g. internal coherence), it could hardly be true.

5   Do Theologians Resemble Managers?

We are now in a position to weave the different partial evaluations together into an overall-evaluation of Den Heyer's proposed conceptual innovation on the basis of Schwöbel's criteria. We have seen that both from the perspective of systematic theology and from the perspective of historical theology and from the perspective of practical theology, reasons can be adduced for a positive as well as for a negative appraisal. In part this was the result of the fact that Den Heyer's proposal could be interpreted in either of two ways. But even when we weighed both interpretations separately, the results were equally inconclusive. What shall we conclude from this fact? Perhaps it shows that Schwöbel's criteriology is not refined enough to result in a decision, at least not in this particular case. Or perhaps it shows that Den Heyer's case should be improved and amended in a number of respects in order to become a candidate for replacing the classical doctrine. Or perhaps – and that would be the most striking conclusion – it shows that the issue of change and continuity in religious traditions just is not the kind of thing which can be adequately managed by theologians, because theologians cannot exclude their own subjective spirituality and theological preferences from playing a decisive role in their evaluation of concrete proposals.

Let us try to explore these things further by taking into account the considerations on change in practice which we put forward above. First of all, is the doctrine of atonement an 'element' on its own, or is it related to other important parts of the doctrinal heritage of the Christian tradition? Clearly the latter is the case. How we shape the doctrine of atonement not only depends upon our moral sensibilities, but also upon our image of God, our anthropology, and upon our estimation of the seriousness of sin. Usually it is not the case that when people change their doctrine of atonement, *as a result* their thinking about God, human nature and sin is altered. It is rather the other way round: the pressures which are exerted on the classical doctrine of atonement betray that below the surface our thinking about God, human nature and sin has changed. Therefore, if we accept Den Heyer's proposal to change the doctrine of atonement, this has much more far-reaching consequences for the future of the Christian tradition than may be thought at first sight.

Secondly, is the doctrine of atonement relatively important or unimportant in the Christian tradition? Again, the answer is not difficult. To many Christian believers of all ages the belief that Jesus has reconciled us with God by his sacrificial suffering and death belongs to the very heart of their spirituality. As to the

Roman Catholic tradition, the fact that Christ's sacrifice is daily represented in the eucharist is indicative in this respect. But also in the protestant tradition the salvific significance of the Christ-event for our relationship to God is absolutely central; one only has to read the texts of the most popular hymns in order to check this. Songs like 'What a friend we have in Jesus' belong to the most well-known hymns all over the earth; they have an ecumenical potency and range which exceeds the appeal of many official institutions for the advancement of ecumenism. One may indeed wonder if, when this salvific significance of the Christ-event is denied, we are still continuing the same Christian tradition – or whether a *metabasis eis allo genos* has taken place.

Of course that depends in part, thirdly, upon what the proposed successor of the classical doctrine looks like. We have seen that this need not be a doctrine which squarely opposes or denies the classical doctrine. It may be that partial adaptations are being proposed, or a novel interpretation which highlights some interesting aspect that thus far was not spelled out explicitly, but that may be crucial in a new cultural context. Can Den Heyer's proposal be conceived in this way as a new interpretation or a partial adaptation of the old doctrine? At first sight this may seem so. Den Heyer does not argue that the church should dispense with the classical doctrine. He only pleas for tolerance and understanding towards those who don't see their own belief reflected in the formulations of the old creeds and doctrines concerning atonement. Upon further consideration, however, it is clear that he advocates a radical departure from the classical doctrine. His emphasis on the plurality of voices on atonement in the New Testament leads him to the rejection of the classical doctrine as a legitimate interpretation or expansion of the biblical texts. Rather, he sees no positive relation at all between the two, and he considers the classical doctrine to be irreparably wrongheaded.

In sum, if we evaluate Den Heyer's proposal from the perspective of our further considerations, the result is much more unambiguous. All three considerations point into the same direction: the proposed innovation involves a taking leave of many beliefs, including important ones, in a way which is as radical as to threaten the identity of the tradition. So we should reject it. The question is, however, whether we can manage this. One limitation of depicting theologians as the managers of change and continuity is in any case, that this metaphor obscures the extent to which theologians are *themselves* involved in processes of change. Usually they do not stand over against the proposals which come up in order to judge them from a safe distance. Nor do they create their own innovative proposals out of nothing. Rather, like other people, they *find themselves* believing or not believing or no longer believing particular things and doctrines. In this way, Den Heyer has found himself no longer believing the classical doctrine of atonement – and his theological work on atonement seems little more than an attempt to justify this situation.

Now why do people find themselves believing or not believing or no longer believing particular things? This is perhaps one of the most difficult questions of all. But it seems that the role of theology is a modest one in this respect. In any case, it is not an *independent* role. If people sometimes find themselves believing other things than before because their theologians say so, these theologians usually say so not because they are 'treating the tradition to its best advantage,' but because they themselves are influenced by a changing cultural and spiritual climate. Therefore, the question is whether verbs like 'to manage' and 'to decide upon' (viz. the change/identity issue) are not in the end too active to be of much use in illuminating the role of theology in religious traditions. Even if in a religious community theologians have the power and the authority to enforce changes in doctrinal beliefs and so to manage the tradition – like some theologians in the Roman Catholic Church – doctrinal development is hardly due to the innovative work of these theologians. For example, it was the religious life of monastic communities and not the decision of theologians which gave rise to the Mariology encapsulated in the term 'theotokos'; and it was the pressure of popular piety which, still in 1950, led to the dogma of the assumption of Mary.[11] It is we who are subject to changes in belief patterns, rather than these changes being subject to our will or decision.[12]

If this is how it is, what implications follow for our evaluation of the phenomenon of change in the Christian tradition as such? At this point, I part company with Schwöbel. Schwöbel tries to give a theological underpinning of the necessity of ongoing change in the Christian tradition, by arguing that this change is entailed by the very character of the Christian religion as a missionary religion. Expanding on some insights of Carl Heinz Ratschow, Schwöbel says: 'The rationality of Christian theology is therefore [i.e. because of the missionary character of Christianity, GvdB] always a form of contextual rationality. If Christian theology is to remain true to the identity of Christian faith as rooted in the Christ-event it must change when it moves from one cultural context with its particular forms of rationality to another' (175; but throughout the paper, there is much emphasis on this point). Certainly this is an attractive view. For on this view changes in our patterns of belief are no longer the kind of things which we should accept grudgingly because they imply a confession that what we believed in the past was wrong. Nor should we opt for changing the tradition only if all attempts to maintain the tradition have been found wanting. Rather, we should welcome such changes as new possibilities for

11   Cf. Jaroslav Pelikan, *Development of Christian Doctrine: Some Historical Prolegomena* (New Haven/London 1969), 95-119; Alister McGrath, *The Genesis of Doctrine* (Oxford 1990), 11.

12   Cf. Vincent Brümmer's observation in an analysis of the nature of religious belief, in his *Theology and Philosophical Inquiry* (London 1981), 157: 'Becoming convinced is something that happens to us, not something we can decide to do.'

spreading the Christian message. Far from feeling guilty about our changed beliefs (or about our short-sightedness in the past), we should rejoice in the fact that precisely these changes show that we are good Christians!

However, this picture presupposes what is at best a very one-sided picture of the missionary character of Christianity. When Jesus says: 'Go, then, to all peoples everywhere and make them my disciples'(Matth. 28:19), the suggestion is not that the disciples should adapt their message to the particularities of all peoples, but rather that they should try to change these particularities in such a way that they become subordinate to the Gospel. And as to Paul, his becoming a Greek to the Greeks was not an exercise in changing his beliefs, but was meant to 'take every thought captive and make it obey Christ' (2 Cor. 10:5).[13] Of course there is a two-way traffic here. In order to attain commensurability the Christian message must be translated in the specific conceptualities of different cultures. But it is important to see that in this process the Christian message has its specific forms of plausibility and rationality in itself, and that the best way of witnessing to it is to enact these forms of plausibility and rationality. It is a well-known fact that all *Vermittlungstheologie* from Schleiermacher onwards has perhaps made the Christian message less offensive to cultured man, but has hardly yielded any new disciples. Rather, the line of influence went the other way round, and the thought forms of many a theologian became more and more secularized. To extend the sports-metaphor that Schwöbel uses in this connection: away-matches are more easily and frequently lost than home-matches!

6   *Intratextuality and the Inversion of the Hermeneutical Relation*

George Lindbeck concludes his influential study on the nature of doctrine with some intriguing observations that can also be endorsed by those who (like the present writer) are not completely convinced by the cultural-linguistic theory of religion which he expounds in the bulk of the book. In the final chapter Lindbeck argues that if systematic theologians want to fulfil their tasks in a way which is faithful to their own tradition, they should use what he calls an 'intratextual' as opposed to an 'extratextual' method. He especially relates this terminology to the role of holy scriptures in theology, stipulating that the extratextual method locates religious meaning outside the scriptural text, whereas the intratextual method locates it inside the

---

13   See for an interpretation of the confrontation between Christianity and non-Christian philosophies from this perspective, J. Klapwijk e.a. (ed.), *Bringing into Captivity Every Thought* (Lanham 1991).

religion's basic text. Instead of the 'text' we can also read, for our purposes, the basic *message*. Both theological methods are aimed at continuing the religious tradition by interpreting the message and bringing it in relation to contemporary culture, but 'It is important to note the direction of interpretation.' The intratextual method does not want

> ... believers to find their stories in the Bible, but rather that they make the story of the Bible their story. The cross is not to be viewed as a figurative representation of suffering nor the messianic kingdom as a symbol for hope in the future; rather, suffering should be cruciform, and hopes for the future messianic. More generally stated, it is the religion instantiated in Scripture which defines being, truth, goodness and beauty ... Intratextual theology redescribes reality within the scriptural framework rather than translating Scripture into extrascriptural categories. It is the text, so to speak, which absorbs the world, rather than the world the text.[14]

To me it seems crucially important to see the distinction which Lindbeck draws here. In contemporary theology, the hermeneutic task of theology is often without much reflection conceived of in the extratextual way: the direction is *from* the text (or the message) *towards* the world. It appears from Schwöbel's paper, that he is in line with this fairly common view. Following Lindbeck, however, I would advocate a reversal of this hermeneutical direction. The problem with the externally directed hermeneutics is that the conceptual categories of a specific culture or philosophy easily become the basic framework of interpretation. In this way, in the case of Gnosticism Hellenism became the interpreter rather than the interpreted – and the same happened in parts of mainstream Christianity (e.g. when, despite the credal formulations, Jesus became depicted as a semipagan demi-god). Seeking to christianize a foreign culture presupposes an integrally Christian framework into which the foreign categories are to be drawn (rather than the other way round).

Lindbeck's reminder is especially acute in a time and culture that rapidly alienates itself from its Christian heritage. For especially when a religion becomes a foreign text it is tempting to translate this text into currently popular categories rather than reading it in terms of its intrinsic sense. Churches, and perhaps especially theologians, fearing to marginalize themselves, tend to accommodate to the prevailing culture rather than to shape it from a distinctively Christian perspective. Instead, they should see to it that they become or remain intensively socialized into

---

14   George Lindbeck, *The Nature of Doctrine: Towards a Post-Liberal Theology* (Philadelphia 1984), 118.

coherent religious languages and communal practices. For the primary way of transmitting the faith down through the centuries and of fulfilling the missionary task of the church was not to accommodate the Christian message to contemporary sensibilities or to redescribe it in new concepts, but to teach the alien language and practices of the faith to potential adherents, and of course to enact these language and practices both in one's own personal life as well as in the communal life. Still, only an intimate and vivid familiarity with the world of faith makes it possible to experience the whole of life in religious terms.[15]

From this perspective, the phenomenon of *changes* in the belief contents of the Christian tradition – the possible necessity of which I do not deny – should be assessed more critically than Schwöbel does. The inversion of the hermeneutical relation implies a priority of continuity in the Christian tradition over change. To quote Lindbeck one final time: 'Theology should ... resist the clamor of the religiously interested public for what is currently fashionable and immediately intelligible. It should instead prepare for a future when continuing dechristianization will make greater Christian authenticity communally possible.'[16] Pointing as a theologian into this direction, it seems to me, is treating the tradition to its best advantage.

---

15   Cf. Lindbeck, *Nature of Doctrine*, 133.
16   Lindbeck, *Nature of Doctrine*, 134.

12. Tradition as a Dynamic Force for Positive Change

David Brown (Durham, UK)

1 Introduction

Vincent Brümmer's contribution to this volume has two principal concerns, to
locate some of the forces for change within a religious tradition and to reflect upon
what then gives identity to the tradition over time. These questions are also part of
my focus here. But instead of discussing the matter in general terms which I have
done elsewhere,[1] it has been suggested that on this occasion I reflect on the issues
by tackling some specific cases of a developing tradition. Accordingly, to do so I
shall consider one example from the Old Testament and one from the New: changing attitudes to innocent suffering as reflected in differing hermeneutical understandings over time of the book of Job, and secondly changes in how the nativity
stories have been read.

Contemporary biblical scholarship exhibits frequent tensions between two
rather different approaches to Scripture – the historical and the literary. Both I think
are indispensable. In the case of the former, not only is historical investigation
essential in establishing the foundations on which the Christian faith must in the end
stand or fall, it is also, though less commonly noted, crucial in securing our distance
from the text. For taking a text seriously must surely mean willingness to allow it
to say things very different from what we expect and sometimes not at all what we
want to hear. Though obviously not always recoverable, where at all possible we
must allow the original authors and community their integrity as much as, and no
less than, we insist on our own. But the historical is by no means all that matters. No
less relevant is the question of what the text itself can say to us today, and the power
of its narrative to engage our attention. That is one great strength of the more recent
literary approaches, though unfortunately sometimes spoilt by those who use such
methods as a means of circumventing difficult historical questions. Though the
contrast is too crude, in more recent times revelation has often been seen in terms
of one or the other: either God disclosing himself through the historical events that

---

1   'Did Revelation Cease?', in: A.G. Padgett (ed.), *Reason and the Christian Religion* (Oxford 1994), 121-141.

biblical criticism recovers or Christ speaking through the text as it now stands.[2] I would want to opt for neither exclusively, but claim a place for both.

However, it does not seem to me that these are the only two points where we may speak of revelation. What happened historically and how the text speaks to us today both need to be measured against the history of interpretation that links the two. Inevitably, any interpretation is conditioned by the assumptions which we bring to the text, and so it is important that twentieth century prejudices should not always have the final say. We need also to hear other assumptions and possibilities. It is commonplace to find earlier hermeneutical assumptions rejected out of hand as constituting too radical a departure form the text, but on the other side needs to be set the question of how far it is the written word that should in any case have control over the final shape of the narrative. Barth is famous (or notorious, depending on your point of view) for refusing to equate revealed Word with the written word. So in making such a claim I am hardly suggesting something totally novel. But my concern is quite different. What I shall do in what follows is observe and assess why it is that communities of faith can come to form versions of a narrative that diverge substantially from what appears on the written page and make this the hermeneutical grid through which that page is read.

Philosophers have in my view been over-concerned with consistency and coherence in their analysis of theology, and so Vincent Brümmer's stress on other additional criteria for the appropriateness of change is most welcome. Consistency and coherence suggest that religious belief is a purely intellectual system whereas it is obviously much more than that, in particular a way of life that engages one's imagination and emotions, and whether it succeeds or not in this depends at least in part not merely on its internal fit or consistency but also on the success of its applicability to the circumstances and issues thrown up by the wider society within which it is set. Of course, in theory the text could have within itself an infinite range of options with which to deal with all possible scenarios, but what in fact I suggest sometimes happens is the imposition of fresh grids drawn in part from outside to ensure continuing relevance. Such grids could be viewed as undermining the authority of the biblical text, as arbitrary impositions from outside the ambit of revelation, but that is not the only possible interpretation. They might also be seen as God's way of continuing to ensure the relevance of the Christian dispensation.

But why change at all? For me one great advantage of the historical method is the way in which it can expose not only foundations but also a text's limitations and so the reasons why there is pressure to go beyond the written word. It is not that the limitations are seen at the time, but that in retrospect from later in the history of

---

2   One might contrast those who follow Pannenberg and those who follow Bultmann.

interpretation we can identify what factors there were which led to a retelling of the story in a different form. Newman's criteria for identifying a true development have few admirers today. Rather, his achievement was to explode once and for all the adequacy of appealing to purely logical interference as an account of how doctrine develops beyond Scripture.[3] Instead, at most we can detect what I shall call trajectories, possible directions implicit there at the beginning, where we may perhaps speak of an implicit invitation to further development, though the adequacy of such development would then need to be judged not by reference back to the original context but to the deposit of revelation as a whole. Perhaps I should add that by the latter I do not mean simply Scripture as a whole since the final shape of Christian belief is not a matter of the Bible alone, but also of other factors such as reason and experience. Apart from 'trajectories,' the only other piece of jargon which I would like to introduce is the notion of 'triggers.' I do not believe in the social determination of human thought but it does seem to me heavily conditioned, and so whether even ideas inspired by God will come to consciousness appears in part dependent on the degree of receptivity of particular societies and their culture.

Because we are not a very historically conscious age it is very easy for us to fall into the trap of supposing that certain ideas or ways of looking at things have always been around. We then impose those ideas on the biblical text as the only possible way of reading it, and we never realise how widely our own particular notions in fact diverge from the author's intention. I shall provide some examples in what follows, but perhaps a classical analogy will help. Everyone knows the Delphic injunction 'know yourself,' but how many appreciate that it had originally nothing to do with a summons to self-reflection (our own natural way of reading it) and everything to do with knowing one's proper place in society? Or again, to take a still more fundamental case of possible misunderstanding, numerous generations of European schoolchildren have been moved and inspired to identify with the various characters in Homer's *Iliad*, but if Bruno Snell is right, Achilles and Patroclus, Hector and Andromache would all have had a hugely different sense of their identity from what we have, with activity assigned to different parts of the body without any notion of an overall, unifying consciousness.[4] Worlds very different from our own may thus be lurking beneath texts, and so we need to take their historical situatedness with maximum seriousness. But enough of preamble, and so to the first of my two examples.

---

3   The contrast is well indicated in O. Chadwick, *From Bossuet to Newman* (Cambridge 1957).
4   B. Snell, *The Discovery of the Mind in Greek Philosophy and Literature* (New York 1982), esp. 1-22.

Here I must begin by emphasising that my concern is only very indirectly with the wider philosophical issue. Instead, the focus is upon the practical, religious question of how suffering can be lived through and a relation with God still maintained. The two are of course not unconnected, but there is an important difference. For it is one thing to ask, why suffering at all; quite another, why this pain is now befalling me, and what am I to make of it. Given the form of its narrative about a particular individual suffering, the Book of Job is in my view most naturally interpreted as having that later focus. Some will disagree, and in support point to the more theoretical concerns of the author, in his sustained attempt to undermine alternative 'solutions' to the problem of evil advocated elsewhere in the Old Testament canon. But in response, one may note the way in which these too could have a practical dimension. As Ernest Nicholson has observed: 'For an ancient Israelite it was a comfort to know, when misfortune struck, that the fault lay in oneself and that repentance would bring forgiveness and restoration of well-being from a merciful God, or that such misfortune was divine "testing" which would be followed by renewed blessing for one whose heart was proved true to God.'[5]

Either way, the book must certainly be seen as a dialogue of disagreement with an already existing tradition. That it in turn was not to be allowed the final word is, I suggest, the only possible conclusion that can be reached once we examine the narrative's subsequent hermeneutical history. The canonical work opened up three trajectories, each of which were in the long run to have a profound effect on how the story of innocent personal suffering would be told. This is not to say that these trajectories were intended by the author, only that the shape and character of his text made such developments possible. Of the three I am about to mention, two relate to common ways in which the book is read today, though in both cases I want to challenge the historical adequacy of those modern readings. First, God's answer from the whirlwind is commonly interpreted as intended to foreclose all further investigation, and at one level that is exactly the right interpretation. Job is told very emphatically that he has been raising questions beyond his competence.[6] Yet the text as a whole invites a rather different interpretation, since somebody who has spent almost forty chapters investigating an issue can hardly turn round and say that anyone trying to do better is necessarily doing something wrong. He could talk of the certainty of failure perhaps, but not of the illegitimacy of the act per se, since that was precisely the exercise in which he himself had engaged. Moreover, there

---

5   E. Nicholson, 'The Limits of Theodicy,' in: J. Day, R.P. Gordon & G.M. Williamson (ed.), *Wisdom in Ancient Israel* (Cambridge 1995), 71-82, esp. 73.

6   As Job himself acknowledges in his response, 42:3

are hints throughout the text of continuing questioning, with all three of the major Jewish traditions subject to challenge and critique: law, prophets and wisdom.[7] So, there is a sense in which the text, so far from foreclosing all further investigation, invites the process to continue. Secondly, many commentators have found in the presence of God in the whirlwind God's answer in an experience of himself and his care.[8] Once again, however, I find this implausible, since there is none of the personal interaction and descriptive detail that makes some accounts so obviously experiential such as Moses at the burning bush or Isaiah in his vision in the Temple. Nonetheless, by opening just a little the possibility of such an experiential answer, the trajectory for a fuller development was thereby set in place. Finally, central to the narrative is of course Job's claim to innocence. But the portrayal is at such length and given with such self-righteous confidence that inevitably later generations were to ask how adequate it indeed was as a depiction of virtue, and this too opened up pressures towards change.

The result is development in all three areas. Here all I can offer are some sample illustrations, but the point I want to stress is that such accounts in many cases became so influential that in effect the story of Job was quite transformed, and a very different tale told, one which the later community of faith regarded as more adequate to its own life and experience. In due course I shall come to what I regard as the deepest and most satisfactory transformation, but let me first provide some indicators of stages on the way as it were, as each of these three trajectories opened up new avenues for depicting Job and the experience of the innocent sufferer. First then, on exploring other possible answers, consider how crucial life after death came to be in later readings of the book. All of us are familiar with Handel's setting of the famous words from Job 19,[9] as also with the common scholarly conviction that there is no such reference to the afterlife in the passage in question, nor indeed elsewhere in the book. Yet so deep did such an answer resonate that everywhere the Fathers find references to life after death. Ambrose, for instance, can even read, as one such indicator, 'Let the day perish wherein I was born,' interpreting it to mean: 'he wished that the day of his birth might perish that he might receive the day of the resurrection.'[10] Nor should such an answer be dismissed too summarily as incom-

---

7   For law, cf. the implied reference to Sinai, 19:23-4; for prophets, Elihu (a variant of Elijah) speaking under inspiration, 32:18-22; for wisdom, generally but also the parody of Psalm 8 at 7:17-18.
8   A recurring theme in the twentieth century, as reflected in A. Peake (1904), Oesterley and Robinson (1934), and H. Rowley (1963): N.N. Glazer (ed.), *The Dimensions of Job* (New York 1969), 197-205, 205-214, 123-128.
9   Job 19:25; Handel, *Messiah* Part III.
10 Job 3:3 (A.V); Ambrose, *De excessu fratris sui Saturi* 2.32 (trans. from *Library of Post-Nicene Fathers* X, 178).

patible with the general tenor of the canonical work. After all, the prose epilogue speaks of the offer of a new status before God, and in a similar way heaven promises that, if not before, greater intimacy will at least eventually supervene on present suffering.

Then consider what happens with the question of innocence. The reference to the patience of Job in James is familiar,[11] its source less so. As an account of the historical figure's constant grumbles it is singularly inapposite. Calvin, for instance, compares Job unfavourably with David's more accepting response, as presented in the Psalms.[12] Almost certainly, therefore, James is either explicitly referring to a first century BC work, *The Testament of Job,* or employs hermeneutical assumptions similar to those employed in this work. The modification of Job's complaints had in fact already begun with the Septuagint which consistently softens Job's tone. With the *Testament* virtually all hint of anger has gone. In consequence it is tempting to dismiss the work, as many scholars do, as without value, as exhibiting merely superficial piety, but that is to ignore its positive merits. The author may have failed to see the legitimacy of anger against God, but he did at least see the pointlessness of it being quite unyielding, for suffering is surely merely intensified if one remains permanently angry at the lot that has befallen one. Not only that, the author has noted the way in which Job's repeated claims to innocence actually undermine those very claims, and so subtly altered the portrayal of what in fact makes Job virtuous. So, for instance, to give but one example, whereas the biblical Job boasts that his doors always stand open for the wayfarer, the *Testament* expands this into a description of how any who are in need of alms can obtain them surreptitiously without being embarrassed in the process.[13] Concern for others, including wife and family, is made much more explicit, and any hint of arrogance towards others is gone.[14]

However, the most marked change is undoubtedly the experiential one. Much of the work is devoted to a form of Merkavah mysticism under which Job is granted a very much deeper sense of the reality of God through his suffering, which he can then pass on to his children. Indeed, the very reason for him suffering is described as lying not as such in any arbitrary, unknown imposition by Satan but because Job has himself crossed Satan, and decided to oppose him on God's behalf. Though the *Testament* was rejected by Pope Gelasius (d. 496) from having any definitive role in Christian interpretation and the text then disappeared for most of Christian history, it continued to exercise a substantial indirect influence, one illustration of

---

11 James 5:11.
12 Calvin, *Sermons on Job* 12:52. Psalm 22 is taken to be a reflection on David's experience, and to show him a 'mirror of patience.'
13 Job 31:2 & *Testament* 9:8.
14 Contrast the unpleasant sides of Job's character that sometimes emerge: e.g. Job 30:1 & 31:9-10.

which is the key role given to music and to Job's wife not only in much earlier writing and art but even as late as the etchings of William Blake with which I shall end this brief survey. It was all part of the attempt to create a more sympathetic figure, as moral attitudes changed.

Perhaps nowhere is this more marked than in Pope Gregory the Great's influential commentary in the *Moralia,* where not only does Job become a focus for moral reflection but also identified with Christ, and thus of necessity someone in continual communion with God throughout his suffering. Gregory himself suffered much,[15] and there is little doubt that he identified with Job. The Job he identifies with, however, is far removed from the canonical presentation, and instead is someone who in his innocence became Christ-like through suffering. In fact, this is one of the great changes that we must note in the history of the text's hermeneutics. Both morally and experientially Job moves from what might be called an externalist position to an internalist. Thus on the question of experience he moves from one solitary encounter with the external voice of God to continuing and intimate interaction, while morally he moves from general lists of things he has done to the specificity of commitment and compassion for identifiable individuals. The love of husband and wife is perhaps the most obvious case, but there are many more that could be quoted. Though a tradition of blaming her does continue alongside the alternative more positive approach, more typical is the Islamic transformation where, for her urging Job to curse God, God enjoins a beating so light that she will not notice it,[16] while within the Jewish and Christian tradition we find her begging on his behalf and caring for his sores. Job has become a loving individual, which is hardly the first – or even fifty-first – adjective that springs to mind to describe the canonical character.

If we ask what triggered this greater internalism both morally and experientially, as part of the answer one might point to the pattern of Christ himself, but it is also surely not without significance that it reached one of its most intense and influential expressions within the monastic tradition with Gregory the Great. The requirement of hours of prayer and self-reflection inevitably helped generate a rather different view of what might be possible from that suggested by the canonical work.

A still greater change was to be effected in modern times. Apart from conceding that suffering did not necessarily indicate guilt, the one aspect of the Old Testament argument which everyone in the later tradition did accept was the book's implicit assumption that everything which happens must in some sense be willed by

---

15   He suffered from bowel problems and fevers, as well as pessimism in part generated by the extremely unsettled times through which he lived.
16   Cf. A.Y. Ali's edition of *The Holy Qur'an* (Leicester 1975), 1227, n.4202.

God. So the story of individual suffering was developed through a more detailed account of particular providence rather than its rejection. Thus Gregory, for instance, presupposed that God must always bring on suffering for a purpose, whether to upbraid the guilty or to challenge the innocent, but always that thereby intimacy with himself might be deepened, and it is that view that one also finds in Aquinas and Calvin. However, from at least the Renaissance onwards such assumptions about the inevitability of detailed divine planning have sat less and less easily with what Christians believe about other features of the modern world, with increasing stress being placed on the appropriateness of us taking matters into our own hands and so acting responsibly on our own initiative. Numerous examples spring to mind, from changing attitudes to the authority of the state to a specific issue like contraception. One way of putting the contrast would be to observe that modern society – and with it to a large degree the Christian community also – has moved from a world of natural law to one of natural rights, a pattern laid down by God in relation to which one must conform giving place to one where assertion of entitlements becomes the order of the day. If in our own century the focus of that change has largely been in wrestling with biological issues such as contraception and abortion, just as in the nineteenth it was with economic, so in the eighteenth the nature of the question mainly revolved round the issue of suffering and the extent to which it might be seen as God-given. The contributions of Leibniz and Voltaire are so familiar as scarcely to require any mention here. What is often forgotten, though, is that in England discussion was largely conducted through commentaries on the Book of Job, among which one might mention those of Warburton and Sherlock, as well as Pope's two poems on the subject.[17] From the previous century one might also observe that even the title of Hobbes' *Leviathan* is no accident.[18]

What in effect seems to happen is that the engineered view of particular providence loses ground as the community of faith seeks to assert its own right, with God's help, to give point to the suffering rather than allowing it to be seen as something entirely imposed from without, even if that 'without' happened to be God. Kant's change of mind on the matter is symptomatic of a more general change of attitude,[19] but if an English example is preferred, one might note what happens in Blake's handling of the issue in his series of etchings designed to illustrate the story of the book. Significantly, substantial reinterpretation occurs, with an initially self-

---

17 As well as the famous *Essay on Man* one should not forget his *Epistle to Lord Bathurst,* esp. lines 339-402.

18 As Hobbes himself admits: *Leviathan* (rpt. 1962), 2,28; 284.

19 For the contrast between the earlier and later Kant, A. Loades, *Kant and Job's Comforters* (Newcastle 1985), 101-158.

satisfied Job presented as choosing to learn through his suffering and thus in this way to become more Christ-like and so in deeper communion with God.[20]

The above has been the very briefest outline of some of the enormous changes over history to which the interpretation of Job has been subject. Because the Church of our own age is perhaps less interested than any other in its own history, it is not a history with which the contemporary Church is particularly familiar, and so I would not wish to claim in any case that this is how the text is currently being read. What I would claim is that if such trajectories are rejected, Christianity will be the poorer as a result. For to my mind such rewritings can provide a more adequate version of the story of the innocent sufferer than what the original canonical work affords. To justify such a claim is hardly a matter of a brief paragraph, since involved are extensive issues such as the superiority of an internalist to an externalist morality and the Enlightenment notion of responsibility as against the more engineered account of providence that earlier treatments of the story assumed. Arguments could be offered, but this is not the place to provide them. What it is important to say is, I think, twofold. First, the yardstick against which such changes should be measured is not the Bible itself but a Christian conceptual scheme that has long since advanced well beyond Scripture, and continues to change across the centuries. That might initially suggest complete subservience to secular thought, but need not, since the reshaping of Christianity through the adoption of elements drawn from secular triggers does not occur in isolation, but through interaction with the already existing tradition, and so both are changed as Christianity reshapes itself in such continuing dialogues. Secondly, and perhaps still more importantly, let me once again stress that what I have been sketching here is not at all the development of a philosophical solution to the problem of evil. That raises quite other issues. My concern here has been for a 'story' to live by, a telling of what happens to someone like Job that could engage the emotions and commitments of suffering individuals and thereby deepen their relation with God. The question is thus in some ways more imaginative than intellectual. This will be still more true of my second illustration, the nativity stories.

3   The Nativity Stories

The nativity stories in Matthew and Luke are a particularly interesting case to take as our New Testament example, for theologians and clergy alike regularly display embarrassment about the way in which the tradition has developed into the present

---

20   Here I follow S.F. Damon, *Blake's Job* (Providence, R.I. 1966).

practices associated with Christmas: the holly and the ivy, Christmas trees, ships sailing into landlocked Bethlehem and the like, and often as with Barth the point is made that there can be no proper celebration of Christmas without explicit acknowledgement of Calvary.[21] Added embarrassment is caused for those who think the entire childhood tale midrash in any case, and so devoid of any historical truth. The extent to which that is so is too complex an issue for us to consider here.

Instead, I want to begin by making a number of quite simple points, all connected with the question of truth, which I hope will help provide a proper context for the discussion of post-biblical developments which follows. First, even the most conservative Christian when faced with comparative criticism across the synoptic gospels must acknowledge that the evangelists were prepared to adapt Jesus' original words in order that they might speak more effectively to their own time, and that this meant not only changes in style but also at times in content. Matthew's treatment of divorce is a case in point, as is Luke's attitude to eschatology.[22] This is the great strength of the work of the Form critics. Scholars are divided over whether John worked in conscious awareness of the synoptic tradition or not, but, either way, despite occasional exceptions such as John Robinson it is hard not to see John's work as anything other than a considerable development and refinement of the synoptic christology, with great speeches put into Christ's mouth about his significance for the world which almost certainly the historical Jesus never uttered and indeed might well have found utterly incomprehensible. The implications of all this for truth claims is clear. Theological truth and the historical truth about Jesus cannot possibly be simply equated if we wish to defend the kind of initiatives in change that the gospel writers were themselves already taking.

How the development towards a fuller incarnational doctrine might be defended I have already indicated at some length elsewhere.[23] Here I want to apply the point to the infancy narratives. The incongruity of treating them as pure history can forcefully be brought home to any reader who attempts to read them as a preface to Mark's Gospel rather than in their present setting. Not only does the hostility of Jesus' family become incomprehensible but alos Jesus' own reticence, including the whole strategy of the messianic secret that is such a prominent theme in that gospel. But the difficulties of course lie deeper, with Luke allowing, for instance, no space for Matthew's flight into Egypt.[24] The fact that some of it must thus be midrash,

---

21 As in his early Christmas meditations: *Christmas* (Edinburgh 1959), e.g. 11, 13.
22 With Matthew's inclusion of the 'unchastity' exemption (Mt. 5:32), and Luke's downplaying of an imminent eschatology (Lk. 22:69; contrast Mk. 14:62).
23 *The Divine Trinity* (London 1985), 101-158.
24 Within forty days the child is being presented in the Temple, hardly the action of parents worried about the child's safety.

assertions of Christ's significance mediated through reflection on Old Testament verses or themes, need not of course mean that it all is, and even as stupendous a claim as the virgin birth might still be historically true. My intention here is not to arbitrate which aspects are and which not, but rather to observe that even where false historically they can still be true theologically. So, for example, the flight into Egypt may never have happened, but what the story implicitly claims can still nonetheless be true: that Christ is in fact the new Moses who will lead his people out of the captivity to sin and oppression which is Egypt and into the promised land of being the specially favoured children of God. That said, I hope that it becomes easier to see why further elaborations of the story in the post-biblical period need not be automatically dismissed as without truth. Indeed, I want to go further and suggest that at times they embody more truth than their original biblical basis.

Some biblical scholars who favour the current literary approach to the gospels over against the historical sometimes give the impression that all that is now required of the Church is acceptance of the story as it stands, as though story escaped any similar kind of challenge as that mounted by historical criticism. But as the issue of feminist criticism well illustrates, it is possible also to evaluate story as better or less well told, and that can have as profound an impact as historical difficulties on how easily the account might be appropriated in our own day. Most obviously we can ask how well it succeeds in its own terms, but one can also question whether or not it successfully embodies dimensions of existence which the later Church thinks important. I want to give an example of each, once more using my language of trajectories and triggers.

First, then, an evaluation of the two evangelists' intentions on their own terms, where I shall take as my example the familiar stories of the wise men of Matthew and the shepherds of Luke. Matthew's wise men are pagan astrologers, and there seems little doubt that their role is to point to the relevance of Christ for the Gentiles in much the same way as he uses quotations from the Old Testament to indicate the fulfilment of Jewish hopes. Though nowadays we are used to thinking, almost automatically, of the shepherds as a sign of the significance of Christ for the poor and marginalised, to my mind those biblical critics are right who observe that any evidence for seeing the shepherds as a despised class is late. Old Testament imagery had in fact given them high praise, with their profession regularly used as a metaphor for God or for the rule of the king, and so much more likely is the suggestion that they are intended to underline Jesus' role as Son of David, with a greater shepherd of souls now here than that earlier individual from Bethlehem who had also cared for sheep.

If this is a correct account, the trajectory of which I am about to speak would seem only to emerge once the New Testament is treated as a unity, for it is only then that the contrast between wise men and shepherds could begin to emerge, and even then only somewhat incidentally. The wise men became symbols of the relevance of the gospel to the rich because of the costly gifts they bring, while simply by contrast the shepherds then begin to appear poor and ordinary. Indeed, some of the Fathers do not hesitate to criticise them for their failure to bring gifts. The relevance of the gospel to the Gentiles in any case became a less appropriate point to make, the more the known world became evangelised. The notion of the wise men as kings quickly developed under the influence of Psalm 72 (v.10). It took longer for them to be assigned to the three different ages of man, and to the three different races, but this too eventually happened, and one finds this reflected in numerous works of art, a particularly fine example coming from Dürer.[25] Nonetheless, how slowly tradition sometimes moves is reflected in how long it was before related developments occurred in respect of the shepherds, in particular for them to be represented iconographically at the crib, as it is not until the fifteen century that we find them generally there in art instead of in their former accustomed position, receiving the annunciation of the angels in the fields.[26] However, the details of the history concern me less, than the point which could now be made through the medium of the modified story: the relevance of Christ to all sorts and conditions of humanity, rich and poor, young, middle-aged and old, black, oriental and white. And, to address a contemporary challenge and concern, despite their absence from the biblical narrative of the crib even women found their place, in part through the presence of midwives, and in part through women being numbered in the company of the shepherds, sometimes with themselves in that specific role.

My contention then is that so far from tradition undermining the gospel account, it actually offers a better, fuller and richer version of the story. Historically, of course it fails, as in all probability does the original, but to make that the sole ground of one's objection is to support a very narrow view of truth. If Jesus is indeed the Saviour of all humanity, then the story at its deepest level remains fundamentally true. Because its truth is in part parasitic on historical foundations which must be justified from elsewhere, the more intellectualist in their view of truth may be inclined to dismiss it as a not very significant form of truth, but that would be a huge mistake. For religion is not just a matter of the perception of truth but whether that truth succeeds in engaging our hearts and minds, and here I would argue that this is one major reason why the tradition as developed will continue to shape our celebrations of Christmas no matter how much biblical scholars might try to return us to the original, less effective and less powerful, though biblical, meaning.

---

25 Now in the Uffizi gallery in Florence.
26 There are only very few earlier examples, such as one by Taddeo Gaddi from 1340.

One reason why the move of the shepherds from the fields to the crib took so long was because for most of the Church's history the infancy narratives were treated in the same way as the evangelists themselves intended, not as significant in their own right but as anticipatory of a significance that was still to be made explicit, namely in the death and resurrection of Jesus. As Raymond Brown has remarked of Luke's account, it functions in much the same way as the prologue of a Greek tragedy in anticipating what is yet to come,[27] and therefore there is less reflection on the events themselves in their own right than one might otherwise have expected. The fact that this is so brings me on to my second and final example of a trajectory in this context, and that is the treatment of the infant Jesus himself. So much do our present festivities at Christmas focus upon the celebration of children in general that it is easy to forget that this kind of interest in children is essentially a modern phenomenon, and that the focus of the biblical narrative is thus quite different.

Putting this issue bluntly, there is nothing in the two narratives to suggest any interest in the infant Jesus as such as distinct from what he will achieve as an adult. Thus we are given no description of anything he does, unless one includes Luke's incident in the Temple and even there the point is the precociousness of the child who behaves just as if he were an adult. Nor does that emphasis change markedly during the first millennium. Iconographically, the point can be made very effectively by observing that the crib is repeatedly made to look like an altar and the child more often than not simply a mini-adult in his expression and gestures. In comprehending such an attitude one needs not only to recall how strongly theology centred upon cross and resurrection but also the very different attitudes to children which prevailed in the ancient world – a world where parental power was absolute in both pagan and Jewish thinking. All that, however, began to change from towards the end of the thirteenth century onwards, with the generation of the imagery with which we are now so familiar of child and mother in intimate interrelation and interaction.

Almost certainly, it took more than one trigger to generate the change. One of these may have been the revolution in philosophy occurring at the time, and the resultant increased interest in empirical observation. The child now needed to be observed rather than theories simply applied to him or her. Of relevance too was the new forms of piety in relation to Mary. The liveliness of Bernard of Clairvaux's interactive piety with Mary in the twelfth century had helped focus greater interest on Mary's relationship with her child, and so indirectly as a consequence came greater interest in the child himself. But perhaps the most important factor of all was

---

27   R.E. Brown, *The Birth of the Messiah* (1977; rpt. London 1993), 620. Similarly, Brown describes the first two chapters of Matthew as intended to 'anticipate the theology of the rest of the Gospel' (585).

the search at this time for more individualistic forms of piety. Argument continues about the significant moments in history that contributed to the growing sense of the individual with which we are so familiar today, but the social change of the twelfth century is commonly taken to be one such moment.[28] In terms of religious practice, it meant that theories that spoke in terms of appropriate social role were now no longer deemed adequate, and there was search for a much deeper, more intimate relation with Christ. Imaginatively, that was mediated through expansions of the story, and so we find the nativity retold in ways in which individuals, both men and women, could envisage themselves as participants. One highly influential example of this approach is Pseudo-Bonaventure's *Meditations*, where, for example, in respect of the infant Jesus the reader is urged to 'pick him up and hold him in your arms. Gaze on his face with devotion and reverently kiss him and delight in him.'[29]

The result was now a child valued in its own right, rather than just for what he would bring as an adult, and in consequence the incarnation seen as the valuing of our own infancy as well. That is important to stress, since, though we sing at Christmas 'he is our childhood's pattern,'[30] it is important to acknowledge that this was no part of the original meaning of the gospels. Instead, it was something which came to be seen and appreciated much later. One could of course argue that it all comes from 'Suffer the little children' and related passages, but one must avoid historical solecisms. We have no reason to believe that the rights of children would ever have entered Jesus' consciousness, and at most what is being expressed in such passages is a valuing of an attitude (simple trust), not childhood as such. Instead we need to see the value of God's identification with humanity in the incarnation projected back into childhood, once the full significance of that particular period of our lives was in due course seen.

4   Conclusions

What my two examples from the Old Testament and the New have sought to do is illustrate the way in which tradition, so far from being always the dead-weight of conservative reaction, can in fact sometimes be a radical and dynamic force for positive change. Not only that, it builds upon methods and assumptions also present within Scripture itself. The biblical view of truth was not of something static, but of something that could be frequently subject to modifications which might even

---

28   C. Morris, *The Discovery of the Individual, 1050-1200* (London 1972).
29   I. & R.B. Green (eds.), *Meditations on the Life of Christ* (Princeton 1961), 38-39. The work probably dates from the early fourteenth century.
30   From verse 4 of Frances Alexander's hymn of 1848: 'Once in royal David's city.'

sometimes include the jettisoning of its historical dimension if this was the best way of securing a deeper truth. Later tradition cannot therefore be condemned for its methods and assumptions without condemning the Bible itself. Of course, many will dislike any suggestion that the truth of revelation is not contained by the biblical text itself and will long for some simple model of logical deduction, but can we really go on pretending that the biblical text stands totally outside of all cultural history? Culture does impose some limits on what can be perceived at various periods of human history, and if that is so, why should we think the Bible immune? Attitudes to particular providence and to children are hugely different in the twentieth century from what they were in the first millennium and we should not pretend otherwise, nor deny that in part current Christian attitudes have been shaped not only by Scripture but by the wider cultural context of which we are inevitably part. To acknowledge that debt is not to devalue the Bible or God but to recognise his continuing activity within our world, and the importance of his relevance to it.

One last observation. Not all the changes to which I have drawn attention require appeal to some wider cultural consideration in order for their trajectories to be entirely intelligible. The reshaping of the story of the shepherds and the wise men is a case in point. Psalm 72 was already available to Matthew, but there is no evidence he thought of the wise men as kings. If with me you think the later version an improvement, that seems to require the admission that even the final version of the biblical text was not always the best available at the time. But is that too dreadful an admission to make? God in the incarnation submitted himself to human limitations in the most fundamental way possible; so why not also more widely elsewhere?

13. Can We Change the Fatherhood of God?

The Hermeneutical Implications of Change in the Tradition of the Interpretation of the Bible

Hendrik M. Vroom (Amsterdam)

1   Introduction

Traditions change: the heritage (*traditio*) of each tradition is constantly applied in varying contexts and in continual exchange with other worldview traditions. Religious traditions have some basic insights which are passed on to later generations in the form of narratives and rituals. Within these narratives the basic insights of a tradition are interwoven with one another in ways that cannot be conceptualized. For example, the Gospels interweave the human story of Jesus with insights into God's initiative and his presence in the person of Christ. In the various narratives the basic insights are implicitly given a thousand qualifications because the stories have often been shaped in order to show different aspects of the divine and of human life in a paradigmatic way. Moreover, the Bible offers many 'theological' reflections within which basic insights are presented in metaphors (as in, for example, the words 'I am ...') and reflections. As far as I can see, such basic insights cannot be 'translated' fully into clear-cut concepts. They constitute our insight into reality itself, and reality, especially the reality of God and God's history with humankind, is too multi-faceted to allow for concepts that are *clare et distincte*. We may therefore speak of *models*, as Vincent Brümmer does, and try to preserve the openness of the biblical metaphors while analyzing concepts in order to understand the meaning of the biblical witness, to become more adept in explaining it, and to answer the various questions we ourselves have and which, if we would not ask them ourselves, would be raised by unbelievers and people of other faith traditions.

The fatherhood of God is such an idea, which is produced by adding 'hood' to the metaphor 'father.' In our day and age, discussion has arisen as to whether such a masculine metaphor actually helps people to understand who God is and whether such a patriarchal image is suitable for establishing a right relationship with God. Should we not therefore dispense with this masculine term and instead use more inclusive language for the God who loves humans and cares for them? Such a proposal involves (fundamental) hermeneutical questions. In the first place, there are questions as to the nature of religious use of language and the meaning of metaphors. In the second place, questions as to the nature of biblical authority and the right of the church to change what God has revealed arise. Can we change the images of God that are given in revelation itself? Has God not revealed 'him'self as Father, and was not the faith of Jesus himself as the Son characterized by trust in God as his Father in heaven? The idea of God as our Father in heaven is certainly one of the most basic insights of the Christian tradition, as evidenced by Christianity's central prayer, the Lord's Prayer. What exactly is it that would change if we were to drop the title 'Father' when we refer to God? If we were to do this, however, on whose authority could we use a different name? Would Christian faith remain the same if we dropped this central piece of its heritage? Some have even said that changing the fatherhood of God would create a new religion.[1]

2   Examples of Deliberate Change

Before I deal with these complicated and quite central questions concerning the Christian idea of God, I would like to describe some other changes which have occurred in mainstream churches in the Netherlands as well as in a number of other countries, and examine how such changes have been defended theologically. Some central issues on which opinions have changed in my own denomination, the Reformed Churches in the Netherlands (RCN), are the relation between creation and evolution, women in office, homosexuality and, as a result, the nature of biblical authority. Behind this lay a change with respect to ideas of God and the creational order, moving from more static ideas toward more dynamic and relational ideas. The RCN's origin can be traced to two secessions from the existing Reformed public church of the Netherlands in 1834 and 1886. These were motivated largely by a rather liberal theological climate in the church. Two leading theologians, Abraham Kuyper (d. 1920) and Herman Bavinck (d. 1921), returned to the sources of Calvinism and stressed both the sovereignty of God and biblical authority. Kuyper states that in reading Scripture one cannot ignore its mystical background without falling into an abstract rationalism. However, he also displays a more rigid line of thought when he requires an obedience to Scripture comparable to the obedience of soldiers to their general.[2] Herman Bavinck acknowledges already in his four-volume *Reformed Dogmatics* that science, modern exegesis and historical evidence introduced some important questions concerning the relation between the text of the

---

1   Alvin F. Kimel, 'The God who Likes his Name,' in: Alvin F. Kimel (ed.), *Speaking the Christian God: The Holy Trinity and the Challenge of Feminism* (Grand Rapids 1992), 208.

2   A. Kuyper, *Encyclopaedie der Heilige Godgeleerdheid* (Encyclopedia of Sacred Theology) III, rev. ed. (Amsterdam 1909), 69; *Dictaten Dogmatiek* (lecture notes) I, 65.

Bible and modern insights that could not be easily solved. The Bible is apparently not a handbook for geology, astronomy, geography or history.[3] The 1926 Synod left no room for people who did not accept a literal reading of the story of the Fall; they were expelled from the church. Nevertheless, the *interbellum* was a period of restoration. After World War II, developments in society, science and the life of the churches themselves led people to rethink the traditional understanding of Scripture. Among the major elements in this process of becoming more open to new developments in these churches – the Dutch Roman Catholic church went through a similar process! – were the modernization of society, the role of the media (through which people became increasingly more acquainted with other denominations) and membership in the World Council of Churches since 1969. In 1967 the Synod of the RCN revoked the statements made in 1926 concerning the exegesis of Genesis, thereby breaking through the literal interpretation of scripture in general.[4] In the sixties the Synod also decided to accept women as deacons, elders and ministers.

Characteristic of such a period of change is uncertainty as to the correct interpretation of Scripture, of which I will give two examples. After a series of earlier reports and discussions, the Synod of 1967/8 decided to admit women to the offices of the church. The report by a synodical committee, which had to write a proposal on the basis of the reports of the task force committee, is remarkable. According to the synodical committee, this report had not done full justice to all 'data given in the New Testament concerning church offices.' It thereby opened the debate on the use of Scripture.[5]

In times of change the application of Scripture will *necessarily* be uncertain as long as people disagree about the contextual application of Scripture. Behind such changes lay differences in relation to basic insights into human life which support the views on the issues at stake. The change in the case of women in office occurred alongside societal developments which in the long run had the effect of questioning the patriarchal views on women and men and their roles in church and society. The traditional insights into the differences between male and female have been reinterpreted from a more egalitarian perspective. It should not be forgotten that it was

---

3   Herman Bavinck, *Gereformeerde Dogmatiek* (Reformed Dogmatics) I, 5th ed. (Kampen 1967), 381.

4   See J. Veenhof, 'Honderd jaar theologie aan de Vrije Universiteit,' in: W.J. Wierenga *et al.*, *Wetenschap en rekenschap* (Kampen 1980), 44-104 for the developments that occurred over a century in the Faculty of Theology at the Free University of Amsterdam. Cf. also his 'Geschiedenis van theologie en spiritualiteit in de gereformeerde kerken,' in: M.E. Brinkman (ed.), *100 jaar gereformeerde theologie* (Kampen 1992), 32ff., 35ff.; on the revocation, see 67.

5   *Bijlagen bij de Acta* of the General Synod of the RCN 1967/8 (Kampen 1968), no. 81b, 540; cf. the advice 543; see the *Acta* themselves, §§ 336, 351, 365.

generally held to be evident that women had a different role to play in society from men and that these roles were based not only in Scripture but also in a God-given creational order. These insights have been very basic indeed, as evidenced by the prolonged, emotional and keen discussion on 'headship' (over women in the church) in some North American churches. In their context as well as in Scripture, people have seen, in the words of Abraham Kuyper's commentary on the *Heidelberg Catechism*,

> the divine ordinance, that the man is the head of the woman. Whoever stands on the Word of God *must* acknowledge the priority of the man above the woman, not in spiritual value, but in natural ability [or: gifts] and position and their reciprocal relationship.[6]

Kuyper thinks that it is both scriptural and natural. However, changes of insights into human existence are introduced by text *and* context, both in Scripture and in the changing cultural values and ideas.

In the meantime various topics became subjects of discussion. Doubts arose as to the justification of nuclear arms; the peace movement of the seventies and eighties had strong roots in the churches. The results of historical and exegetical research occasioned a debate on the authority of Scripture. In a situation of conflict concerning a wide range of issues, all of which had a bearing on the explanation and application of Scripture, the Synod decided in 1975 to establish a standing committee on Church and Theology. Its task was to write a report on the use of Scripture, which was published in 1981.[7] Its subtitle, *On the Nature of Biblical Authority*, is an indication of its intention not to dispute the authority of Scripture but to understand its nature in a new way. Essentially, the role of the church in the explanation and application of Scripture acquired more importance than is customary in traditional Reformed theology.

Since 1969 several committees discussed the issue of homosexuality without being able to reach a clear consensus.[8] In 1979 a synodical committee was insti-

---

6   Abraham Kuyper, *E Voto Dordraceno* IV (Amsterdam 1905), 165.
7   The title was *God with Us: On the Nature of the Authority of Scripture* (Reformed Churches in the Netherlands, Leusden 1982). More than 70,000 copies were sold within a short time, not including the translations into other languages. See my 'Scripture Read and Interpreted: The Development of the Doctrine of Scripture and Hermeneutics in the Gereformeerde Theology in the Netherlands,' *Calvin Theological Journal* 28 (1993), 352-371.
8   See Henk B. Weyland, 'Om de heelheid van een mens: Gereformeerde synoden over de plaats van homofiele leden,' in: R. Kranenborg & W. Stoker (eds.), *Religies en (on)gelijkheid in een plurale samenleving* (Apeldoorn 1995), 177-188.

tuted to advise the Synod on the issue. This committee went through an intense process by which it reached the conclusion that homosexual orientation should not be condemned and, further, that decisions made by homosexual couples concerning their sexual life should not be judged by others but left to their own conscience *coram Deo*. After good and intense discussions the Synod decided to accept loving and faithful homosexual relationships. It was clear, however, that more studies should be done on the use of Scripture, since Scripture had always been understood as condemning homosexuality. The Synod therefore instructed the Committee on Church and Theology to study the meaning of texts on homosexuality and their application. After intense discussions the Committee submitted a report on *The hermeneutical presuppositions of the use of Scripture on the question of homosexuality* (1982).[9] In this report the *loca probantia* which have been understood to condemn homosexuality are explained within their scriptural, historical, cultural and religious context. The report states that the nature of homosexuality as an inherent sexual preference (rather than a temporary variation in conduct and promiscuity) was not known either in the purity laws or in the letters of Paul. The report deals with the use of Scripture, pointing to the centre of the Gospel and the central commandments of love for God and one's neighbour, from which new questions, which inevitably arise as time goes on, can be approached, praying for the guidance of the Holy Spirit. Love is the centre of Christian ethics, and this love should permeate all conduct. Moreover, there are all kinds of nuances in the New Testament letters with regard to the value of prescriptions – not all moral rules and advices stem from Christ himself (see especially 1 Corinthians 7:10, 12, 25).

The tone of this report is 'relational.' The idea of a natural or creational order, which can be known both through nature and Scripture and has been established forever, has made room for an approach in which the saving presence of God among humans is central. God *in se* has moved more to the background and God *quoad nos* to the foreground. Compared to the balance in the traditional 'framework of interpretation,' the basic insights into the static and eternal elements in nature, which were central in classical scholastic theology, have receded into the background and the insights into God's saving acts have become more prominent. As a result, the contextuality of the biblical moral rules could be accepted.[10] In the new approach the self-evidence of heterosexual relationships is no longer a primary insight, but the quality of human relations: trust, faithfulness, love and justice. From that per-

---

9   *Homophilia: A Report on the Biblical Data* by the Committee on Church and Theology for the General Synod of the Reformed Churches in the Netherlands, Synod of Bentheim 1981 (Leusden 1982). The report has also been translated into German and Polish.

10   Cf. for a more traditional approach the Catholic encyclical *Veritatis Splendor* (1993); see § 43 on the natural law as the human expression of the eternal law of God.

spective an opening could be made for accepting homosexual relationships in love and faithfulness.[11]

The Synod accepted this report unanimously and submitted it to the churches to be studied. Moreover, it used the report as background for the decision taken in 1979. Since that time, quite a number of homosexual ministers have been accepted by local churches, although males encounter more resistance than their female counterparts do when it comes to accepting partners in the vicarage.

One point in the discussion within the Committee is relevant for understanding changes in the tradition. One of the Committee members pointed out a difference with respect to the discussion on women in office. In that discussion Scripture provided a central insight by which the other texts could be interpreted: the well-known text by Paul in Galatians 3:28: '... there is no longer male and female; for all of you are one in Christ Jesus.' Taking this as a central insight, the New Testament rules concerning the roles of women and men in the church can be reinterpreted as conditioned by a patriarchal culture. Scripture does not provide such an explicit point of departure in the discussion on homosexuality; hence, the acceptance of homosexuality goes much more against the grain of the biblical texts than the acceptance of the liberation of women does.

On the basis of these examples we see that we must distinguish between two kinds of change: *contextual change* and *deliberate change*. Contextual changes are changes that occur when people understand the content of faith from the perspective of the context within which they live. Contextual changes occur more or less 'automatically' when people appropriate the tradition. As Gadamer expresses it, to understand is almost always *to understand differently*.[12] Here one should keep in mind the theory of the fusion of horizons as it developed in general philosophical hermeneutics. In addition to contextual change, there is deliberate change, a conscious changing of the tradition that arises from the decision not to adopt certain elements in the tradition. Such decisions affect various areas, such as doctrine, life and the organization of the church. On the basis of a few practical cases we have seen how complex such a process of change is. The complexity arises from the clash between the tradition and those who renew it, which is accompanied by a period of

---

11 In order to illustrate the disagreement in times of change it is of interest to know that the Committee on Church and Theology consisted of ten members. Although seven of them were in favour of accepting homosexual relationships (although not hetero- or homosexual promiscuity), in order to prevent the possibility of a minority report, it was decided to begin the report with an introduction consisting of four opinions of Committee members, beginning with an acceptance of the homosexual orientation without praxis and proceeding to a full acceptance of homosexuality, leaving the decision with regard to their sexual life to conscience of the homosexual brothers and sisters before God Himself.

12 H.-G.Gadamer, *Wahrheit und Methode*, 2nd ed. (Tübingen 1965), 280.

division. The complexity is linked with the normativity of Holy Scripture, with the processes of making decisions and the implementation of changes – in short, with the role of the tradition that interprets the Scripture, the entirety of the official and informal 'rules' by means of which a religious tradition interprets and contemplatively applies its heritage and adapts to changing circumstances.[13]

In the following, I will examine what changes in the concept of God occur if people no longer want to call God Father. Many questions would arise as a result. If we were to stop speaking of God as Father, would we not be changing one of the most central insights of Christianity? If the term 'Father' depicts a reality, can that expression be changed? Is there a starting point in Scripture that would legitimate such a change? Let us delve into these questions in theological hermeneutics, which are even more complex than questions in philosophical hermeneutics because of the normativity of Scripture and the deliberate changing of tradition.

3   Is God a Father?

One of the clearest objections to speaking of God as Father is that if God is male, then the male is God.[14] If God is actually a father, then men could claim an almost divine authority or, in any case, a much greater authority than that of women. In the context of our more egalitarian and emancipated culture, we must not only implicitly interpret the father image differently but dispense with it and replace it with other images. A 'contextual change' of the tradition in the sense of a father image that slowly changes is not enough; what is needed is a 'deliberate change,' through which we distance ourselves from the traditional image of God and thus also from the traditional concept of humanity and the relationships between women and men. Some argue for complementary images of God (God as Mother as well), others speak of God as Parent and still others wish to dispense with all metaphors that are borrowed from family life. But if God *is* a father and has revealed himself as the Father of Jesus Christ, can this metaphor with the reality it is intended to depict be abandoned? It seems that whoever no longer calls God Father mutilates the identity of the Christian tradition to such a degree that another tradition arises.[15]

A number of *loci* in dogmatics, philosophy of religion and feminist theology converge in this problem: the concept of God, the doctrines of Scripture and tradi-

---

13   See my 'Scripture Read and Interpreted,' 35ff.; more fully elaborated in 'De gelezen Schrift als *principium theologiae*,' in: M.E. Brinkman (ed.), *100 jaar theologie*, 96-160.
14   Thus Mary Daly in *Beyond God the Father* (1973), often quoted; see, for example, Kune Biezeveld, *Spreken over God als Vader: Hoe kan het anders?* (Baarn 1996), 15-61.
15   See footnote 1.

tion, and patriarchy. In relation to our theme – identity and change in tradition – I will discuss the following two subjects: the meaning of metaphors in a religious tradition (4, 5) and the normativity of the biblical images of God (6).

4 Father as a Traditional Metaphor

'God as father' is a metaphor or model. The discussion about metaphors is carried on predominantly in terms of a philosophical analysis. In religious hermeneutics, the religious and traditional dimensions should be analyzed more carefully. In religion we are often dealing with 'traditional metaphors.' A traditional metaphor is a metaphor that was coined by a religious tradition and is used in that tradition to speak about transcendence. In the Christian tradition, such a metaphor is therefore used to speak about God. However, we will first examine some notions about metaphors in general.

A metaphor rests on the interaction between the subject about which someone speaks and the meaning of an unexpected term by which he or she refers to the subject. The effects of new metaphors are rather open; poetic metaphors and many of the terms coined by a market dealer have in common that they are unexpected, and invite us to look at reality differently. The reader of a poem associates certain things with the subject to which the metaphor applies and other things with the utterance of the metaphor. Through interaction both sets of associations bring about an understanding that would otherwise not or probably not arise. The meaning of a new metaphor cannot be translated in the sense that it cannot be described without a loss of meaning. Janet Soskice and others thus rightly dismiss the substitution theory of metaphors, which says that a metaphor can be translated into other, more literal terms.[16] It is important to see the unique nature of metaphors. Metaphors are often distinguished from comparisons because comparisons (God is as *caring* as a father; Hercules is as *strong* as a lion) are not open but specify what they concern. Nevertheless, it is possible for some comparisons to be closely related to metaphors. Sometimes in a metaphor the word 'as' can be added or left out without any change of meaning. The meaning of 'Hercules is a lion' does not differ greatly from the meaning of 'Hercules is as strong as a lion.'[17] The difference must not be made

---

16 Janet Martin Soskice, *Metaphor and Religious Language* (Oxford 1985), 24-26; J.J. van Es, *Spreken over God* (Amsterdam 1979), 71-73.

17 J.J. Van Es, *Spreken over God*, 69, distinguishes between literal and metaphorical comparisons. Cf. Soskice, *Metaphor*, 59. See also Johanna W.H. van Wijk-Bos, *Reimagining God* (Louisville, KY 1995), 35, 108, nt. 1.

absolute, for there are many kinds of metaphors and comparisons. There are dead and living metaphors. Examples of dead metaphors are referring to a chair leg as a 'leg' and to the section of pavement in the middle of a wide street as an 'island.' Living metaphors are created with new expressions such as the 'Queen of hearts,' 'news hunters' and 'head-hunters.' The distinction between dead and living metaphors can be nuanced by imagining a sliding scale from worn, dead metaphors through established metaphors with a relatively defined meaning to completely new metaphors.

Words that are used in metaphors do not, strictly speaking, have a metaphorical meaning but are used metaphorically by a speaker within a certain context. In agreement with Van Es and Soskice I believe that a metaphor arises only if someone uses words.[18] A subject is spoken of in words that are normally used to refer to another subject.[19]

The examples given make it quite clear that some images are adopted within the conventions of language: head-hunter has become a well-known term for a personnel advisor. Because many metaphors have become common expressions in everyday language, their meaning is well-defined. Thus metaphors form a spectrum that runs from dead metaphors with meanings that are so defined that they can often be described as literal, to new creative metaphors, the meanings of which are still open. Between these two extremes a linguistic community has standing metaphors that are meant and understood as metaphors but which still have a relatively well-defined meaning. It can be difficult to state the meaning of standing metaphors in different words, as every translator knows. While the meaning of standing metaphors is largely established, these metaphors are more suggestive and open-ended than words used literally.

Thus the distinction between dead and living metaphors is not very clear. In fact, there are many grades of metaphoricity. Some long-established metaphors have become so common that they are viewed as literal. The line between literal language and dead metaphors is far from clear-cut, as can be seen in the example of the table leg: one person would say that this is literal language and another would call it a dead metaphor.[20] The use of the term 'island' for a section of pavement on a busy road is less 'dead' than 'refuge.' If someone is almost run over and just manages to reach the island, its meaning easily becomes obvious. Through the contamination of expressions standing metaphors can acquire new meaning, for example, if one says: 'News hunters are wolves who do not lose sight of their prey for one moment.'

---

18   Van Es, *Spreken over God*, 48; Soskice, *Metaphor,* 52f., *passim.*
19   Soskice, *Metaphor*, 49.
20   Cf. Soskice, *Metaphor*, 72.

Thus between dead and living metaphors there are many standing metaphors for which the range of associations is not open but limited through their customary use. Standing metaphors have conventional meanings which are actualized in their concrete use. 'John is a wolf' is an actualization of a standing metaphor. The associations which a standing metaphor evokes in speaker and listeners are established through convention. We could call a boy who has been pursuing a girl for months a terrier but not a wolf. If we call people herd animals we are not speaking about wolves (which also have a clearly defined social structure) but cattle. A standing metaphor is therefore a *metaphoric expression* that is established but which can be modified in a concrete situation and which then becomes an actual metaphor. 'X is a wolf' is an expression, whereas 'Dick is a wolf' is a metaphor.

Within a language community people become familiar with the meaning of such expressions even though their meanings remain relatively open and other associations can suddenly become actual. Standing metaphors do not have a fixed meaning. Like many words and concepts, they can acquire other meanings with the passage of time.

Standing metaphors are very important for the language of faith. When standing metaphors are supplied by a tradition, I will call them *traditional metaphors*.[21] These are not dead metaphors, but neither are they new ones. An example of a traditional metaphor is 'God is Father.' Because it is not a new metaphor but a traditional one, its meaning is more or less established. In the discussion on God's fatherhood, the term 'father' is sometimes meant metaphorically and sometimes intended as a model. A model is a standing metaphor that lies in the centre of an entire web of metaphors.[22] Soskice also calls the fatherhood of God a model that makes all kinds of metaphors possible, such as 'God cares for his children.'[23] She uses the term 'model' when one thing or state of affairs is seen in terms of another and the term metaphor when one thing or state of affairs in language is suggestive of another.[24] A model can be a thing, such as a small plane, but it can also be linguistic.[25] Soskice stresses the fact that a metaphor describes something for the first time, so that a new meaning arises which can subsequently be conveyed by that

21   Cf. Sallie McFague, *Models of God* (London 1987), 34, 39.
22   Sallie McFague, *Metaphorical Theology* (London 1983), 23: God the father has moved from being a metaphor to being a model which classifies the use of other metaphors and, as a model, lies between metaphor and concept.
23   Soskice, *Metaphor*, 55.
24   Soskice, *Metaphor*, 50f., *passim*.
25   Soskice, *Metaphor*, 55, cf. 102.

metaphor.[26] In the transferral of metaphors within a literary or religious tradition a complicated process of use and reinterpretation of metaphors takes place.

What McFague and Soskice call a model comes close to what I would call standing imagery and standing metaphor. Insofar as a metaphor is passed on within a religious tradition, I would prefer to call the standing metaphor a *traditional metaphor*. I have difficulty calling the fatherhood of God a model because it is linked with the most well-known prayer in Christianity, the Lord's Prayer.[27] The idea of 'fatherhood' is also too multi-faceted to serve as a model. Ricœur's warning, that 'the father figure is not a well-known figure whose meaning is invariable ... it is a problematic figure, incomplete and in suspense,' should be taken to heart.[28] The meaning of a standing metaphor is never invariable; it is always defined by the speaker, the listener and the context. The person who is addressed understands the expression on the basis of his or her own associations. Van Es rightly states that two people who both call God father need not necessarily mean the same.[29] But one may also have difficulty in understanding the meaning of a standing metaphor because of one's own associations. Thus, it is possible to misunderstand traditional metaphors. The Christian tradition passes on the expression 'God is our Father' with the intention of using it within the correct context. At one time this expression was new, but it has now matured and has several meanings – I will return to this in more detail later.

God as Father, God as Creator, Israel as child and Jesus as Son are not new metaphors because they already exist in contexts that determine the meanings that one may associate with them. As we have already seen, every culture and community has such conventions. If we see a crowd of people pouring through gates and someone says, 'People are just like sheep,' we do not think of 'woolly' people but of group behaviour. If, within the Christian faith community, someone says thoughtfully, 'God is a father,' then the intention of the speaker and the meaning of her words are largely determined by the insights of the tradition. Through analysis of the biblical context within which the terms have arisen we can determine precisely what is meant by them – as distinct from the associations that a new listener would have with this expression based on her experiences. Here one must, of course,

---

26   Soskice, *Metaphor*, 90, cf. 156ff.
27   I am leaving out of consideration here the fact that the terms used with reference to the Trinity have at times become somewhat technical; in those cases one could speak of a model. These terms are often not reflected upon thoroughly, as when the Father is identified within the Trinity with God.
28   P. Ricœur, 'Fatherhood: From Phantasm to Symbol,' in: P. Ricœur, *The Conflict of Interpretations* (Evanston 1974), 468.
29   Van Es, *Spreken over God*, 169.

consider the use of the imagery in the history of the church, for we have no immediate unbiased access to the past. Thus the explanation of a traditional metaphor is much different from that of a new metaphor. If a poet uses a completely new metaphor and no one is able to ask him about his meaning, then we have only our own associations with the subject and the metaphors used within the context of the poem to work with. But in the case of a religious tradition we are dealing with two contexts – that of the tradition and the contemporary context. Without a more detailed explanation with regard to the intentions of the tradition it is not possible to understand the meaning of the metaphor within the tradition. An example from another tradition will make this clear.

The statement 'The Buddha is enlightened' is a metaphor. An archaic meaning of 'enlighten' is to 'shed light on.' Someone who knew only of this meaning and was standing in the centre of an old and large city would likely think of a floodlight and, based on his set of associations, wonder if there was a statue of the Buddha somewhere in the city that had spotlights trained on it. From within the Buddhist tradition one would explain that here enlightenment refers to the insight that arose after the darkness of ignorance. The statement 'The Buddha achieved insight' is also more or less metaphorical, for it does not involve acquiring insight into something nor a theory that the Buddha developed but the emptiness that the Buddha realized, and 'emptiness' is also used metaphorically for an 'insight' that could also be called completeness or radical openness. As we stated earlier, it is not possible for religious metaphors to be translated into other terms without a loss of meaning, but this intranslatability does not exclude a more detailed definition of the meaning.

Together, religious metaphors form a network of meanings that collectively indicate and open up the particular way of experiencing and living that the tradition intends to pass on. Let me give two examples of this. In Buddhist literature authors often have the habit of circling around a subject in several ways rather than using strict argumentation and furnishing proofs. In his book *Religion and Nothingness*, K. Nishitani circles around the core Buddhist insight from the perspective of various themes in the successive chapters.[30] His discussions of the themes religion, self, nihilism, transcendence, time and history all ultimately refer to 'emptiness.' Thus a web of meanings arises which, in its coherent totality, provides insight into the Buddhist view of transcendence that cannot be defined. The meaning of time, history, self, etc. gradually becomes clear. The explanation is actually a *guidance toward* something.[31] The biblical traditions are not concerned with 'emptiness' but

---

30 K. Nishitani, *Was ist Religion?*, tr. D. Fischer-Barnicol (Frankfurt aM 1982).
31 See my *Religions and the Truth*, tr. J. Rebel (Grand Rapids 1989), 301-314 on the first and well-understood doctrine.

with acquiring insight into living before God. Here, too, poetry, narratives and reflections form a web of meaning in which the nuances of one term can determine the meaning of other terms. A good example of this is the word justice, which is not directed toward formal justice and equality in the eyes of the law, but toward contextual justice, which is closely connected to peace, mercy and wisdom. Meanings are explained by means of synonyms, related words and their opposites. Words are a part of the language games that determine their possible meaning. Which elements from among these possible meanings are actualized depends on the concrete statement made by someone within a certain context. Klaus Koch rightly speaks of the semantic fields of words:

> Every lexeme belongs to a field of verbal associations – often to several different fields – which is to be accentuated through an investigation of the widely-scattered linguistic material, because it has been filtered, according to the viewpoint of the replaceability of words, in a syntagma and the exploration of synonyms, antonyms, hyponyms and semantic fields.[32]

The juxtaposition of words that mutually explain one another is characteristic of Hebrew poetry; this figure of speech is called *parallellismus membrorum*. Through the coordination of related expressions and the opposition of contrasting expressions the meaning becomes explicit. Thus Isaiah speaks of God as father:

> For you are our father,
> though Abraham does not know us
> and Israel does not acknowledge us;
> you, O Lord, are our father;
> our Redeemer from of old is your name (Isaiah 63:16).

The opposition between God and the patriarchs Abraham and Israel accentuates the fact that God knows 'us' while the parallelism specifies the father as our Redeemer. Traditional metaphors also exist within a semantic field. If one would confine oneself to saying that we could understand the expression 'God is Father' by allowing what we associate with the word 'God' to interfere with what we associate with the word 'father,' then one overlooks the fact that the meanings of both 'God' and 'father' are defined within the Christian tradition by the biblical narratives about God. The meaning of the metaphor 'God is our Father' is defined by the Bible and

---

32   Klaus Koch, *Was ist Formgeschichte? Methoden der Bibelexegese*, 3rd ed. (Neukirchen 1974), 326.

the tradition. Thus it is not the case that the associations that one has with 'God' are determined by tradition and that the associations that one has with 'father' are determined by one's own experiences in life. Both of the terms in the metaphor, 'God' and 'father,' acquire new meaning as a result of their being used within the web of metaphors and other expressions provided by the tradition.

The meaning of metaphors within the tradition is largely determined by the classic texts. Besides the biblical texts that introduced the designation of God as 'father,' the use that has been made of this metaphor in the Christian tradition plays a major role. Insofar as the fatherhood of God has become a standing model for the Christian image of God, its meaning has sometimes become rigid. Vincent Brümmer has, like others, pointed out that the standing, conceptual metaphors of a tradition can become rigid, causing other aspects of the image of God to become obscured. He rightly warns that summarizing all of the statements about God by means of one particular model exacts a high price.[33] In order to indicate the various aspects of God several metaphors must be used.

Alongside the mutual supplementation of the various images for God, it is also necessary to test the metaphor as it has developed in the course of time against the original texts. Theology must continually examine which meanings were originally attributed to the metaphor 'father' in Scripture so that one-sided developments can be corrected. Biblical metaphors are based in revelation and therefore retain their normativity, and their meaning may not be completely separated from Scripture.[34] This means that the Bible must not only be recited but reflected upon anew and sometimes articulated anew.[35]

The insight that the meaning of traditional metaphors such as 'God as father' is chiefly defined by the biblical writings does not affect the possibility that a person who encounters a metaphor for the first time has no other choice than to introduce his own associations (for example, with fathers), because one learns the things that are meant by words through experiences that one has gone through. This brings us back to the phenomena of historicity, the fusion of horizons and 'contextual change' within a tradition. Scripture is understood differently in one period than in another because people approach it from a different framework, live within a different

---

33 Vincent Brümmer, *The Model of Love* (Cambridge 1993), 14f., 21, 29.

34 Cf. G. Green, 'The Gender of God and the Theology of Metaphor,' in: Alvin F. Kimel, *Speaking the Christian God*, 57, considers it theology's task to explore and elaborate 'the biblical paradigm so that its meaning and implications can be heard in the present'; in the Christian tradition, 'Father' always refers to the Father of Jesus Christ (59).

35 See E. Schüssler Fiorenza, *Bread not Stone* (Boston 1984), 13f.; McFague, *Metaphorical Theology*, 54-66; McFague, *Models of God*, 40-45.

horizon and have different experiences. This is one of the causes of the plurality that is so typical of religious traditions and culture in general.[36] The fact that traditional metaphors have a meaning defined by the tradition thus implies that their meaning is not entirely open. We do not construe our description of reality on the basis of our own desires but on the basis of experiences that we feel are typical of how reality is. Colin Gunton has rightly introduced this as an argument against Sallie McFague's one-sided emphasis on our construction of images of God at the cost of the other aspect, i.e., the description of reality.[37] If the meaning of a traditional metaphor is not established to a certain extent, it is impossible to know what is meant by it and it is useless to speak metaphorically. But precisely because metaphors in traditions form a network within which they have their meanings, it is possible to adopt the meanings proposed – leaving aside the difficulties that can arise from one's own experiential horizon. It is exactly here that feminist circles object to speaking about God as Father.[38] These objections cannot, in my opinion, be answered adequately by referring to the meaning that is attributed to 'God as father' in the Bible. Because the metaphor of father in the Bible is patriarchal and the patriarchal elements in the image of God have been stressed for centuries, a real problem exists here. But if one acknowledges that the meaning of a traditional metaphor has been established to a large extent and that its original meaning can be studied through exegesis, then one has a starting point for the renewal of our language about God. If exegesis demonstrates which meaning the metaphor of God as father had in the Old Testament and which elements were significant for Jesus in his speaking to God as his Father, then it is possible to stress these elements apart from the metaphor of father. True, the metaphor would then be lost, but much of its intended meaning would remain. One cannot substitute other terms for a metaphor without shifting its meaning to some degree. Inasmuch as we can in this way avoid authoritarian characteristics in the metaphor of God as father, this loss of meaning is acceptable. By listening to the Bible texts people can acquire a deeper understanding of the biblical metaphor, and as a consequence correct the associations which 'father' has for them. However, the juxtaposition of original meaning and contemporary associations can also lead them to push the father-meta-

---

36   See my *De Schrift alleen?* (Kampen 1978), 191-201, 232-250.
37   C. Gunton, 'Proteus and Procrustus: A Study in the Dialectic of Language in Disagreement with Sallie McFague,' in: Alvin F. Kimel, *Speaking the Christian God*, especially 73; cf. my *De Schrift alleen?* on the subjective and objective moment in knowledge and in theology, 222-270.
38   Cf., for example, C. Halkes, 'De motieven van het protest in de feministische theologie tegen God de Vader,' *Concilium* 1981, no. 3, 105-112; Kune Biezeveld, *Spreken over God als vader*, chapter 1.

phor into the background in favour of other predicates and images, that emphasize other qualities of God.

Thus, on the one hand, the meaning of the fatherhood of God has been relatively established, and speaking of God as a heavenly, truly good Father can correct human images of fatherhood. On the other, a patriarchal culture and bad examples of fatherhood can make it difficult for people to speak about God as Father.

5 God's Fatherhood as a Traditional Metaphor

The meaning of a traditional metaphor is defined by its source and by the meanings that have been ascribed to it throughout the centuries. In the case of the father-metaphor, that source is the Bible.[39] Speaking of God as Father is not specifically biblical, but Jesus' trust in God is characteristic for his relationship with the father, and the father-metaphor in the Bible has connotations of trust and concern. In popular representations in the ancient Middle East the king was depicted as God's son, and his coronation was seen as procreation. It is this representation that lies behind the prophecy of the coming king who will throw off the yoke of the oppressors:

> For a child has been born for us,
> a son given to us;
> authority rests upon his shoulders;
> and he is named
> Wonderful Counsellor, Mighty God,
> Everlasting Father, Prince of Peace.
> His authority shall grow continually,
> and there shall be endless peace
> for the throne of David and his kingdom.
> He will establish and uphold it
> with justice and with righteousness .... (Isaiah 9:6f.)

The king as the son of God is a powerful and good king. Where in the background God is seen as the father of this child, the king is in turn called father. In Psalm 2:7 the king is explicitly called the child of God. In a later text the sonship of the king is explicitly stipulated. In 2 Samuel 7 the prophet Nathan is commanded by God to

---

39 Cf. for example, Kune Biezeveld, *Spreken over God als vader*, 116-135; H. Ringgren, 'Ab,' *Theologisches Wörterbuch Zum Alten Testament* I (Stuttgart 1973), *s.v.*

speak to David. He must speak about the faithfulness of God toward David's kingly house, but the father-son relation entails conditions:

I will be a father to him,
and he shall be a son to me.
When he commits iniquity,
I will punish him with a rod such as mortals use,
with blows inflicted by human beings. (II Samuel 7:14)

The image of the father-son relation thus expresses that the king is like a son of God and that this father will judge him according to the norm of justice. The relation of God to the king is interpreted in the Bible as a relation of God to his people, the children of Israel. God is a father who continually liberates his children, whereas the people constantly turn away from him. Nevertheless, God has mercy upon his people again and again; He is bound to his people as a father or mother is bound to his or her children:

Woe to anyone who says to a father:
'What are you begetting?'
or to a woman, 'With what are you in labor?'
Thus says the Lord,
the Holy One of Israel, and its Maker:
Will you question me about my children,
or command me concerning the work of my hands? (Isaiah 45:10f.)

I will not attempt to summarize the broad discussion on the biblical metaphor of God's fatherhood but will only mention two things. First, the fatherhood of God is encompassed within the framework of his mercy and redemption and his desire for his people to live in peace and justice. Second, it concerns the fatherhood of God, the Maker of heaven and earth, the Creator of human beings, the Creator of his people. As Henry Jansen has shown, the point of the relational qualities is that they are attributed to God.[40] 'God is love' makes sense if and only if 'God' has meaning without love. God's goodness is not a necessary goodness but a free goodness.[41] The metaphor of God's fatherhood intends to say, among other things, that the One who has created all things is 'bound' to his children and cannot abandon them. That

---

40   Henry Jansen, *Relationality and the Concept of God* (Amsterdam 1995).
41   Cf. Vincent Brümmer, *The Model of Love*, 175-178; cf. my 'God and Goodness,' in: Gijsbert van den Brink, Luco J. van den Brom & Marcel Sarot (eds.), *Christian Faith and Philosophical Theology: Essays in Honour of Vincent Brümmer* (1992; Kampen ²1996), 244-248.

God disciplines his children as a father indicates that this love exists within the framework of his salvific will, so that his love is expressed in terms of salvation as well as discipline. He wants to set his children on the right path. Thus the image of God as father stands for parental love and parental authority – not a detached authority but an authority that is connected to the norms of the Kingdom of Peace. If one should separate God's mercy from God's authority, one loses God's salvific will as a critical norm for human authority and the abuse of power.

In the New Testament as well, God's fatherhood is a critical norm for what people make of their parenthood. Klaus Berger links the emphasis on God's fatherhood with the fact that early Christianity was a religion of radical conversion.[42] People turn to God and join the Christian community; they radically abandon everything. This radicality is expressed in Jesus' words about hating one's father and mother and the priority of following him above burying one's own father (Matthew 8:21f.). In God Christians find security, concern and faithfulness. In Berger's opinion, the metaphor of God as father is not derived from relationships as they have been depicted in the richer classes but to the daily interaction of parents and children in the poorer classes.[43] Berger points out that, while God is depicted as caring, Jesus brings a very demanding message. He presents humans with a crisis, calls people to abandon hearth and home, and compares himself with those who believe they can borrow status from their intimacy with God. It seems to me that one could say that the fatherhood of God stands for love, faithfulness, good will, concern and the will for salvation and thus entails elements of upbringing, correction and discipline.

Throughout the history of Christianity the image of God as father has undergone other developments. In the discussion on God as Father the doctrine of the Trinity plays a major role: the Father is actually the Father of the Son, and *vice versa*. Because the Father is actually the Father, the fatherhood cannot be changed and thus neither can the way we speak of God as Father be changed. At the same time, it is also clear that God is not an ordinary father, for the tradition confesses that the Son is begotten of the Father before all worlds and yet says nothing about a mother. This language with respect to God as Father is also metaphorical; it describes the relation between the Creator and Christ in terms of a father-son relationship. In principle, the metaphor of mother could have been used here as well. In speaking of Father and Son it would also have been possible to indicate which elements of the father-son relationship are activated. Because the meaning of this metaphor has largely been established by tradition not all of it can be translated, but

---

42   K. Berger, *Theologiegeschichte des Urchristentums*, 2nd ed. (Tübingen 1995), 30f.
43   Berger, *Theologiegeschichte*, 30f.

it can for the most part be explained and it is possible to indicate the core elements in this unique Father-Son relationship.

None of this alters the fact that the tradition speaks of God as Father and not of God as Mother. In the context of a patriarchy, speaking of God as Father was more obvious than speaking of God as Mother. Speaking of God as Father has sustained a patriarchal society. And yet there is no lack of maternal images of God in the Bible.[44] With regard to Jesus' intentions, Berger feels that Jesus' critical words passed on by Matthew are too often overlooked:

> But you are not to be called rabbi, for you have one teacher, and you are all students. And call no one your father on earth, for you have one Father – the one in heaven .... The greatest among you will be your servant. All who exalt themselves will be humbled, and all who humble themselves will be exalted. (Matthew 23:8-12)

The typical Christian use of metaphors is not only the 'is and is not' that often appears in the discussion on metaphors. McFague points out that the approach to metaphors enclosed in these words is not a modern version of the *theologia negativa*: a denial that what we say really applies to God.[45] A positive statement is also made: God is a father and is not a father. In my opinion, this dichotomy of 'is and is not' also contains a third way of speaking about God: the *via eminentiae*.[46] This way of attributing meaning is as follows: God is a father, not as humans understand it but in a much superior way. This is clear in the above quote in the words 'the one in heaven' and in the text:

> Is there anyone among you who, if your child asks for a fish, will give a snake instead of a fish? ... If you then, who are evil, know how to give

---

44 See, for example, Johanna W.H. van Wijk-Bos, *Reimagining God*, 50-65.

45 McFague, *Metaphorical Theology*, 19, cf. 13, 28. For the 'is and is not,' cf. also a quote from Dionysius in Thomas, *Summa contra Gentiles* I, (tr. A.C. Pegis) (1955; rpt. London 1975), 139 (I 29,4): 'The same things are both like and unlike God.' Cf. for a discussion of analogy, especially in Thomas and Barth, Vincent Brümmer, *Speaking of a Personal God* (Cambridge 1992), 43-52.

46 Cf. the emphasis on *eminentia* in Thomas, *Summa Contra Gentiles* I 30,4 (p. 141): 'Now, the mode of supereminence in which the above-mentioned perfections are found in God can be signified by names used by us only through negation, as when we say that God is *eternal* or *infinite*, or also through a relation of God to other things, as when He is called the *first cause* or the *highest good*.' See also Wolfhart Pannenberg, *Systematic Theology* I, tr. G.W. Bromiley (Grand Rapids 1991), 343f. and Herman Bavinck, *Gereformeerde Dogmatiek* I, 87-107.

good gifts to your children, how much more will the heavenly Father give the Holy Spirit to those who ask him! (Luke 11: 11, 13)

The way of attributing meaning in 'if you then, ... how much more will the heavenly Father ...' is a classic Jewish way of reasoning, closely related to the emphasis that Karl Barth places on the fact that the words with which one refers to God acquire their meaning from God's revelation.[47] Images of God such as father and mother are qualified by capitalizing them and adding 'qualifiers' such as 'in heaven.'[48] This qualification is not included in 'and is not' because it entails a reference to eminence.[49]

6   Can we Change the Fatherhood of God?

Thus speaking of God as Father must be amended. Images can be very powerful, and the meaning of a traditional metaphor can be difficult to understand by those who have had bad experiences with earthly fathers.[50] What must be changed is not the fatherhood of God but the way in which we speak about God's nearness, authority, love, discipline, etc. After all, God is not a literal, natural – that is, human – father but is known through the metaphor of fatherhood. We cannot change God but we can change the way we speak about God. Because this also changes our knowledge of God, it entails a comprehensive change in the tradition. It entails a change in our image of God and thus also in our concept of humankind, for the image of God and the concept of humankind are always related to each other. Insofar as a conscious change in the tradition is entailed here, it is not simply a contextual change but a deliberate change.

---

47   The 'kal wachomèr,' cf. M.J. Mulder, 'Functie en uitleg van de bijbel (Oude Testament) rondom het begin van onze jaartelling,' in: G.J.D. Aalders *et al.*, *Bijbels Handboek* IIB (Kampen 1983), 263. I think that McFague does Barth an injustice when she writes that Barth's doctrine of the *analogia fidei* means that 'our language refers to God only as God from time to time causes our words to conform to the divine being,' *Metaphorical Theology*, 13. Cf. K. Barth, *Church Dogmatics*, I/1, tr. G.W. Bromiley (Edinburgh 1975), 243: human knowledge of God is transformed into the divine knowledge of humans; in this relationship there is a 'likeness of the known in the knowing.' It is here that Barth speaks of *analogia fidei*. Cf. G.C. Berkouwer, *De triompf der genade in de theologie van Karl Barth* (Kampen 1954), 171f.

48   I.T. Ramsey, *Religious Language* (London 1957).

49   Cf. W. Pannenberg, 'Analogy and Doxology,' in: Pannenberg, *Basic Questions in Theology* vol. 1, tr. George H. Kehm (Philadelphia 1970), 227f.

50   See Janet Soskice, 'Revelation and Gender,' in: Vincent Brümmer & Marcel Sarot (eds.), *Revelation and Experience* (Utrecht 1996), 72-92.

An important question is how this change in the traditional way of speaking of God as Father can be legitimized. The reason for this change in the patriarchal image of God lies in the context of opposition to the role of women and men that has arisen and the resulting social subordination of women, with many far-reaching consequences for the way our culture has been organized. Many of the changes that the Christian tradition has undergone began outside of the tradition, although always some Christians have started to support these changes. A few examples are the abolition of slavery, subsequent democratization, a different explanation of the doctrine of creation, etc. Even though these processes of change were introduced by minorities, the initiative for change was usually external. Changing the tradition was embedded internally by searching for starting points for the changes within the tradition itself. At the beginning of this contribution I gave examples of changes, such as opening church offices to women in Protestant churches and accepting loving and faithful homosexual relationships. In both cases we saw that the changes were legitimized from the perspective of central ideas. These were appealed to in order to eliminate discrimination against women and homosexuals. This was followed by the question of whether dispensing with the patriarchal way of speaking of God could be defended from the perspective of central elements of the tradition.

On the basis of the above analysis of the traditional metaphor of God as father I think that we can answer this question affirmatively. Actually, the same procedure is followed here: from the perspective of central notions in the father image of God and the image of God in general, the patriarchal tendencies in the image of God are corrected. It may not be possible to translate a new metaphor into other terms – at least, not without losing some of its meaning – but with a standing or traditional metaphor the meaning is much more defined, which makes it easier to express it in other words. Exegetical research and the study of church history plays a major role here. The most central characteristics of the metaphor of God as father can be rendered in other words.

Central and essential to the Christian image of God is the fact that the relation between God and humans is a personal relation, which is why personal metaphors are irreplaceable. God may be viewed as supra-personal or more than personal but not as impersonal in the sense of being an object.[51] Because God has entered into a relationship with humans, relational metaphors will be dominant. This entails that God is introduced through images borrowed from humans. Because humans are female as well as male, one will have to speak of God as a woman or a man, a she or a he. Because inclusive language is often regarded as impersonal, there are meta-

---

51 Cf. Bavinck, *Gereformeerde dogmatiek* I, 269; L.J. van den Brom, *Creatieve twijfel* (Kampen 1990), 68ff.

phors in which one can choose between speaking about men or women, but a better alternative might be to alternate between the two. In the Bible metaphors appear in clusters. God is the Maker, the Master, the King, the Lord and *the Mother who bears*. Each metaphor makes other metaphors possible and brings with it its own associations. By using more metaphors one is able to avoid speaking of God too rigidly and also to avoid a patriarchal image of God.[52]

At last, then, we arrive at an answer to the question: can we change the fatherhood of God? First, we must state that God himself cannot change her fatherhood. In creating humans, he became their Maker. Secondly, the same thing can be said about God as Mother: God cannot change his motherhood. Thirdly, if more female metaphors of God are included in speaking of God, human experience is broadened so that the web of metaphors linked to these female metaphors expresses other aspects of the relationship between God and humans.[53] Fourthly, in the metaphors of God as father and mother there is an indissoluble relationship. After God had mercy on humans, he continued to be associated with them. The father in the parable of the prodigal son describes God as if He could not change. That unchanging element is lacking in metaphors such as friend and partner, although this aspect could be inserted by the addition of adjectives such as 'eternal.' Fifthly, when we improve the way we speak of God, we do not change God but that which we say about God and therefore change our knowledge of God and ourselves, and thereby the relationships among humans. If we do this well, it is an improvement. Sixthly, the argument that the Bible's authority forbids us to add to speaking of God as Father by speaking of God as Mother is not tenable because the living tradition has undergone 'deliberate changes' on other points as well. Seventhly, and finally, there remains the fact that Jesus taught his disciples to pray 'Our Father, who art in heaven.' This name of God, however, does not exclude the name of God as Mother. Those, whether female or male, who think of God as a truly good father will not be disturbed by the obviously patriarchal nature of this reference. Those who do find it disturbing can avoid speaking about God as Father. Thus whether we use it or not says something about ourselves at the same time.

---

52   As Kune Biezeveld, *Spreken over God als vader*, 300, concludes.
53   It is not the intention of this contribution to analyze these metaphors and their basic elements but only to analyze the legitimacy of changing the way of speaking about God. For intrinsic meanings and comparison with images of fatherhood and parenthood, see, among others, McFague, *Metaphorical Theology*, 174ff.

Index of Names

243

Contributions to Philosophical Theology

Edited by Gijsbert van den Brink, Vincent Brümmer and Marcel Sarot

Svante Lundgren

Fight Against Idols

Erich Fromm on Religion, Judaism and the Bible

Frankfurt/M., Berlin, Bern, New York, Paris, Wien, 1998. 193 pp.
ISBN 3-631-32757-9 · pb. DM 65.–*
US-ISBN 0-8204-3557-0

Erich Fromm (1900-80) was a famous psychoanalyst, social critic and author of bestsellers like *Escape from Freedom* and *The Art of Loving*. But he was also very interested in religion. Having been brought up as an orthodox Jew he abandoned institutionalized religion as a young man. But he was influenced for life by the Talmudic studies of his childhood. Later in life he met and was enriched by Buddhism and mysticism. In this book the author analyzes what Fromm thought about religion, how he expressed his ambiguous feelings about Judaism, and his radical interpretation of the Bible. This is a book about a fascinating man with views that challenge both believers and atheists.

Contents: Erich Fromm · Psychoanalysis and religion · Idolatry

Frankfurt/M · Berlin · Bern · New York · Paris · Wien
Auslieferung: Verlag Peter Lang AG
Jupiterstr. 15, CH-3000 Bern 15
Telefax (004131) 9402131
*inklusive Mehrwertsteuer
Preisänderungen vorbehalten